The Politics of Kathy Acker

The Politics of Kathy Acker

Revolution and the Avant-Garde

Emilia Borowska

EDINBURGH
University Press

Edinburgh University Press is one of the leading university presses in the UK. We publish academic books and journals in our selected subject areas across the humanities and social sciences, combining cutting-edge scholarship with high editorial and production values to produce academic works of lasting importance. For more information visit our website: edinburghuniversitypress.com

Edinburgh University Press Ltd
The Tun – Holyrood Road
12(2f) Jackson's Entry
Edinburgh EH8 8PJ

Typeset in 11/13 Adobe Sabon by
IDSUK (DataConnection) Ltd, and
printed and bound in Great Britain.

A CIP record for this book is available from the British Library

ISBN 978 1 4744 2465 3 (hardback)
ISBN 978 1 4744 2466 0 (webready PDF)
ISBN 978 1 4744 2467 7 (epub)

Contents

List of Illustrations

Acknowledgements

I owe my deepest thanks to Tim Armstrong for his expertise, mentorship and support throughout this research project. I have benefited immensely from the constructive readings of earlier drafts by Robert Eaglestone, Alex Houen and Jane Elliott. For their directions for improvement of later versions, I am indebted to my anonymous reviewers; their suggestions have strengthened my work in numerous ways. This project arose out of my doctoral dissertation, and I would like to extend my gratitude to the English Department at Royal Holloway, University of London for fostering a vibrant research community.

I wish to express my heartfelt thanks to all editors at Edinburgh University Press who supported and worked on this book: Michelle Houston, Ersev Ersoy, Camilla Rockwood, Adela Rauchova, Rebecca Mackenzie and James Dale. I am also very grateful to Matias Viegener, Acker's literary executor, for his great kindness and generosity in allowing me to reproduce the illustrations. My appreciation and gratitude also go to Jacqueline de Jong for email correspondence and her permission to reprint *The Situationist Times* material. I am indebted to the librarians and archivists: for enabling me access to the Kathy Acker Papers, thanks to Laura Micham and Kelly Wooten at the David M. Rubenstein Rare Book and Manuscript Library, Duke University; for assistance in obtaining reprints of *The Situationist Times* I would also like to thank Kevin Repp and Rebecca Aldi at the Beinecke Rare Book and Manuscript Library, Yale University; thanks to staff at Kingston University Library for a welcoming research and writing space. Chapter 3 previously appeared in *Contemporary Women's Writing* (10.3 November 2016, pp. 373–93), and I thank the editors of the journal for permission to reprint it with slight alterations. Paul Schmidt's translation of 'Democracy' by Arthur Rimbaud is reproduced here with the permission of HarperCollins Publishers.

I would like to thank fellow Acker scholar Spencer Dew for sharing his work and exchanging ideas. For the stimulating discussions, inspiration and helpful comments on my work in various stages of the project I thank Pirkko Koppinen, Andrew Purssell, Albertine Fox and Xavier Marcó del Pont. I remain indebted to the late Andrzej Antoszek; his passionate teaching and scholarly work will always inspire me. I am also grateful to Patrycja Antoszek and Zofia Kolbuszewska for their support prior to commencing my studies in the UK. Thank you to my parents, Krystyna and Ireneusz, and to my close family and friends for their loving support and faith in me. My last and warmest thanks go to Cormac Browne, for his kindness, love, and his unceasing enthusiasm for my work.

Abbreviations

Works by Kathy Acker

BB   *The Burning Bombing of America*, in *Rip-Off Red, Girl Detective* and *The Burning Bombing of America*

N   *I Dreamt I Was a Nymphomaniac: Imagining*, in *Portrait of an Eye*

TL   *The Adult Life of Toulouse Lautrec by Henri Toulouse Lautrec*, in *Portrait of an Eye*

DQ   *Don Quixote: Which Was a Dream* (New York: Grove Press, 1986)

ES   *Empire of the Senseless* (New York: Grove Press, 1988)

MI   *In Memoriam to Identity* (London: Pandora, 1990)

Works by other authors

OR   Hannah Arendt, *On Revolution* (Harmondsworth: Penguin, 1990)

BE   Alain Badiou, *Being and Event*, trans. Oliver Feltham (London: Continuum Press, 2010)

LW   Alain Badiou, *Logics of Worlds: Being and Event II*, trans. Alberto Toscano (London: Continuum, 2009)

AO   Gilles Deleuze and Félix Guattari, *Anti-Oedipus: Capitalism and Schizophrenia*, trans. Robert Hurley et al. (Minneapolis: University of Minnesota Press, 2000)

TP   Gilles Deleuze and Félix Guattari, *A Thousand Plateaus: Capitalism and Schizophrenia*, trans. Brian Massumi (Minneapolis: University of Minnesota Press, 2005)

BP   Michel Serres, *The Birth of Physics*, trans. Jack Hawkes, ed. David Webb (Manchester: Clinamen Press, 2000).

Abbreviations

Works by Kathy Acker

Works by other authors

Introduction

A revolution is like a fever that temporarily grips the patient. Such was the observation of Crane Brinton in his seminal work *The Anatomy of Revolution* (1938).[1] Not all revolutions, Brinton observed, run the full course of the fever; many are suppressed prematurely. But for others, the initial delirium typically subsides into a convalescence that, ultimately, ends in a restoration of the pre-revolutionary order. So it is that many a revolution observes the same process: the overthrow of the old regime is followed by a brief 'honeymoon' period, which lasts until 'contradictory elements' arise among the revolutionaries.[2] Finally, the new revolutionary body collapses, devouring itself in a spectacle of political terror. 'Revolution, like Saturn, devours its children': Brinton quotes Pierre Vergniaud's prophecy that the French Revolution will end in despotism.[3] The end result? Revolutionaries come out of the experience untransformed, often sadder, sometimes wiser, and most likely to renounce their revolutionary passion. This final reaction 'comes as naturally to societies in revolution as an ebbing tide, as calm after a storm, as convalescence after fever, as the snapping-back of a stretched elastic band.'[4]

Revolutions in Kathy Acker's novels evoke variations upon this Saturnian refrain. While her fevers often differ in their course, involving different revolutionary agents, different variations of a fundamental phenomenon, each of them either fails to reach their ultimate goal, or heavily compromises that goal in the process. In Acker's final full-length novel, *Pussy, King of the Pirates* (1996), a fortune-teller in pre-revolutionary China evokes a solemn warning: 'the revolution, which was just about to happen, had to fail, due to its own nature or origin'.[5] In the cards laid before them, the Chinese soothsayer sees the end of dreaming and the beginnings of revolution's nightmare: 'As soon as it [the revolution] failed, as soon as sovereignty, be it reigning or revolutionary, disappeared, as soon as sovereignty ate its own head as if it were a snake, when the streets turned to poverty and decay, but a different poverty and decay'.[6] Revolution is presented as if fixed upon a wheel of fortune; fated to return full circle to what had come before, like a snake consuming itself. Like Saturn devouring his young before being resurrected in the form of yet another revolution, with its own unrealised promise of a better world ahead.

The sobering morning-after of revolutions – a realisation of their failure to deliver the promise of freedom; their cycle of fervour replaced by terrified conservatism; their only change being the shift in leaders' names – has led many postmodernists to consign the revolution to the dustbin of history. They view them, along with ideas such as truth and progress, as an outdated and dangerous model of change. Instead, poststructural theorists and postmodern writers offer a new kind of ethic. This usually involves the writer putting forward a persistent critique, and a conscious undoing of teleological narratives. They then put their efforts into articulating alternative calls for decentred subjectivity, usually accompanied by a desire for the ending of dualistic structures of oppression.

Yet while the perceived failures of revolutions have caused many intellectuals to eschew such political ambitions altogether, the ideal of a revolutionary transformation still lives on, like a resilient virus, in much postmodern thinking. Acker, for instance, is deeply concerned with the progressive use of the revolutionary past, and she focuses upon the idea that history is sometimes born from the will of the masses, and can take the form of rapid, novel political action.

This tension – between realising that revolutions are ultimately doomed to failure, and yet are still able to persist in the imaginations of writers such as Acker – is central to this book. My aim is to explore and reveal Acker's revolutionary merit, while also confronting the fact that, in her work, revolutions, not unlike the romantic relationships in her novels, follow an invariably Brintonian cycle of attraction and disappointment. But I will also show that, to a surprising extent, Acker positively wills revolution into being, while simultaneously depicting it as repeatedly failing.

Acker has long been regarded as one of the most prominent writers of the postmodern avant-garde. Since the publication of her trilogy of novels, *The Childlike Life of the Black Tarantula by the Black Tarantula* (1973), *I Dreamt I Was a Nymphomaniac: Imagining* (1974) and *The Adult Life of Toulouse Lautrec by Henri Toulouse Lautrec* (1975), her writing has been pored over by poststructural critics, and her shifting representations of sexuality and gender continue to fascinate feminist studies.[7] This book takes for granted such alignments with postmodernism, and that movement's broadly understood political dimension, but it seeks to depart from earlier scholarship by focusing singularly on her commitment to a revolutionary transformation. Whereas other scholars have looked at the political value of Acker's experimental work, they regard it mostly as overlapping with the political implications of poststructuralism. How Acker puts the historical context of revolutions and the historical avant-garde to work within her political agenda, though, remains largely unexamined.

This monograph is a response to that. It posits that Acker's writing shares an affinity with the theories underpinning the revolutionary event as seen in thinkers such as Gilles Deleuze, Félix Guattari, Alain Badiou, Hannah Arendt, Michel Serres and others. In part, my reading is propelled by Acker herself. She once urged her readers directly to relate her stylistic disruptions to a radical political vision. In a 1988 interview with Ellen Friedman, Acker expressed her concern that the label of 'experimental' literature is too often applied 'to hide the political radicalness of some writers', and the implication is that artists 'have nothing to do with politics'.[8] When asked the question: 'What hasn't been noticed about your work?', Acker admitted that 'my work with language and postmodernism – that's been noticed about my work', but suggested that an isolated postmodern analysis of her work is not sufficient to bring out its radical dimension.[9]

Acker has long been associated with a wide variety of ostensibly postmodern literary strategies and concepts such as appropriation, transgression, pastiche, the destabilisation of gender, the decentralisation and fragmentation of self, and nonlinear narratives. As the shock value of Acker's experimental, often pornographic prose is waning, and seeing that much has been done to highlight the sophistication of Acker's political strategies akin to the tenets of poststructuralism, the more recent readings, which I am engaging with and building on, increasingly identify the need for a new line of enquiry. In the hope of unpacking the dimensions of her political vision beyond the parameters of postmodernism, they turn their attention to the issues of community and potentiality as well as the intertextual, spatial and historical contexts of her work, and even attempt the recovery of Acker's humanism.

In telescoping Acker's engagement with revolution across and beyond the Western world, my book shares affinity with the transnational approach adopted by critics in Polina Mackay and Kathryn

Nicol's edited volume *Kathy Acker and Transnationalism* (2009). As my Introduction and the following chapters will make clear, Acker's figuration of the political is directly informed by the global character of the revolutionary explosion of the 1960s and 1970s that eclipsed youth movements all over the world to fight oppressive governments and ideologies. Despite the American New Left's intense connection to the international protests of the symbolic year 1968, there has been a tendency to view the American counterculture and its writers in isolation, as something quintessentially specific to America. A study of the radical dimension of Acker's politics must account for its conscious crossings of barriers between nations and historical periods: the importance she attaches to links and overlaps between international revolutionary movements, past and present. Acker herself coined a perfect term that explains the sometimes unexpected collisions of distant geographies and histories in her works: 'topological revolutions',[10] those unceasing foldings, unfoldings and refoldings of the revolutionary script that are meant to inscribe new potentials into the present.

In his book *Postmodernism and Its Others: The Fiction of Ishmael Reed, Kathy Acker, and Don DeLillo* (2006), Jeffrey Ebbesen argues that although Acker incorporates poststructuralist theory into her work and many of Frederic Jameson's claims about postmodern writing can be applied to Acker, her political project in many ways exceeds the flattening effect he detects in postmodern art. Rather than erasing historical referent, Acker, writes Ebbesen, 'wants to see history as alive, in process, and in the present'.[11] Thus Ebbesen encourages us to uncover the aspect of Acker's politics located in history. This, in my view, calls out for further consideration and the development of an interpretative framework that will supplant poststructural readings, and my book is a response to that challenge.

Spencer Dew's discussions of Acker's affinities with Marcuse, Arendt, Goya, Rimbaud, Blanchot and others shed light on Acker's extensive pedagogical programme which provides her readers with a set of critical tools for understanding reality while offering practical models of new relations between humans. 'It is through pedagogy', Dew argues in his *Learning for Revolution* (2011), 'that Acker's attempts at politically functional literature find their most elaborate development.'[12] Dew conceptualises Acker's relationship with the authors she borrowed from in terms of 'textual friendships' between 'pedagogical partners' who strive towards a new community. I similarly intend to show how Acker's appropriation of other texts serves revolutionary ends. My emphasis, however, is on how the appropriated texts constitute for Acker a point of entry into revolutionary history which she hopes to put into progressive use through their creative textual transformation. My study also sketches an affinity with critics who relate Acker's writings on the body with political concerns. In his *Powers of Possibility* (2012), where Acker is discussed next to Allen Ginsberg, Amiri Baraka, William Burroughs and Lyn Hejinian, Alex Houen theorises a literary practice of potentiality in order to analyse the relationship between social activism and literary art. According to Houen, the art of potentiality involves a performance of feeling and possibility that can elicit meaningful action from the reader. Houen posits that whereas 'Writing fictions about revolution will not automatically catalyse revolution in the world', Acker's 'fiction and the "languages of the body" can reconfigure how one is affected by the world, and in doing so they also rewrite one's capacities for feeling and action'.[13]

Kathryn Hume has made 'modernist' claims about the more coherent, humanist voice that can be heard beneath the 'background babble' of Acker's writing.[14] Hume notes that Acker's alliance with feminist and poststructuralist theories has led many critics to trust and perpetuate Acker's self-proclaimed denials of having a literary voice of her own. She had consistently spoken against her authorial self in interviews and essays, and further destabilised the presence of this authorial self in her fiction by decentring and multiplying the identities of her protagonists. In an interview with Larry McCaffery in April 1990, Acker recollects that during her teenage years she was encouraged by the Black Mountain Poets to seek her unique authorial self. She was told that 'when you find your own voice, then you're a poet'.[15] In her essay 'A Few Notes on Two of My Books' (1989), she claims that creativity and originality, rather than serving as expressions of the genuine artistic self, are in fact aspects of bourgeois ideology based on ownership and a phallocentric literary canon – hence her statement 'I hated my fathers.'[16] For Acker, literary plagiarism – that is, refusing to own and use one's own voice – becomes a central strategy in combating these ideologies. According to Hume, however, these plagiaristic strategies do not erase her individual persona because 'reading all the novels [. . .] makes this persona much more prominent, and it stays in the mind when the postmodern pastiche characters based on Heathcliff, Pip, and Jane Eyre have become indistinct or are themselves taken over and made to sound like that voice'.[17] A coherent aim of her wild, homeless and androgynous characters is a hope for a better world, summarised by a utopian comment at the end of *Empire of the Senseless*: '[O]ne day, maybe, there'ld be a human society in a world which is beautiful, a society which wasn't just disgust' (*ES*, 227). There is, then, an undeniable humanist impulse in Acker's writing, whose authorial persona has revolutionary dreams and desires a friendlier world. Indeed, in an interview with Sylvère Lotringer given towards the end of the 1980s, she admits that 'If you scratch hard, you find that I'm a humanist in some weird way.'[18]

The recent centenary of the Russian Revolution of 1917 revived intense reflections in the Western world on that decisive event that changed the course of modern history – on its triumphs, betrayals, failings, and ongoing significance, depending on one's persuasion – while provoking larger questions about revolutions as a means to change. The year 2017 also marked the twentieth anniversary of Acker's death, with numerous publications emerging around it, including the publication of Acker and McKenzie Wark's correspondence in the volume *I'm Very into You* (2015); Chris Kraus's critical biography *After Kathy Acker* was published in 2017, and the biography by Jason McBride, *Kathy Acker: Her Revolutionary Work and Life*, is forthcoming. In *Kathy Acker: Writing the Impossible* (2016), Georgina Colby undertook the investigation of modernist roots of Acker's experiments with language, further consolidating a reorientation of Acker scholarship away from the postmodern territory.

While political criticisms have tended to discuss Acker's own politics in broad terms, this book situates her work in the revolutionary tradition, bringing the revolutionary event to the forefront of her political concerns. The revolutionary Acker that I argue for in these pages is not intended to replace other 'political Ackers', such as the ones identified by critics working within the fields of language, genre, gender and sexuality. Rather, my aim is to uncover the previously neglected aspects of her politics. The central claims on which the argument of my book is founded are: Acker uses history as a potent source for revolutionary transformation of the present; it is important for Acker to establish transhistorical and transnational links; her politics is founded on an evental understanding of revolution, broadly understood as a moment of possibility; her politics can be characterised as anarchist; the evental dimension permits Acker to restore the revolutionary agenda of the historical avant-gardes; she develops a truth-based model of political subjectivity; and finally, that she elaborates a full conceptualisation of artistic responsibility.

In what follows, using Arendt's *On Revolution* (1963) as my point of departure, I trace the development of the meaning of revolution. Different meanings of revolution emerge from this analysis: the pre-modern as repetition; the modern as novelty; the postmodern as failure; and finally, the creative re-configuration of revolution which I identify in Acker – revolution understood in terms of the event, as theorised by critics such as Badiou, Deleuze and others. I then situate her work within the avant-garde tradition, and suggest that contrary to the recurrent pronouncements of the death of the avant-garde and the charge that the neo-avant-garde is politically bankrupt, Acker's work is representative of how the revolutionary spirit of the historical avant-garde lives on.

Acker, Arendt and the potentiality of history

In 1995, Acker wrote an essay that she called: 'Writing, Identity, and Copyright in the Net Age'. In it, she explained how, when confused about her writing, about its purpose and methods, and when she is perplexed by those recurring questions of 'why?' and 'how to write?', she would turn to 'older writing'.[19] To give an idea of what she meant by that, she cited Hannah Arendt's essay 'On Humanity in Dark Times: Thoughts about Lessing' (1968). Arendt delivered this essay as a lecture in her acceptance of the Lessing Prize of the Free City of Hamburg in 1959.

Perhaps finding inspiration from this talk, Acker is resolutely critical of the copyright laws established by the publishing industry. Instead, she believes that writing is an open-ended, communal act; not one based upon the ownership of text, but rather on the free exchange of countless human initiatives across space and time. 'I do not write out of nothing, or from nothing, for I must write with the help of other texts', she opines.[20] Such a pronunciation would, no doubt, have found favour with Arendt, a writer who regarded the texts of others and her own writings as a public arena of unexpected hidden potentialities of change. Arendt and Acker both viewed writing as an engagement within a common humanity and not as an individualist enterprise. On the one hand, they criticised writers who abandoned political commitment for the sake of disinterested inwardness or profit. On the other hand, they valued those authors who did not ignore reality, even though in their work they often take '[f]light from the world in dark times', constructing a world that would be an alternative to the present condition.[21]

Writing, Acker maintains, 'restores meaning to a world which hardship and suffering have revealed as chaotic and senseless'.[22] Acker's mode of writing is an affirmation of Arendt's argument that 'Power arises [. . .] only where people act together, not where people grow stronger as individuals.'[23] Acker also writes that Arendt's thinking is 'deeply embedded in the historical',[24] and her ideas resonate with the cultural and political dilemmas that humanity faces today. Navigating between her own commentary and passages from Arendt's 'On Humanity in Dark Times', Acker demonstrates that their methods, ideals and dilemmas are part of the same literary endeavour. In the eyes of Acker, Arendt becomes a shining beacon for responsible writing in hard times – writing, in other words, that engages with committed human action, driven by a will to change.

Acker and Arendt also share their understanding of history as a potent source for action in the present. Acker asserts that: 'If we throw history away, we are depriving ourselves of potentialities, potentialities for actions. Models and paradigms for actions. Potentiality is kin, and I am talking politically, kin to the imagination.'[25] Arendt's humanist views on history, community and writing all clearly inform Acker's own oeuvre when she writes: 'The loss, not of art, but of community, the loss of history and of writing as the ground of history – that loss in this world is a kind of death'.[26] The connection between community, history and writing is central to Acker's definition of living art, and its political engagement in the world. Rather than consigning revolutions to dusty archives, Acker sees them as brimming full of potential towards the transformation of the present.

In his introduction to Arendt's *On Revolution* (1963), Jonathan Schell writes of the confusion of the reader who struggles to comprehend that *The Origins of Totalitarianism* and *On Revolution* are the works of just one author.[27] In *The Origins*, Arendt sought to understand the rampant evil embedded in the totalitarian movements of Hitler's Nazism and Stalin's communism, and how such evil remained a threat to the modern world. Accordingly, she grappled with questions such as: '*What happened? Why did it happen? How could it have happened?*'[28] In a totalitarian world, Arendt suggested, the space for spontaneity, and the capacity to begin anew, had both been extirpated. In 1963, Arendt continued her critique of totalitarianism with her book *Eichman in Jerusalem*, but then she published *On Revolution* the same year. In it, her attention turned away from the totalitarian consequences of modernity, to something else: to modernity's democratic impulses that she identified in the true 'action in concert' she saw in revolutionary movements.[29]

How can we explain this change in focus? While the historical circumstances that prompted *The Origins* are clear, Schell occupies himself with tracing this new spirit, which was first put on display in Arendt's *The Human Condition* (1958) and blossomed into a full-blown analysis of collective action a few years later in *On Revolution*. Schell suggests that this change can best be understood against the backdrop of the 'fresh event' of the Hungarian Revolution in 1956 against the Soviet-installed Hungarian communist government. These events helped 'crystallize' the new strands of thought in Arendt's work.[30] For Arendt, Hungary's spontaneous revolt against Soviet rule was a relief; it inspired a far-reaching hope in human action capable of heroic resistance against totalitarianism. While cautious in her enthusiasm, as she immediately started to think of the possible repetitions or new forms of totalitarianism within the triumph of liberal democracy, the Hungarians' revolutionary spirit offered to Arendt a strong model of 'true action in concert'.

The Hungarian October was preceded by the Polish June. This movement was recounted by Acker in her book *My Death My Life by Pier Paolo Pasolini* (1983). 'As a result of the city communications and Cegielski factory workers' unfulfilled demands, the Poznan riots broke out,' she wrote as she told the story of the workers' bloody uprising in Poznan in June 1956, the first instance of the Eastern Bloc rebellion against Soviet rule.[31] The Poznan revolts caused a major political crisis, but were soon brutally suppressed. Within weeks, the world's media attention was to turn away to the more radical Hungarian uprising in October, which during a few days established a new government in the place of the Soviet one. The Hungarian effort was also crushed, but, as Arendt insists, it remains 'a true event whose stature will not depend upon victory or defeat; its greatness is secure in the tragedy it enacted'.[32] The revolt had not only restored Arendt's hope in the survival of elements of the human condition such as spontaneity, collectivity and the desire for freedom in a totalitarian setting, but also inspired her to reflect on other episodes of revolutionary action. Although she never ceased worrying about the evil of totalitarianism – its origins and its threat of return – with *The Human Condition* and most explicitly in *On Revolution*, Arendt had now become actively engaged with the origins and potentialities of revolution. *On Revolution* was part of Arendt's project to revive the democratic spirit of revolutions, and she hoped to inspire its revival in revolution-fearing America. She found the emerging civil rights movement to be rich with revolutionary potential which she strove to inspire.[33]

When Arendt wrote that 'The Hungarian Revolution had taught me a lesson',[34] she suggested that events offer the most provocative foundations for contemporary action, rather than theoretical normalisations of a social reality by the social and political sciences. Her essay 'Totalitarian Imperialism: Reflections on the Hungarian Revolution' (1958), written in the aftermath of events in Hungary, explores this position: 'Events, past and present – not social forces and historical trends, nor questionnaires and motivation research, nor any other gadgets in the arsenal of the social sciences – are the true, the only reliable teachers of political scientists, as they are the most trustworthy source of information for those engaged in politics.'[35] In order to understand how such revolutionary events are a crucial aspect of Acker's politics, it is important to first establish what a revolution is, and how its meaning has evolved over the course of Western history.

The meaning of revolution

The modern understanding of revolution owes much to the French Revolution, with its radical project of inventing new, specifically republican forms of community in a society shaped by a monarchical past. Since 1789, revolutionary action has promised the prospect of irreversible historical change. Noel Parker defines modern revolution as 'an exemplary instance of the *modern experience of change*', namely, a powerful tool for bringing about a new social order.[36] The defining features of a modern revolution include a 'sudden, profound, deliberately provoked crisis about legitimate power over a society, tending to produce an upheaval and change in both the political and social spheres'.[37] In the modern sense, revolutions connote a violent, often uncontrollable rupture with the past, new social and political beginnings, and the capacity of the human will to reconfigure the future. Yet, the word 'revolution' has a striking etymology that is worth investigating in more depth in order to understand its postmodern articulations more fully. Its original meaning has its roots in astronomy, and it was later used as a metaphor in political discourse, implying the opposite of what revolution is understood to mean by many today.

Until the end of the eighteenth century, 'revolution' referred simply to a rotation, from one state of affairs to another, which could be perfectly repeated from time to time.[38] The word revolution derives from the Latin *revolvere*, 'to turn, roll back', and was originally applied to the cyclical movement of celestial bodies. As Arendt notes in *On Revolution*, 'revolution' developed as an astronomical term indicating a recurring, cyclical movement that metaphorically described the restoration of monarchical power. The word gained increasing importance with Copernicus's radical treatise *De revolutionibus orbium coelestium* (1543), which saw the Earth displaced as the centre of the universe. The inherent Latin meanings of regularity and repetitiveness beyond human control were retained to describe the 'Glorious Revolution' of 1688 – the overthrow of the Stuart dynasty under James II of England in favour of William III and Mary. Despite its name, this event 'was not thought of as a revolution at all, but as a restoration of monarchical power to its former righteousness and glory', as Arendt explains (*OR*, 33).[39] Arendt argues that understanding what revolution meant to the ancient Greeks, Romans and early modern Western culture is the key to learning about the political significance of the French and American Revolutions. Arendt notes that:

> Modern revolutions have little in common with the *mutatio rerum* of Roman history or the στάσις, the civil strife which disturbed the Greek *polis*. We cannot equate them with Plato's μεταβολαί, the quasi-natural transformation of one government into another, or with Polybius's πολιτείων ἀνακύκλωσις, the recurring cycle into which human affairs are bound by reason of their always being driven to extremes. Antiquity was well acquainted with political change and the violence that went with change, but neither of them appeared to it to bring about something altogether new. (*OR*, 11)

The modern association of revolution with novelty and political violence begins as recently as the late 1700s: 'It was only in the course of the eighteenth-century revolutions that men began to be aware that a new beginning could be a political phenomenon, that it could be the result of what men had done and what they could consciously set out to do' (*OR*, 37).

The semantic shift from the old astronomical meaning to the new political metaphor Arendt identifies in a famous exchange on 14 July 1789 between Louis XVI and his messenger, the Duke of Rochefoucauld-Liancourt. On hearing about the fall of the Bastille, the king exclaimed: 'C'est une révolte' ('Is this a revolt')? His messenger corrected him: 'Non, Sire, c'est une révolution' ('No, sir, it's a revolution') (cited in *OR*, 38). When the king declares the storming of the Bastille 'a revolt' he assumes he can 'use his power' and mobilise support to suppress the defiance of authority. However, although Liancourt uses the term 'revolution' in its old political sense – indicating the mirroring of the movements of stars – he suggests that the movement 'was irrevocable and beyond the power of a king' (*OR*, 38). Here, for perhaps the first time, revolution was used 'without any connotation of a backward revolving movement' (*OR*, 37). The emphasis was no longer on the cyclical nature of the event, but its unstoppability (*OR*, 38).

During the French Revolution, Arendt notes, the imagery of celestial bodies was replaced by an entirely new 'watery' and elemental vocabulary. The actors and witnesses of the Revolution coined such metaphors as '*torrent révolutionnaire*', 'the mighty current', a 'stream of "progressing violence"', flowing in the same direction with an ever-increasing rapidity', 'the majestic lava stream', or 'that mighty storm-wind' (*OR*, 39). These metaphors suggest the extent to which the revolutionaries were not in complete control of the new political situation they had created and whose future could not be safely predicted. Observations of the watery, stormy and supernatural landscapes of the French Revolution had led Arendt to link them with the Hegelian rectilinear concept of history as progress, and no longer as a cyclical, ever-recurring movement. The proliferation of weather-related metaphors highlights the strong awareness of change, in contrast with the relatively stable and predictable solar system.

Although the French Revolution's grand aim was to establish equality and liberty for humanity, the gain was not shared by many in the French society. The bourgeoisie grew in power, while the working classes and the peasantry's dissatisfaction increased, spurring attraction towards socialist ideologies. Marx witnessed first-hand the terrible working and living conditions of the Manchester working classes, which he saw as a consequence of the capitalist system. In the climate of brewing radicalism, Marx and Engels outlined their vision of transformation in *The Communist Manifesto* (1848). The text enjoyed only limited readership at that time. Most of the European revolutions of 1848 were suppressed within a year, and the real impact of *The Communist Manifesto* was truly felt from the 1870s revolutions onwards. It conceived the French revolution as a class struggle between the bourgeoisie and the land-owning aristocracy, which resulted in the transition from feudalism to capitalism. The capitalist system, they argued, should then create possibilities for the greater proletarian revolutions to occur, which would abolish private property and establish global communism.

Marx's design of the future revolution to come and the vision of society that followed it differs from anarchist thinkers with whom he was in conflict. The classical anarchists, including Pierre-Joseph Proudhon, Mikhail Bakunin and Peter Kropotkin, proposed a complete abolishment of authority and state and of centrally organised forms associated with them, such as class and the party. The anarchists considered Marx's elaborate talk of revolution happening in stages – with the vanguard proletarian party seizing power, after which the state would supposedly 'wither away' – unrealistic and dangerous, arguing that the revolution would only replace one regime with another. They called instead for the state to be dismantled in a huge upheaval carried out by the broad masses.

The Russian anarchist Bakunin took an active part in the 1848 uprisings, rejecting the notion of a revolutionary professional who designed revolutions from the library. For Bakunin and his followers, revolutions were a result of a spontaneous will of the people rather than being predetermined by historical laws, such as those outlined by Marx. Whereas Marx endorsed the centrally organised proletariat as the revolutionary force, anarchists recognised insurrectional capacity in any oppressed social group, including peasants, students and intellectuals. Bakunin advocated a complete elimination of centralised power, economic or political, proposing in its place voluntary federations of communes and cooperative organisations. 'The urge to destroy is also a creative urge' is his most famous dictum, placing him at the violent, bomb-wielding end of anarchist tradition. The idea was not only to eliminate all governments but also to construct creative spaces for cooperation, about which, like other anarchists, Bakunin was intentionally vague. Bakunin's thinking is fraught with contradictions – while upholding un-hierarchical society as an ideal, he created his own disciplined secret society based on dictatorial rules.[40] These paradoxes aside, Bakunin's anarchist message became a vital source of inspiration for multiple worker movements during the nineteenth and early twentieth centuries. A new wave of interest followed in the years after the Second World War, when Bakunin's faith in the spontaneous rebellion of the people, his faith in the potential of the lumpen proletariat as a revolutionary force, and his rejection of science deeply impressed the young rebels in 1960s America.[41]

Marxists and anarchists both concentrate their efforts on the overthrow of power. As a result, both offer an imprecise vision of a future society. Arendt reverses their emphasis by alerting us to the realities of post-revolutionary order. For Arendt, the tragedy of many revolutions is the waning revolutionary spirit and the inability to sustain the freedom that the revolutionaries strove to assure. For the revolution to be successful, Arendt asserts, there needs to be work towards 'institutionaliz[ing] a freedom which [is] already an accomplished act'.[42] Arendt shifts focus from the social question and class restructuring prioritised by Marx towards political innovation, which leads her to favour the American Revolution over the French one. Unlike America's efforts towards building a constitution, Arendt maintains, the French Revolution was overtaken by the mission to eliminate poverty, to the detriment of creating lasting institutions that would allow democracy to flourish. The challenge was to make the spontaneous revolutionary spirit durable, by preserving it through institutions and incorporating it into the human experience.

This apparent celebration of the American Revolution with its political concerns was considered a controversial step by many scholars, who accused Arendt of conservatism and elitism for ignoring the underprivileged. Moreover, Marxist historians tend to interpret the American and French Revolutions as driven by bourgeois self-interest, viewing their constitutions as documents securing property rights of the elite uncommitted to democratic outcomes. But according to Arendt, Marxists neglect the politically creative elements of the American Revolution, which, in her mind, in the long run are more radical than the socio-economic restructuring that took place in the French Revolution and the communist revolts modelled on it. The sociological and Marxist approach, Arendt argued, was too obsessed with the social causes of events, and predetermined people's behaviour in response to social forces. Instead, Arendt was interested in areas where people can think and act independently of the social situation. In the words of Daniel Gordon, for Arendt 'The purpose of revolution is to forge an open political and dialogical space in which the revolutionaries and their heirs can exercise free thought and action.'[43] According to Arendt, the American Revolution has been excluded from the revolutionary tradition for not having grown out of the same social questions that drove events in France. Arendt saw in the American Revolution an ultimately unfulfilled opportunity to establish a lasting institutional space as a basis for freedom in which citizens could participate. Yet this '[f]ailure to remember' the American Revolution, Arendt maintains, 'is largely responsible for the intense fear of revolution in America' (*OR*, 208).

The French Revolution marked the shift towards a linear understanding of revolutionary change, but, like the modern revolutions that followed it, it remained haunted by the drama of repetition. As Lynn Hunt has noted, the French revolutionaries were simultaneously shaped by voluntarism and determinism. Although they 'believed they were breaking with the past and thought that they could mould the future in accordance with their new principles', Hunt maintains, the 'events also showed that this voluntarism would inevitably run into the obstacles thrown up by social inertia. The future, it turned out, had many deep connections to the past despite the desire for rupture.'[44] What the revolutionaries feared and sought to suppress was precisely the cyclical return to the original point of historical rupture. When the new French society named their babies after classical heroes, and rechristened the centres of the rebellion employing symbols from antiquity, their intention was not to revolve back to and restore the Roman Empire but to replace the emblems of the Ancient Regime.[45] Hunt writes: 'The festivals employed costumes, symbols, and ceremonial forms from Antiquity, not in order to link up with the past but in order to jump over the French past to a time of new beginnings, of innocence, and authenticity.'[46]

The drama of repetition is reflected in two orders of temporality in Marx: a linear unfolding of the communist idea laid out in *The Communist Manifesto*, and the repetitive temporality of bourgeois revolutions he describes in *The Eighteenth Brumaire of Louis Bonaparte* (1852), in which Marx mocks the ability of the bourgeois revolutionaries to make an absolute break with the past. The present is compelled to repeat the past, not as tragedy, but as farce, wrote Marx. Marx writes that the 'social revolution of the nineteenth century cannot create its poetry from the past', like the previous revolutions did, 'but only from the future'.[47] From the beginning, then, modern revolutions have been 'haunted by the ghost of revolution in its pre-modern sense',[48] as Peter Starr has observed. The drive for novelty, rebirth and total transformation appears to be accompanied by the shadow of an abortively cyclical return to an old regime which could re-emerge in different forms. As a result, the French Revolution produced a contradictory legacy, having given birth to both democracy and terror.

While the French Revolution became a prototype for other modern revolutions, the revolutions that followed often differed in nature, involving diverse historical agents. The spread of communism and battles for liberation in colonised areas instigated further mutations of the revolutionary 'script'. The more recent studies of revolutions follow Arendt in their rejection of the sociological approach indebted to Marx. The contributors to the volume *Scripting Revolution: A Historical Approach to the Comparative Study of Revolutions* (2015) agree that sociology overemphasises the socio-economic conflict as a basis for revolution, while neglecting to account for what propels revolutionary imagination. They suggest that the historical studies have largely ignored the impact revolutions have on each other, failing to consider 'a defining feature of revolutions and of revolutionary history – namely, the self-conscious awareness with which revolutionaries model their actions on those of revolutions past'.[49] They propose instead to approach revolutions as 'a script played and replayed, improvised upon and extended in different times and places, but nevertheless possessing a degree of narrative continuity and analytical identity'.[50] Thus the revolutions that followed the French revolution improvised on the original revolutionary theme: 'Marx rewrote the script of the French Revolution; Lenin revised Marx; Mao revised Lenin; and so on and so forth,' and so 'the script can be replayed indefinitely, but also be changed, adopted or even subverted'.[51]

1968: revolution in the revolution

'Run, comrade, the old world is behind you!' is one of the slogans that marked the walls of Paris during the May revolts in 1968. It draws on the writings of the Situationist International, a group of radical Leftist thinkers and artists active between 1957 and 1972 who played a significant part in the events of 1968. The Situationists and their collaborators frequently employed the phrase 'old world' to refer to the 'spectacular' world of consumerism, oppression, dehumanisation and alienation that they rejected.[52] This wall-writing typified the atmosphere of spontaneous, utopia-driven insurgency by students and blue-collar workers who filled the streets of Paris in mass protest. The social upheaval was propelled by the genuine belief of the participants in the total upheaval of the established regime. The vocabulary used to describe the events conjured up familiar supernatural and catastrophic images of the 1789 Revolution when the revolutionaries spoke of lava, fire, hurricanes and the whirlpools of revolution. It was the 'year of the first cracks' in the wall of de Gaulle's regime, as Pascal Ory and Jean-François Sirinelli have described it,[53] as it marked a significant interruption in the grand narrative of post-war history, when a modern democratic nation courted the possibility of a Leftist revolt by staging the longest general strike in twentieth-century Europe.

The French May was part of a worldwide revolutionary movement, which almost simultaneously erupted elsewhere in Europe, parts of North and West Africa, across the United States, Latin America, Vietnam, China and Japan.[54] Nineteen sixty-eight – the year of the surprise Tet Offensive in Vietnam, the Chicago Convention, the Czech Prague Spring, the March student protests in Poland, the height of the Cultural Revolution in China, the beginning of the Troubles in Ireland – signposts a series of extraordinary, dramatic or tragic events crowding around it and far-ranging social, political and cultural transformations that passed through it. They shared their unexpectedness, dramatic character, anarchist rhetoric and lack of planning and organisation. As observed by Mark Kurlansky, 'people were rebelling over disparate issues and had in common only that desire to rebel, ideas about how to do it, a sense of alienation from the established order and a profound distaste for authoritarianism'.[55] Looking back at the events a decade later, Eric Hobsbawm systematised the tumultuous era as occurring in three zones: the uprisings of the capitalist West, the revolutions in socialist nations, and the 'anti-imperialist' struggles of the 'third world', represented respectively by France, Czechoslovakia and Vietnam.[56]

Acker's work is preoccupied with all three zones of the global context of the 1960s and its legacy, giving expression to these events' global, kaleidoscopic and cross-inspirational character. The Algerian War, the Cultural Revolution in China, the anti-communist uprisings of Polish students and workers: these are just some of the more distant locations that Acker brings into proximity with rebels at American campuses. Not only were the 1960s movements in the West inspired by the revolutionary movements of the third world such those in Vietnam, Cuba and China, but they also recycled the long revolutionary script, modelling themselves, in political aspirations, on the 1848 revolutionaries, the Parisian Communards and Russian and Spanish anarchists. The third-world nations, in turn, recycled scripts from the European revolutionary past – the communist leader Mao Zedong, the leader of the Cultural Revolution in China, made direct references to the Paris Commune.

Raising expectations of a groundbreaking social and political transformation, the 1960s revolutions started off in a strictly modern sense, entailing the rejection of the 'old world' in order to give birth to 'a new world'. The vocabulary used to describe the events continues to be dominated by the familiar images of unstoppable powers of nature. Yet for all its quintessentially modern beginnings, 1968 marks a significant modification in revolutionary form: it was 'a revolution in the revolution'.[57] The sixties radicalism decomposed the modern revolutionary script of the Old Left faithful to Soviet Marxism and the Soviet Union, in which change was centred on the acquisition of power and subsequent requirement of conformity. Orthodox Marxism's sweeping visions of history and one-directional programme of transformation – with its prioritisation of the working class, elevation of the hierarchical party as an organisational model and leader-oriented projects – gave way to the turbulent dynamic of new politics embraced by the formations of the New Left, which favoured anarchism, spontaneity, reflexivity, immediacy, experimentation, self-organisation, diversity, locality and individual freedom. The Beat writers' ideas of peace and love, alternative ways of life, free sexuality and experiments in mind-expanding drugs influenced many, fuelling the cultural revolution in post-war America. The young activists of the decade no longer believed that it was enough to acquire power to bring about lasting change, but a more profound re-evaluation of social and political values and culture was needed. Moving beyond the Old Left's concerns, the radicals reacted against the authoritarian structures of society, alienation, economic injustice, the prevailing ideologies of the government, educational institutions, corporate America and military forces. The Old Left's grand scheme of transformation gave way to multiple concurrent narratives of anti-war, feminism, gay rights, immigrant and environmental movements, for which the civil rights movement provided a blueprint. Todd Gitlin points out that 'without the civil rights movement, the beat and Old Left and bohemian enclaves would not have opened into a revived politics', instead remaining a mere 'transitional subculture of the young, a rite of passage on the route to normal adulthood'.[58]

The New Left activists took up ideas of Herbert Marcuse, the Frankfurt School philosopher, who theorised emancipatory possibilities and called for rebellion against bureaucracy in his essays and best-selling books such as *Eros and Civilisation* (1954) and *One-Dimensional Man* (1964). Marcuse's view that modern, consumption-oriented people had lost their ability to rebel and control their lives struck a chord with the American counterculture of the 1960s. Acker acknowledged her defiant political stance as indebted to Marcuse and considered him her mentor and inspiration. She stated repeatedly in interviews that in order to continue their academic relationship she followed him from Brandeis University to the University of California, San Diego.[59] There she joined the Students for Democratic Society (SDS). It was the first and the most visible movement of the New Left, whose manifesto, the Port Huron statement, laid out the ethos of 'participatory democracy'.

Left-wing radicalism was met with hostility from the conservative authorities, which Ronald Reagan orchestrated. He supported America's war in Vietnam, opposed women's liberation and confronted radical students and their radical tutors. Before capturing the White House, while serving as governor of California, he crudely mocked the folk aesthetics of the sixties in an attempt to reduce them to a student frenzy towards sexual liberation and to associate them with America's enemy. He was quoted as calling the Berkeley university campus in California (which became a centre of radical political activism of the late sixties) 'a haven for communist sympathizers, protesters and sex deviants'. Stirring into violent action, on 15 May 1969, then-Governor Reagan sent police officers into People's Park near the Berkeley campus to quell the protesters. At that time Marcuse kept receiving death threats, and eventually lost his position as a lecturer at the University of California, after being denounced by Reagan for 'complicity in campus violence'.[60]

Acker would fictionalise these events in *My Death My Life by Pier Paolo Pasolini*, where the government's suppression of American protests is discussed alongside anti-Soviet worker and student protests of 1956 and 1958 in Poland. 'All Polish students think about is sex',[61] the narrator provokingly asserts, and tells us how in both contexts – capitalist America and Soviet-occupied Poland – brutal propaganda campaigns were employed to reduce the revolts to mere spectacles of the workers' uncivilised provocations and students' irresponsibility in order to strip them of political significance. Marcuse and his student followers are dismissed as criminals: 'In San Diego: Marcuse lived in fear of his life. Whenever we were in a car, the cops stopped the car because, they said, we were bank robbers.' In effect, the philosophy and sociology departments were closed and 'The ruling elite stuck its own people into the now vacant university positions.'[62]

Marcuse was the most active member of the Frankfurt School in terms of relating critical theory to political practice, and rebellious students chanted 'Marx, Mao, Marcuse', linking him with the world's most influential revolutionary figures. In his affirmation of the global student revolts of the late sixties, he wrote that they represented 'a protest against the entire system of values, against the entire system of objectives, against the entire system of performances required and practiced in the established society'.[63] Whereas, as we have seen, orthodox Marxism championed the working class as the revolutionary force, Marcuse recognised the instruments of radical social change in new minority organisations, outsiders and radical intelligentsia. Oppositional proletariat, Marcuse argued, lost its transformative potency, because they had a vested interest in the capitalist system.[64] Therefore, models offered by Maoism, third world movements and anarchism provided an alternative inspiration to the New Left. By the late seventies Marcuse had revised his glorified view of the counterculture, accepting its limitations and recognising that the involvement of the masses, and the mobilisation of the working class in particular, was necessary for total revolutionary upheaval to take place.

The morning after

During the events of 1968, new politics and alternative ways of living seemed achievable. However, the revolutionaries did not manage to escape the 'old world' for longer than several months to a couple of years. In France, the tide had turned with the re-election of the de Gaulle government and subsequent restoration of the previous order, inaugurating a lasting period of disenchantment with revolutionary politics and a subsequent shift to post-Marxism.

The perceived failure of the 1960s revolts in the Western world produced a further re-evaluation of the Marxist model of revolution and the political vision of the world that had crystallised around it – a dissident tendency which has come to be associated with postmodernism. In *The Condition of Postmodernity* (1990), David Harvey identifies the events of 1968 as proto-postmodern: a full-blown, bifurcating, incoherent anti-modern movement that culminates in 'the global turbulence of 1968', which, though failing to bring the expected revolution, must be 'viewed [. . .] as the cultural and political harbinger of the subsequent turn to postmodernism'.[65]

The overall reception of this mass 'street theatre', to which it is now often reduced, has been negative. Conservatives in America and France have persistently argued that the 1960s brought the social order into abysmal anarchy as the revolutionaries focused merely on the destruction of institutions, while lacking any clear goals for reform. Ardent critics of the events have also stressed the nihilistic, individualistic and anti-political tendencies of the 1960s revolts and have pointed out that the participants achieved the opposite of what they set out to achieve.

The academic left has attempted to formulate its own coherent model for understanding the collapse of the New Left's movements and the counterculture generally. One argument is that government repression caused the decline of the New Left. Another is that the movements fragmented into a number of factions which lacked cohesion and a common goal. But David Barber points out that the success of the government's intervention depended on the movements' weaknesses. The New Left movements also had multiple practical divisions from the start, and the real reasons for the defeat are to be found elsewhere. For Barber, the defeat had more to do with the white New Left radicals' failure to challenge their white middle-class attitudes towards race, gender, homosexuality, class and nation. They came to mirror the values of mainstream society, no longer representing the 'left'.[66] Acker herself decided to withdraw her membership from the SDS when she realised that it had become 'very elitist'.[67]

The co-optation argument, in turn, relates youth revolt to the market forces. It posits that capital preys on and appropriates the countercultural ethos of individuality, authenticity, antiauthoritarianism and freedom. This is precisely Christopher Gair's point when he describes the way in which corporate co-optation deprived the 1950s and 1960s revolts of their original insurrectionary content – the extensive threat they posed to the dominant conservative order – and turned emblems of youth protest such as subversive music and clothing, and even drugs, into commodities.[68]

But the distinction between counterculture and the capitalist system has never been pure. As Harvey points out, 'Any political movement that holds individual freedoms to be sacrosanct is vulnerable to incorporation into the neoliberal fold.'[69] In Harvey's assessment, the 1968 movement had incompatible objectives: personal freedom and social justice. The two are difficult to combine because the former elevates individual wants and desires and finds the state and institutions oppressive, while the latter requires the sacrifice of personal needs to achieve solidarity, community and institutional change in order to deal with social concerns such as poverty, access to education and health care. The neoliberal rhetoric, Harvey asserts, with its foundational emphasis on individual freedoms, 'has the power to split off libertarianism, identity politics, multiculturalism, and narcissistic consumerism from the social forces'.[70]

Yet for Joseph Heath, Andrew Potter and other ardent critics of the counterculture, the hippie ideology and capitalist economy have been always not in conflict but in harmony: 'The crucial point is that (contrary to rumour) the hippies did not sell out.' Rather, they argue, 'There simply never was any tension between the countercultural ideas that informed the '60s rebellion and the ideological requirements of the capitalist system.'[71] The '68-ers are thus blamed for the spread of rampant individualistic consumerism of the following decades, and for accommodating the spirit of neoliberalism.

For America and Britain, the early 1970s was a tumultuous period of political and socio-economic transition: the wave of political corruption peaked with Nixon's resignation in 1974; the war in Vietnam ended a year later; the revolutionary left was defeated and political thinking took a dramatic shift to the right. The exhaustion of the Fordist model, the series of economic crises originating in oil shocks and deindustrialisation (of which unemployment and stagflation were the symptoms) were the conditions under which neoliberalism developed from a relatively minor theoretical trend to a cultural hegemony, replacing the post-war social-democratic consensus.

Punk is a fuelled response to these transitions.[72] In the mid-1970s, Acker aligned herself with the punks' rejection of what the hippie counterculture stood for. The countercultural ideas of free love and community became exhausted. Their subversion proved not radical enough, and hippies increasingly associated themselves with the corporate world. Turning to punk, Margaret Henderson asserts, allowed Acker to attend to those revolutionary aims that were unaddressed by the US counterculture and associated art practices.[73] Punk becomes the vehicle for Acker to articulate a fierce feminist voice which challenges the mainstream values of the counterculture, and in particular the 'hegemonic and countercultural gender identity, patriarchy, and heterosexual desire'.[74] Acker's short story 'New York City in 1979' makes the counterculture's failings most explicit. Hippies are described here as 'rich' as they arrive in a limousine, hoping to get into a fashionable artists' club.[75] They clearly fail to transcend capitalist consumerism. Rather, their ideas of free love have become fused with it: 'The sex product presents a naturally expanding market. Now capitalists are doing everything they can to bring world sexual desire to an unbearable edge.'[76]

Punk dismisses the countercultural ideal of utopian communities separate from the mainstream as naive. Instead, 'punk accepts that there is no outside to the system, and hence one can either critique it with anarchic disrespect, or attempt to exploit the system'.[77] Richard Hell, one of the founders of the punk music scene that included the Ramones, Television, The Voidoids and Patti Smith, notes that what 'separates Punk from previous anti-establishment youth movements is that Punks were a little cynical themselves from the very beginning, or at least wary of underestimating even their own self-serving impulses'.[78] It is thus hardly surprising that there are many overlaps between Downtown writing, punk poetics and postmodernism, and this shared sensibility offers both possibilities and limitations in reading Acker's politics. Punk is increasingly received not as a raging attack on the conservative culture of neoliberalism, but more as a symptom of it or even a direct contribution to it.[79] Robert Siegle asserts that punks approached their predecessors the Beats with both admiration and caution, all too aware of the vulnerability of the countercultural spirit to corporate co-optation.[80] Just as punk substitutes the utopian component that defined the spirit of the '60s counterculture with the raging anger and negativity of 'no future', Downtown writers apparently give up on grand visions of liberation in favour of what Siegle has described as 'hit-and-run guerrilla action'.[81] Downtown writers abandon utopian imagination, finding alternative worlds no longer conceivable, as there is no escape from reification and repression.[82]

This heightened self-consciousness similarly characterised the Downtown writing scene with which Acker is associated, whose works shared many stylistic traits with punk. In his reading of punk characters in Burroughs and Acker, Lee Konstantinou warns against the trap of reading punk simply as falling victim to the market forces. Because punk opposes administered life by centralised state power, and elevates a self-sufficient self-managing individual outside of institutions, rather than being anti-capitalistic, it ironically 'helped reorganize or reinvent the spirit of capitalism.'[83] The punk enemy was not capitalism as such, but the old kind of capitalism that was bound with the state. 'Far from having no future', Konstantinou argues, 'punk helped make the [neoliberal] future.'[84] Read this way, punk suffers the fate of a hippie, but sells out more inevitably and cynically. Punks' rejection of utopia encapsulated in the slogan 'no future' can thus be seen as not a threat but a contribution towards Thatcher's conservative hegemony of 'there is no alternative'.

By 1984 – the Orwellian year and an oppositional pairing with the hopeful 1968 – the conservative turn was consolidated by Reagan's re-election with his 'Morning in America' campaign. The spread of AIDS was having a devastating impact on the arts community. The East Village was increasingly commercialised. Thatcher and Reagan endowed Britons and Americans with a sense of 'the meaning of the eighties', championing capitalism, facilitating a service economy in place of the manufacturing industry, promoting the individual and the family, authoritarian leadership and hostility towards 'welfarism'. The waves of optimism and economic prosperity connoted with rightist Reaganomics and Thatcherism of the 1980s were a welcome reaction against the now nagging and tiring legacy of the sixties. Most Americans happily buried the 1960s' radicalism, naivety and permissiveness which degenerated into the 1970's despair, defeatism and pessimism.

Things did not fare better for the revolutionary left in France. In the aftermath of May 1968, an uprising which many leading French politicians came to perceive in terms of 'failure', the very concept of politics was redefined and the possibility of a political mobilisation questioned.[85] Following the 1960s revolts, revolution thus underwent further modification, to become connoted with failure. Modern revolutions as 'deliberate pursuits of change', to use Parker's definition, are now commonly seen to end in failure since they do not produce significant change, or because they trigger a series of unintended consequences. Peter Starr, in his 1995 study *Logics of Failed Revolt: French Theory after 1968*, has observed that the central focus of postmodern French theory after May 1968 (represented mainly by Jacques Lacan, Roland Barthes, Julia Kristeva, Hélène Cixous and Jacques Derrida) was now to explain 'the failure of revolutionary action'.[86] With reference to the pre-modern meaning of revolution, Starr proposes that these theorists were fascinated with the ghostly return of revolution as repetition, which ultimately produced little in the way of political change.[87]

In *1968: From Revolution to Ethics*, Julian Bourg challenges the evaluation of the May revolts' energies according to what they promised and what they failed to deliver. Instead, he demonstrates that the cultural memory of the May crisis neglects its less straightforward, unintended consequences, which, he argues, necessarily point to an ambiguous renewal of ethical discourse during the 1970s. Bourg contends that the 1968 revolts changed the concept of revolution by shifting it to the register of ethics. In response to the apparent impossibility of institutional overthrow, intellectual questions no longer concerned changing the world, but how to live in the world that we have, how to transform our relation to institutions, to the state, and to humanity:

> In the years after 1968, France did experience a revolution. In 1968 that word – *revolution* – was on everyone's lips. By the early 1980s and especially by the 1990s, everywhere one turned, there was talk of *ethics*. What had been revolutionised was the very notion of revolution itself.[88]

The fascination with ethics which followed the perceived failure of the May revolts replaced the modern fascination with radical politics and, in part, has led to the de-radicalisation of political intellectual discourse. The theorists who came to prominence in the wake of the May events – usually associated with the label of postmodernism, albeit sometimes unfairly and ambivalently – include Jean Baudrillard, Roland Barthes, Cornelius Castoriadis, Hélène Cixous, Régis Debray, Gilles Deleuze, Jacques Derrida, Michel Foucault, Luce Irigaray, Julia Kristeva, Henri Lefebvre, Jean-François Lyotard, Nicos Poulantzas, and Paul Virilio. Although this group is far from homogeneous, their political and philosophical concerns revolved around issues of power, difference, disintegration and decentring, language, origin, and the valorisation of spatiality and nonlinear desire as opposed to historical progress.

Nick Hewlett similarly argues that since the early 1970s, theory in France has registered a break with the emancipatory tradition. He insists that poststructuralism should be understood as 'part of the process of intellectual depoliticization, of the departure from the tradition of a close relationship between theory and practice'.[89] Although poststructuralism is radical in its methodology, for Hewlett, 'its political consequences are not necessarily radical by any means'.[90] In the postmodern orientation where power is diffused, and the self is fragmented and contingent, human agency and the potency for a real intervention in the material world seem impossible to locate.

In many ways, the intellectual conservatism of poststructuralism's critique of Western rationalism, with its crude rejection of such concepts as authenticity, value and truthfulness, has prepared the ground for a rethinking of socio-political change across post-Marxist contexts. Hewlett observes a gradual restoration of belief in radical transformation among the next generation of post-Marxist thinkers. His *Badiou, Balibar, Rancière: Rethinking Emancipation* (2007) traces a renewal of the radical emancipatory tradition in the early years of the twenty-first century both in France and beyond, which coincides with the growing popularity of thinkers such as Alain Badiou, Etienne Balibar and Jacques Rancière. Their intellectual position continues to be profoundly affected by a strong heritage of human struggle for emancipation expressed through democratising revolutionary events in world history. While these philosophers operate within non-postmodern concepts, reviving ideas of truth, passion, belief, universality, revolution and political subjectivity, their ideas, rather than nostalgic turns to unchecked idealism, remain inflected by the lessons of poststructural critical discourse.

With apparent poststructuralists such as Deleuze and Guattari, they share their fascination with the possibilities occasioned by the event.

Against Thermidorian reaction: Badiou, Deleuze and Guattari on the event

The idea of the event is intrinsic to the fundamental questions of philosophy such as: why do things happen? What is the nature of change? As Iain MacKenzie points out, 'any attempt at a full survey of the role played by the event in philosophy would almost be tantamount to a history of philosophy itself'.[91] Indeed, the endeavour to understand the nature of the event goes back to the change versus being debate of the pre-Socratics, and Heraclitus's famous statement that 'Upon those who step into the same rivers different and ever different waters flow down' – which was taken to mean that everything is in a constant flux. By contrast, Parmenides claimed that 'all is one', and that change and motion are mere appearances of a single eternal reality. Philosophy has considered the event as a foundational concept embedded in these two orientations of change (or becoming) versus being, yet its separate treatment has returned only recently to the centre of philosophical discussion and political theory.

The revival of evental theories in France in the late twentieth century began as a response to the eruption of revolutionary energy during the 1960s and continues to be a vital part of May 1968's ambiguous legacy. In the mid-1970s, many French intellectuals distanced themselves from the May events and turned instead to political conservatism, a group that in turn came to be labelled the *Nouveaux Philosophes*.[92] Badiou compares their renunciation of revolutionary activism to the Thermidorian reaction, a term used to describe Robespierre's infamous reign of terror during the French Revolution. In Badiou's view, a Thermidorian is not just any political reactionary but a distinctive type of conservative, whose passion for the event in which they once believed ceases and is turned back against that event. In contrast to the subject that is 'faithful' to the event, a Thermidorian 'renounces his revolutionary enthusiasm and sells his rallying to the order of proprietors'.[93] Like Badiou, Deleuze and Guattari have never recanted the revolutionary spirit of May 1968, being highly critical of the conservative positions of the *Nouveaux Philosophes* and those who view the uprising as yet another instance of a failed revolt.

The works of Deleuze, Guattari[94] and Badiou[95] are among the most important theoretical-philosophical options currently available for a politics of liberation. Their contributions to the theorisation of the (political) event were each profoundly influenced by the May revolt. However, as Badiou notes in his reading of Deleuze in *Logics of Worlds*, their approaches to the event are fundamentally different and apparently irreconcilable. As Badiou states: 'The notion is central in Deleuze, just as it is in my own endeavour. But what a contrast!' (*LW*, 382). While the Deleuzian concept of the event strictly correlates to the concepts of becoming, the fold and creative repetition, Badiou's event rests on the possibility of a rupture in the order of being, or a radical break with the past. Unlike Deleuze, who thinks 'that the new is a fold of the past', Badiou prefers to think of events as 'absolute beginnings'.[96]

Rather than consider their arguments as disjunction, as if one must decide between what appear to be dramatically opposed formulations of events,[97] I follow Hollis Phelps and other scholars who reconsider their relationship in terms of possibility and conjunction.[98] Keeping in mind the irreconcilable differences between them, it is possible and worthwhile to trace certain paths and options that result from their *rapprochement* with regard to emancipation.

In conjunctural terms, Deleuze, Guattari and Badiou's notion of a political event exceeds the logic of failure and success and the cause-and-effect ordering by historians and political analysts. What Deleuze and Guattari label 'macropolitics' does not account for 'micropolitics' – the non-measurable and nonlinear 'molecular' flows and becomings that accompany events. 'May 1968 in France was molecular', they claim, 'making what led up to it all the more imperceptible from the viewpoint of macropolitics' (*TP*, 216). For Deleuze and Guattari, the power of the event is specified in terms of micropolitics, particularly by opposing history to 'becoming'. They argue that: '"Becoming" does not belong to history. [. . .] What History grasps of the event is its effectuation in states of affairs or in lived experience, but the event in its becoming, in its specific consistency, in its self-positing concept, escapes History.'[99] Deleuze reproaches Thermidorians for being blind to the 'non-historical cloud' of becoming that transcends historical context:

> It's fashionable these days to condemn the horrors of revolution. It's nothing new; English Romanticism is permeated by reflections on Cromwell very similar to present-day reflections on Stalin. They say revolutions turn out badly. But they're constantly confusing

two different things, the way revolutions turn out historically and people's revolutionary becoming. These relate to two different sets of people. Men's only hope lies in a revolutionary becoming: the only way of casting off their shame or responding to what is intolerable.[100]

In Deleuze and Guattari's notion of a political event, becoming is thought of together with repetition which, far from being opposed to the emergence of the new, is the condition for the continuous production of difference immanent in the constitution of events. The key to unravelling the paradox of the new emerging by means of repetition is through the distinction between the two mutually exclusive yet corresponding modes of the real: the virtual and the actual. Deleuze characterises any actual event as containing a virtual dimension which is 'always forthcoming and already past'.[101] Rather than an imperfect incarnation of the perfect virtual form, the actual is the realm where virtual events manifest themselves as novel, singular occurrences, which in his *Logic of Sense* (1990) he calls 'accidents'. He cautions against assuming that accidents are the essences of events. Instead, they are signs indicating that the event has been produced. In the words of Deleuze: 'The event is not what occurs (an accident), it is rather inside what occurs, the purely expressed.'[102] In this sense, repetition is a creative transformation of the event, 'the power of beginning and beginning again'.[103] Thus the virtual dimension always expresses itself in different actualities, such as the French Revolution, or the Russian Revolution of 1917.

With reference to Deleuze's concept of creative repetition, Slavoj Žižek notes that: 'What repetition repeats is not the ways the past "effectively was" but the *virtuality* inherent to the past and betrayed by its past actualization. [. . .] [T]he emergence of the New changes [. . .] the balance between actuality and virtuality in the past.'[104] Since for Deleuze repetition is a transformative, productive process thought of in terms of becoming and not a matter of repeating the same over and again (as in Platonist theory), he calls for the repetition of the event because he sees in this process the possibility of reinvention. This imbues repetition with an explicitly political dimension, because, for Deleuze, the emergence of new events such as the revolts of 1968 inevitably involves the possibility of new social and subjective configurations. Deleuze acknowledges that:

In historical phenomena such as the revolution of 1789, the Commune, the revolution of 1917, there is always one part of the *event* that is irreducible to any social determinism, or to causal chains. Historians are not very fond of this aspect: they restore causality after the fact. Yet the event is itself a splitting off from, or a breaking with causality; it is a bifurcation, a deviation with respect to laws, an unstable condition which opens up a new field of the possible.[105]

While Deleuze's conception of the event explicates an 'origami universe' – at once enfolding and unfolding, connecting and becoming, repeating – the event for Badiou conjures up a world of fireworks.[106] For Badiou, first and foremost, the event is an explosion, a cut, a surprise that comes out of the blue, an incomprehensible rupture in continuity and a separation from being. In other words, the event is the extraordinary moment of rupture which shatters the status quo and in so doing creates the possibility of bringing a different world into being.

Badiou maintains that in order to properly ground the 'intelligence of change' through the event as a rupture in being, one needs to look to set theory, a fundamental branch of mathematics elaborated by Georg Cantor and developed by Zermelo-Fraenkel's axiomatisation in the early twentieth century.[107] One of the central tenets in *Being and Event* is the claim that mathematics has ontological bearings because it helps identify the multiple as properly absolute and thus establish the 'laws of being' (axioms) without resorting to interpretation. Instead of any constituent reference to difference, which comprises Deleuze's method, in Badiou, 'what comes to ontological thought is the multiple without any other predicate other than its multiplicity. Without any other concept than itself, and without anything to guarantee its consistency.'[108] Foreclosed from any other relation, *being* is conceived here as an unlimited pure multiplicity founded on nothing but itself, which leads Badiou to link it with the bare concept of the void. In set theory, the void, also called the empty set symbolised by Ø, is a set that contains no elements and thus cannot be 'presented' in a situation. Presentation is an organising activity of ordering or counting so that the multiple is made consistent by being structured into a collection of sets. The resulting organised product, a 'consistent presented multiplicity, thus: a multiple [. . .], and a regime of the count-as-one [. . .], or structure', Badiou calls a *situation* (*BE*, 522). Thus, ontology provides the rules for the formation of any ordered multiple-ones out of the chaotic pure multiple. According to Badiou, in ontology 'there is nothing [that is, a void] apart from situations' (*BE*, 25). He writes that any situation is founded on the exclusion of the void, and the task of ontology is accounting for the prohibition on the void ever being presented in situations. On a political level, this means that the state, which Badiou deliberately links with the technical term 'state *of the situation*', exists to sustain pre-existing class interests, and is concerned with excluding any possibility of a different, more egalitarian way of being from emerging: '*the State always re-presents what has already been presented*' (*BE*, 106; author's emphasis).

How then, does Badiou relate his notion of the event to a maths-based ontology? He sets out to demonstrate that mathematical formalism cannot account for historical situations which contain events.[109] This is because events are 'points of excess' and are attached to the void of every situation. Since events are outside the realm of ontology, it is philosophy's task to isolate and give support to the emergences of such non-ontological concepts as the event, truth or subject. Badiou departs from the ontological confines of 'being as being', defining the event instead as comprising 'on the one hand, elements of the site; and on the other hand, itself (the event)', thus making the event self-referential (*BE*, 506). However, according to the foundational axiom of Zermelo-Fraenkel set theory, a set cannot contain itself as a member. In these terms, an event would therefore be an abnormal set because it violates this fundamental rule and does not comply with the hierarchical nature of set theory. Moreover, since an event is 'forbidden', 'ontology rejects it as "that-which-is-not-being-qua-being"' (*BE*, 184). For Badiou, what happens in an event such as the French Revolution is thus the 'collapse of foundation, i.e., the insurrection of the unfounded', or a 'destabilization of the ordinary universe'.[110] Above all, an event is 'purely hazardous, and [that] which cannot be inferred from the situation' (*BE*, 193). While the situation is restructured to the procedure of count-as-one, every event is 'supernumerary' (*BE*, 178), absolutely unpredictable and it is impossible to decide whether or not it belongs to the situation, and this is why Badiou often refers to the event as 'the undecidable'. In contrast to the state (of situation), evental politics is committed to the excessive equity that the state suppresses: 'politics stakes its existence on its capacity to establish a relation to both the void and excess which is essentially different from that of the State; it is this difference alone that subtracts politics from the one of statist re-insurance' (*BE*, 110). It is only through the rupture of the event that emerges on the edge of the void that there can be a genuine novelty in being, a chance to begin from scratch, to interrupt the order of continuity and inevitability.

Badiou's theoretical premise rests upon the idea that true politics takes the form of an event, which for him is virtually synonymous with the broad concept of revolution. Invigorated by the events of May 1968, to which he frequently refers, Badiou insists that any radical transformation is inseparable from the interventions in the material world by the collective and rebellious actions of ordinary people. According to Badiou, politics begins in disorder and a sudden rupture in the status quo as part of a three-way process: event-subject-truth. In this case, the truth of the event resides in the subject's militant fidelity to the implications of the event:

> A subject is nothing other than an active fidelity to the event of truth. This means that a subject is a militant of truth. [. . .] The militant of a truth is not only the political militant working for the emancipation of humanity in its entirety. He or she is also the artist-creator, the scientist who opens up a new theoretical field, or the lover whose world is enchanted. (*BE*, xiii)[111]

In political terms, individuals become faithful subjects when they are revolutionaries, meaning when they commit themselves to the unpredictable unfolding of the extraordinary event. Fidelity implies remaining loyal to the new knowledge that has been created in the event, a 'type of rupture which opens up truths' (*BE*, xii). Neither passive spectators nor experts but militants, by declaring their faithfulness to the event, they are also embarking on a process of truth.

However, as Peter Hallward asks: why 'does so rigorously subjective a philosophy need anything like a concept of the event at all? Are not the political agents of any given sequence themselves responsible for what happens?'[112] Badiou argues that radical politics, which he identifies with the event, exceeds and unbinds stable foundations of autonomous agency. Becoming a political subject does not mean identifying oneself with the pre-existing revolutionary ideology such as a political party. Rather than preceding the event, the agents are co-engendered and seized by the event, escaping their individual identities for the new collective 'we'. Recollecting his experience of May 1968, Badiou says:

> we were the genuine actors, but actors absolutely seized by what was happening to them, as by something extraordinary, something properly incalculable. . . . Of course, if we add up the anecdotes one by one, we can always say that at any given moment there were certain actors, certain people who provoked this or that result. But the

crystallisation of all these moments, their generalisation, and then the way in which everyone was caught up in it, well beyond what any one person might have thought possible – that's what I call an evental dimension. *None* of the little processes that led to the event was equal to what actually took place . . . ; there was an extraordinary change of scale, as there always is in every significant event. [. . .] Yes, we are actors, but in such a way that we are targeted by, carried away by, and struck by *[atteint par]* the event. In this sense there can undoubtedly be collective events.[113]

Highlighting the importance of subjective commitment, Badiou's idea of the event has an inspirational quality because it suggests that the unexpected can happen and that change is possible. However, as Badiou's critics have noted, in his theory it is often unclear what qualifies as an event, and a few critics have claimed that his mathematisation of ontology is a redundant step, or even that it does not convincingly translate to political reality. Inspiring as they are, his events are historically rare, short-lived or unexpected, and as such cannot be triggered by a conscious human action. In answer to such charges, Badiou asserts that there is no need to wait for an event to spring from the status quo. He instead proposes that 'Many events, even very distant ones, still require us to be faithful to them.'[114] Elsewhere, he states that his threefold logics of the event-subject-truth and the grounding of ontology in mathematics are a decision. His is a philosophical choice and an intervention aimed at articulating 'the means of saying "Yes!" to the previously unknown thoughts that hesitate to become the truths that they are' (*LW*, 3). Above all, Badiou wishes to rescue philosophy from the blind alley of postmodernism, where philosophy no longer searches for truth but for a plurality of meanings, rendering itself unable to explore properly the realm of politics, commitment and responsibility.

Badiou and Deleuze's theories of the event, although emerging out of different ontologies – with the former's identification of 'being' with the 'void' and the latter's reliance on the repetition of difference – are both engaged with the transformative potential of events, and it is this aspect of their theory that directly informs my reading of Acker's radical prose. The point here is not an attempt to 'understand' Acker's novels by analysing their historical background. Rather, I wish to follow a Deleuzian counterclaim which posits that, as Žižek has put it, 'it is [. . .] the work of art itself that provides a context enabling us to understand properly a given historical situation'.[115] If read chiefly as a postmodern, deconstructive gesture, Acker's fiction would present us with a series of unending and altogether uninspiring terrorist subversions of a sterile capitalist and patriarchal space, within which the idea of the radical politics of emancipation is seen as an obsolete illusion. Yet, as her novels demonstrate, revolution, freedom, responsibility, commitment, subjectivity and novelty are not 'dead' categories within her writing.

To be sure, anyone who lays claims for Acker's revolutionary significance is compelled to confront the fact that in each of her books revolution either fails, or is betrayed or heavily compromised. As she writes in *Empire of the Senseless*:

> I'll tell you about stupidity and business: the Algerian revolution was stupid! Right. Innocent people got killed. But it was good for business. Any revolution, right-wing left wing nihilist, it doesn't matter a damn, is good for business. Because the succession of every new business depends on the creation of new markets [. . .] Disruption is good, necessary for business. (*ES*, 182)

Indeed, Acker's refusal to provide a positive image of revolutionary change, if read literally, leaves no hope for the potency of radical politics and easily leads to the conclusion that Acker's project has itself completely failed. The category of the event will allow us to comprehend Acker's repetition of revolutionary failure as being underpinned by political creativity.

The avant-garde and its afterlives

It was not only revolution that was disqualified as a positive means of transformation of society after May 1968. The apparent triumph of conservatism in the 1980s resulted in a series of proclamations of various deaths and defeats. The avant-garde has also proven to be a failed political concept, and is now often considered dead. In *The Century* (2005), Badiou eulogises the legacy of the avant-garde thus: 'More or less the whole of twentieth-century art has laid claim to an avant-garde function. Yet today the term is viewed as obsolete or even derogatory. This suggests we are in the presence of a major symptom'.[116]

One text which continues to inflect discussions of the avant-garde is Peter Bürger's *Theory of the Avant-Garde* (1974). According to Bürger, the avant-garde artwork formulated itself as an attack against the institutionalisation of art, which was identified with the tradition of aestheticism, and with that tradition's absence of social involvement. The historical avant-garde intended to reintegrate art with everyday life: 'As institution and content coincide [in Aestheticism,] social ineffectuality stands revealed as the essence of art in bourgeois society, and thus provokes the self-criticism of art. [. . .] Instead of being based on ritual, art will now be based on politics'.[117] Rather than creating a 'practical' work with a clear social content, the avant-garde aimed to relate aesthetic experience with the real world, where it can transform everyday life. Ultimately, Bürger claims that the avant-gardists failed to achieve their goal of dissolving the boundary separating art and life, as much of their transgressive methods were recuperated by 'the culture industry' and innovation-seeking capitalist markets. Unsurprisingly, on Bürger's account neo-avant-gardes fail again, not tragically, as with the promethean Dadaists and Constructivists, but as farce: cynically and pathetically.[118]

Donald Kuspit's *The Cult of the Avant-Garde Artist* (1993) proclaims the death of the avant-garde, and casts the neo-avant-garde as its negative imprint. Praising historical vanguards as risk-takers for whom art's primary mission is the healing of social ills, and who express an authentic spirit of creativity and rebellion, Kuspit castigates their neo-incarnations as creatively bankrupt, inherently parasitic, decadent and narcissistic. Kuspit suggests that neo-avant-gardists, often producers of conceptual art and forms of appropriation and copy, have a necrophilian relationship with their past models:

> At the end of this century the avant-garde is a dead cultural tradition, as appropriation art indicates. It turns truisms into pseudo-avant-garde metaclichés. It turns important avant-garde works of art, half-embalmed by history, into wax works, giving them an ironic permanence.[119]

For artists such as Sherrie Levine, Kuspit maintains, 'maleness is simply a signifier and guarantee of success',[120] and appropriation art deadens the avant-garde's revolutionary ambitions, reducing their legacy to an intellectual rhetoric, a reading I challenge in Chapter 3. In his account, postmodern art is reactionary and merely affirms the status quo. Rather than wanting to change society, the neo-avant-garde offers only patchy solutions which can make life more bearable. It relies on extensive use of irony, which for Kuspit constitutes a risk-free, 'comfortable form of criticality'.[121] John W. Maerhofer's *Rethinking the Vanguard* (2009) also addresses the ongoing 'cleansing' of the avant-garde of its political inheritance and its decentralisation in post-war discourse. The question for Maerhofer is whether neo-avant-gardism, as something which takes note of its historical legacy and its failures, can be used as a viable strategy to confront late capitalism and its mechanisms of recuperation, seeing that even when identification with the projects of Constructivists, Dadaists and surrealists occurs in the postmodern discourse, it is often to denigrate their utopianism.[122]

The relationship between the avant-garde and the neo-avant-garde in the postmodern climate is thus largely seen as a strained one. The discussion of the historical avant-garde is often underpinned by melancholic laments about its death and failure; its farcical afterlife as the neo-avant-garde, and the apparent annulation of its political spirit and historical situatedness under the liberal gaze of postmodernism. Hal Foster, whose approach I align with my own, eschews this oft-treaded path and instead considers cultural forms, including the avant-garde and the neo-avant-garde, as always unfinished, incomplete and haunting. In *The Return of the Real* (1996), Foster criticises Bürger for presenting a reductive cause-and-effect, before-and-after trajectory of the avant-garde, moving from '*absolute origin*' to tragic end.[123] Foster writes that even though Bürger insists on the uneven and contradictory development of the avant-garde, the conventional historicity he applies suggests a linear evolution. Foster also challenges Bürger's teaching that the repetition of the historical avant-garde in the neo-avant-garde reverses the original project of connection between autonomous art and the practices of everyday life, turning 'the transgressive into the institutional'.[124] Against the rhetoric of rupture and death, he works with the Freudian terminology of return, delay and deferral. The return Foster postulates does not denote a conservative reworking of the old medium, but rather advances '*a temporal exchange between historical and neo avant-gardes, a complex relation of anticipation and reconstruction*'.[125]

Foster's 2002 essay 'This Funeral is for the Wrong Corpse' invokes in its title a song by the punk band The Mekons, with whom Acker once collaborated.[126] In response to the apparent death of socialism in 1989, the Mekons protested: 'How can something be really dead when it hasn't even happened? [. . .] this funeral is for the wrong corpse'. In this context, Foster accepts the 'aftermath' condition of art and criticism but, speaking with The Mekons, he does not consider the avant-garde project as having been realised and therefore possible to be already over.[127] This insight prompts him to investigate new ways in which the past moments of the avant-garde are 'living-on' in contemporary art. This living-on, the after-life of the avant-garde, writes

Foster, 'is not a repeating so much as a making-new or simply a making-do with what-comes-after, a beginning again and/or elsewhere'.[128] Seen in this way, the project of the avant-garde is not dead, but open to renewal and 'formal transformation that is also social engagement'.[129] Thus the avant-garde project may be regarded by many as a ghost, but Foster seems to perceive it more as a seed.[130]

Acker as a responsible artist

How does Acker negotiate the artist's responsibility towards society? She rejects the route of adopting a condemning pastiche of historical avant-gardes. Rather, her writing repositions, re-politicises and re-materialises the old avant-gardes in innovative ways. This involves developing new forms of the subject's vanguard fidelity to events – past and anticipated ones – where artistic imagination coincides with revolutionary politics. In other words, Acker's return to the avant-garde is also a return to the events around which these avant-garde works were produced. When she revisits Arthur Rimbaud, Blaise Cendrars, Andrei Bely, the Russian Constructivists, the surrealists or the Situationists, for instance, their radical political inheritance – that of revolution – is plainly in sight. In a 1994 interview with Acker, Lawrence Rickels called Acker's strategy of plagiarism 'an improper burial' as a way of keeping something 'secret and alive'.[131] Rather than simply copying, Acker gave the old avant-gardes a new life by transforming them to become fit for revolutionary use here and now, in the present.

In the counter-revolutionary epoch, Acker offers an alternative voice. She calls for an avant-garde which opposes the instrumental use of art and hopes to combine criticality with positive dreaming. 'Dead art' is her metaphor for conformist, right-leaning, monolithic 'high culture' desperate to receive support from the government and please the tastes of a disengaged audience. Instead, she urges us to look elsewhere and does so by providing us with examples of 'living art' I outline below.

In her essay 'Dead Doll Prophecy', Acker clearly defines and defends her writing methods. She rails against the legal repercussions that resulted from her appropriation of elements of Harold Robbins's 1974 novel *The Pirate* into one of her own.[132] In this essay, an artist named Capitol (who returns in *In Memoriam to Identity*, as we shall see in Chapter 5), crafts various 'dolls', which we can take to signify an assembly of ready-mades, where the collected bits and pieces are hooked together, thus replicating Acker's playing around with elements of language and diverse textual material. It is an essay that traces her struggle for survival in the art world while questioning the norms of mainstream culture:

> 'HERE IT ALL STINKS,' CAPITOL THOUGHT. 'ART IS MAKING ACCORDING TO THE IMAGINATION. BUT HERE, BUYING AND SELLING ARE THE RULES; THE RULES OF COMMODITY HAVE DESTROYED THE IMAGINATION. HERE, THE ONLY ART ALLOWED IS MADE BY POST-CAPITALIST RULES; ART ISN'T MADE ACCORDING TO RULES.' ANGER MAKES YOU WANT TO SUICIDE [sic].[133]

The essay looks at what it means to be a responsible artist. '"WHAT IS IT?" CAPITOL WROTE, "TO BE AN ARTIST? WHERE IS THE VALUE THAT WILL KEEP THIS LIFE IN HELL GOING?"'[134] In the eyes of Acker, this means taking – and sticking to – important decisions, such as her own refusal to comply with the teaching of the Black Mountain poets, who insisted that in order to become a fully-fledged writer she needed to find her own voice. Instead, Acker 'Decided that since what she wanted to do was just to write, not to find her own voice, could and would write by using anyone's voice, anyone's text, whatever materials she wanted to use.'[135] Her rejection of the author as god/sole creator is accompanied by further resolutions: 'Decided to use or to write both good literature and schlock. To mix them up in terms of content and formally.'[136] These decisions are part of Acker's larger scheme of artistic responsibility, summarised in the formula: 'Writing must be for and must be freedom.'[137]

Acker's writing is, then, responsible because it seeks to embody freedom by negating the given reality.[138] In her words: 'To copy down, to appropriate, to deconstruct other texts is to break down those perceptual habits the culture doesn't want to be broken.'[139] If the doll is dead, intimating a Romantic predisposition to suicide and transcendentalism, it is only because Capitol considers death 'PREFERABLE TO A DEAD LIFE' and prophesises that 'THEY [Harold Robbins's lawyers, mainstream culture] CAN'T KILL THE SPIRIT'.[140] The practice of deconstruction, Acker suggests, is one way for art to thrive, to live on: 'living art rather than dead has some connection with passion. Deconstructionists of newspaper stories become the living art in a culture that demands that any artistic representation of life be nonviolent and nonsexual, misrepresent.'[141]

In her 1990 article for the *New Statesman and Society* entitled 'Diary: At the Edge of the New', Acker writes about the still pervasive polarisation of the New York art scene into 'uptown' art and 'down-town' avant-garde cultures. As an example of uptown art, which gets funding and financial rewards because it fulfils market demands, she singles out Wendy Wasserstein's play *The Heidi Chronicles* (1988). If Wasserstein undertakes the significant subject of feminism – given its ailing status in the Reagan era – to Acker the play ultimately confirms conservative values and social divisions:

> Here is feminism in New York City on the edge of 1990. And here is important art. At least according to the culture that has money, both those who can afford 40 dollars for a theatre ticket and those who fund, and therefore decide what is, art. [. . .] Rich people and high culture inhabited the upper stratosphere; the poor, underfunded or unfunded theatres, and the avant-garde (considered dead phenomenon) hid in the lower regions of what many think of as hell.[142]

Acker then contrasts the overwhelming deadness of uptown art with Richard Foreman's experimental play *Lava*, which she considers an example of living art. Foreman, Acker writes, 'does nothing to please or captivate an audience. He uses no ironic, clever jokes; in fact he uses only the edges of theatrical characterisation and narration.'[143] Notably, the play engages the audience in its refusal to accept their given existence, and instead invites them to imagine what might be beyond this existence, to a realm where 'the imaginative is made actual or material'.[144] This is evocative of Marcuse's idea that if '[a]rt cannot change the world [. . .] it can make conscious the necessity of change, only when it obeys its own law as against that of reality [and] can contribute to changing the consciousness and drives of the men and women who could change the world'.[145] This belief that aesthetics and imagination can have transformative powers is what lies behind Acker's enigmatic formulation that 'If writing cannot and writing must change things, [. . .] writing *will* change things magically.'[146]

The search for living art continues in 'After the End of the Art World', the essay Acker submitted for the 1995 issue of *Art & Design*. Nicholas Zurbrugg writes of the avant-garde artists who contributed to the volume: 'At the inner margins of the new, and at the outer margins of the old, their work typifies the most significant live-ends of the supposedly dead-end "Post-Modern condition".'[147] Intent on proving that avant-garde art is far from dead, Acker is full of praise for the subversive aspirations of VNS Matrix, the Australian feminist artist hi-tech collective, and the San Francisco all-women cyberpunk band Tribe 8; she considers both artistic groups to be 'signs of birth'.[148]

In contrast to the prevailing myth of individuality, embodied by the sterile figure of the American cowboy, this 'funky feminism' situates community at the core of its practice.[149] Thus the vitality of the contemporary art world resides not only in transformed forms and experiential possibilities, but also in an openness to the outside world and connectivity within itself.

Lynnee Breedlove, the founder and leading figure of Tribe 8, emphasises that Acker strove to make art – and her desire to educate through art – available and relevant to the wider community. The participants of her writing classes in public spaces in San Francisco included both students who paid fees and outsiders – 'punks, queers, whores, strippers, messengers, junkies, survivors'. Acker's aim, Breedlove recalls, was to 'inspire all of us to keep passing on that encouragement: "write"'.[150] To Breedlove and others, Acker exemplified impassioned and inclusive writerly existence: 'She modeled [sic] integrity. And she let us know that punks and academia were not mutually exclusive.'[151] Moreover, in her teachings Acker allowed avant-garde and history to renew and regenerate itself with new formal, political and ethical consequences. Writing is itself a gift passed on to new generations: 'She brought the ghosts of literary heroes into our lives. She brought queer history to life. She lived it.'[152]

Acker is critical of artists who give in to the demands of the market, or who remain in the safety of elitism. Her 1995 essay 'Proposition One' compares Charles Baudelaire, Arthur Rimbaud and Antonin Artaud's relation to society to the literary careers of some contemporary writers. Baudelaire and Rimbaud, writes Acker, 'saw themselves, writers, as dandies, friends of whores, slackers – as anything but powerful'.[153] Acker goes on to cite Baudelaire's contention to go against rather than maintain the values of bourgeoisie literature: 'I . . . saw the city as from a tower, / Hospital, brothel, prison, and such hells'.[154] She also evokes Rimbaud's refusal of the class distinctions of master and worker and his criticism of literary elitism: 'The hand that guides the pen is worth the hand that guides the plough. – What an age of hands! / I shall never have my hand'.[155]

She relates these considerations to Deleuze and Guattari who, she notes, also link the personal, political, theoretical and the artistic together. Like Artaud, these philosophers read mental illness politically. Crucially, they distinguish between schizophrenia as an illness and schizophrenia as a process. They posit that the schizophrenic process, which is categorically different from the debilitating disease, is the matrix of the unconscious and provides us with the model of how desire works: 'schizophrenia is the process of the production of desire and desiring-machines' (*AO*, 24). This replaces the Freudian model of the unconscious or id – viewed as an isolated reservoir of repressed passions and fantasies which pressure the ego – with a productive process which gives rise to machines: assemblages or configurations of non-egoic desire. Mental conditions such as psychosis, neurosis and perversion, they maintain, are all derivations of schizophrenia. However, instead of building connections they become 'territorial' – bogged down and walled off. This is why they claim that 'Schizophrenia is at once the wall, the breaking through this wall, and the failures of this breakthrough' (*AO*, 136).

Acker cites Deleuze and Guattari's discussion of artificial separations between art, politics and theory, and hints at an alternative – a desiring machine:

> What is at stake is not merely art or literature. For either the artistic machine, the analytic machine, and the revolutionary machine will remain in extrinsic relationships that make them function in the deadening framework of the system of social and psychic repression, or they will become parts and cogs of one another in the flow that feeds one and the same desiring machine.[156]

She then asks: 'How can this unhealthy, repressive-because-repressed, stoppage be overcome?'[157] It becomes apparent that Acker, like the authors of *Anti-Oedipus*, diagnoses society as sick. As Mark Seem remarks in his introduction to Deleuze and Guattari's book, 'For we are sick, so sick, of our *selves*!'[158] The message is this: for the artistic body to remain alive, it needs to become part of the assemblage of analytic and revolutionary machines, instead of being fixated on itself. 'A schizophrenic out for a walk', Deleuze and Guattari famously write, 'is a better model than a neurotic lying on the analyst's couch. A breath of fresh air, a relationship with the outside world' (*AO*, 2).

Acker suggests that the models provided by Baudelaire, Rimbaud and Artaud are the rare instances of such a machinic relationship: 'they viewed their writing – every aspect, content and structure, because their very lives, their life-decisions – as politically defined'[159] (though she reviews her stance on Rimbaud, as Chapter 5 will elaborate). Deleuze and Guattari propose that the way not to 'sell-out' is to produce literature 'which places an explosive device in its package, fabricating a counterfeit currency, causing the superego and its form of expression to explode, as well as the market value of its form of content' (*AO*, 134). At present, Acker admits (with regret), even those writers who do not write according to the rules of the market often alienate themselves and their work. Such a writer 'prefers to remain in the non-commercial (the bohemian, the experimental) world, for there she is safe. Safe to be able to write as she sees fit.'[160] But Acker insists that if one commits oneself to write in contrast with the present reality, one 'must make clear the reasons for writing the way she or he does, must make those reasons, which are also and always political positions, present'. With regard to elitism, Acker believes that the younger audiences do reach for the 'difficult' texts, by authors such as William Burroughs, Michel Foucault and Teresa de Laurentis, so 'disjunctive' texts, which are not a conventionally 'good read'.[161]

By the end of the 1980s, Acker grew seriously concerned about the tendency in postmodern academic discourse to disconnect theory and art works from their political motivations and contexts. Theory's ambitious projects of questioning the society that we have, and envisioning ways of changing and revolutionising it, seem to have lost their potency:

> I've seen too many English departments destroy people's delight in reading. Once something becomes academic it's taken on this level – take the case of semiotics and postmodernism. When I was first introduced to the work of Foucault and Deleuze, it was very political; it was about what was happening to the economy and about changing the political system. By the time it was taken up by the American academy, the politics had gone to hell. It became an exercise for some professors to make their careers. You know, it's just more of the same: the culture is there to uphold the post capitalist society, and the idea that art has nothing to do with politics is a wonderful construction in order to mask the deep political significance that art has – to uphold the empire in terms of its representation as well as its actual structure.[162]

A recovery of some of that lost connection is what this book hopes to achieve. In its discussion of Acker's encounter with Arendt, I have already made explicit Acker's belief that a responsible artist is also necessarily one who is connected to history. Such an artist refuses to live only in the present, conceiving of history as a mere chronicle of events. Instead, they return to past events as a resource brimming with potential for transforming the present. In Acker's essays about art we have seen the centrality of an artist's responsibility towards society, along with her highlights of new beginnings in contemporary art. These thoughts are in no way melancholic. In the avant-garde's critical stance, their connection with life, with community, with history, with the intertwining of aesthetic and political dimensions and all its enduring utopian component, means the horizon of emancipation never disappears.

The book is composed of a series of close readings positioned at the intersection of historical, theoretical, artistic and scientific contexts. Acker's work has been often received in the four phases she frequently demarcated in interviews. The first phase deals with her dissociation from the authorial 'I', the second with the 'deconstruction' of other people's writings, followed by a third stage of 'construction', motivated by 'a search for a myth to live by'. The fourth is concerned with the 'language of the body'. But whereas these demarcations are valid, as Dew has suggested, '[t]he membrane of Acker's oeuvre is porous' and invites also a more flexible approach.[163] In order to attend to the previously neglected aspects of her political project, the readings offered here will combine Acker's original demarcations with a new nomenclature: the revolutionary event; the historical avant-garde; political subjectivity, and artistic responsibility. Each chapter in this book weaves together explorations of these key categories while illuminating a specific aspect of Acker's revolutionary politics.

Chapter 1 relates the terrorist turn of late American counterculture that informs Acker's 1970s works to two revolutionary movements: twentieth-century militant Maoism and nineteenth-century Russian nihilism. The chapter traces the development of Acker's early literary configurations of radical politics from the aesthetics of an exploding bomb and the politics of dissolution towards models of political subjectivity based on martyrdom and sacrifice.

Chapter 2 positions *Don Quixote* within modern revolutionary tradition to investigate the problematic relationship between revolution, repetition and cynicism in Acker's work. Her concern with widespread cynicism in 1980s Western societies coincides here with Peter Sloterdijk and Michel Foucault's attempts to recover the subversive forms of ancient Cynicism as a means to combat modern cynical rationality, characterised by a lack of belief in alternatives. The chapter will argue that as an alternative to the pervasive *realpolitik* that is akin to cynicism, Acker adopts the ethics of ancient Cynicism and offers a 'dreampolitik' elaborated through the historical example of Spanish anarchism.

Chapter 3 examines the middle component of *Don Quixote*, a collage of texts entitled 'Russian Constructivism', shedding new light on Acker's relationship with the Russian avant-garde. It argues that Acker's work, along with the visual art of the neo-avant-garde artist Sherrie Levine on which 'Russian Constructivism' is modelled, has been co-opted by a strain of postmodern criticism which sees her as hostile to the utopian project of modernism and traditional notions of authorship and originality, overlooking her profound engagement with the ideas of collaboration, community and transformation. Using the notion of the event and the artistic category of abstraction, this chapter instead posits that Acker's aesthetic borrowings from the avant-garde are part of a utopic and progressive use of the past in order to create new social possibilities in the political present.

From the dark landscapes in *Don Quixote*, and after the alternations of passion and melancholy withdrawal in 'Russian Constructivism', the discussion will focus on proximity to an evental past in *Empire of the Senseless*, the topic of Chapter 4. It will investigate how this novel opens up history by fusing the French events of May 1968, the Algerian Revolution and the Haitian Revolution to create a new global revolutionary space in the present. I will suggest that the politics of proximity in *Empire* is realised through Acker's continuation of the Situationist's avant-garde project and their shared experiments with topology and turbulence, which in my analysis are complexly interwoven with the fluid and the feminine as operators of change.

Whereas in *Empire of the Senseless* Acker projects us back to the event as a moment of possibility, in her 1990 novel *In Memoriam to Identity*, she underscores the role of individual commitment to realise and sustain that promise, as I argue in Chapter 5. While tracking her search for a subject through her work it will become apparent that Acker searches for an open notion of the political subject that exceeds both orthodoxies – the poststructuralist one and the liberal-humanist one. Although Rimbaud proves to be a disappointing model, he nevertheless becomes a vehicle for Acker to explore the becoming of a political subject and a responsible artist. Of particular importance here will be the novel's engagement with the double legacy of the Paris Commune reflected in two universes. In the prosaic universe, the Commune is another failed revolt on the continuum of history; in the universe of becoming and creativity, by contrast, it is a suppressed promise. In *In Memoriam to Identity*, as this chapter elaborates, Acker crafts a portrait of a responsible artist whose role is mediating events and distilling real points of truth from a world in which such choices seem non-existent.

The Conclusion turns to Acker's last work, the posthumously published play *Eurydice in the Underworld* (1997), which will allow me to revisit, reconnect and reflect upon some of the central points discussed in my book. As in Acker's earlier works, the female characters summoned in the play are allotted a special role in challenging the Saturnian cliché, with Acker insisting that women's association with revolution and fidelity to egalitarian ideals is not simply metaphorical. These readings, orientated around the concept of the event and exploring Acker's alternatives to the pervading cynicism and hysterical amnesia, intend to demonstrate that Acker's politics of writing is of great relevance to present historical conjunction.

Notes

1. Crane Brinton's classic work *The Anatomy of Revolution* (1938) is a comparative study of four democratising revolutions: the English Revolution of the 1640s and the American (1776), French (1789) and Russian Revolution (1917).
2. Brinton, *The Anatomy*, p. 112.
3. Pierre Vergniaud, cited in Brinton, p. 149. Vergniaud refers here to the classical Roman mythical god Saturn, who attempts to pre-empt patricide by eating all of his children in succession.
4. Brinton, *The Anatomy*, p. 243.
5. Acker, *Pussy*, p.10.
6. Ibid.
7. See, for example, Jacobs (1989); Pitchford (2002); Martina Sciolino, 'Kathy Acker and the Postmodern Subject of Feminism', *College English* 52.4 (April 1990), pp. 437–45; Katie R. Muth, 'Postmodern Fiction as Poststructuralist Theory: Kathy Acker's *Blood and Guts in High School*', *Narrative* 19.1 (2011), pp. 86–110.
8. Friedman, 'A Conversation with Kathy Acker', p. 21.
9. Ibid. pp. 21–2.
10. As discussed in Chapter 5, the phrase appears in *In Memoriam to Identity* (1990) in Acker's altered translation of Rimbaud's nostalgic musings on lost geographies and histories.
11. Ebbesen, *Postmodernism*, p. 110.
12. Dew, *Learning*, p. 16.
13. Houen, *Powers*, p. 183.
14. Hume, 'Voice in Kathy Acker's Fiction', p. 486.
15. McCaffery, 'An Interview with Kathy Acker', p. 91.
16. Acker, 'A Few Notes on Two of My Books', in *Bodies of Work*, p. 9.
17. Hume, 'Voice in Kathy Acker's Fiction', p. 486.
18. Acker, 'Devoured by Myths', an interview with Lotringer Sylvère in *Hannibal Lecter, My Father*, p. 17.

19. Acker, 'Writing, Identity, and Copyright in the Net Age', in *Bodies of Work*, p. 98.
20. Ibid. p. 100.
21. Cited in Acker, 'Writing, Identity, and Copyright in the Net Age', in *Bodies of Work*, p. 103.
22. Acker, 'Writing, Identity, and Copyright in the Net Age', in *Bodies of Work*, p. 100.
23. Cited in Acker, 'Writing, Identity, and Copyright in the Net Age', in *Bodies of Work*, p. 104.
24. Acker, 'Writing, Identity, and Copyright in the Net Age', in *Bodies of Work*, p. 98.
25. Ibid. p. 99.
26. Ibid. p. 100.
27. Schell, 'Introduction', pp. xii–xiii.
28. Arendt, *The Origins*, p. xxiv; author's emphasis.
29. Acting 'in concert' is central to Arendt's characterisation of power, namely, the potential that emerges between people when they act together: '*Power* corresponds to the human ability not just to act but to act in concert. Power is never the property of an individual; it belongs to a group and remains in existence only so long as the group keeps together.' Arendt, *On Violence*, p. 44; author's emphasis.
30. Schell, 'Introduction', p. xvii.
31. Acker, *My Death*, p. 338.
32. Arendt, 'Totalitarian Imperialism: Reflections on the Hungarian Revolution', p. 5.
33. Gordon, '"The Perplexities of Beginning": Hannah Arendt's Theory of Revolution', p. 125.
34. Cited in Young-Bruehl, *Hannah Arendt*, p. 202.
35. Arendt, 'Totalitarian Imperialism: Reflections on the Hungarian Revolution', p. 8.
36. Parker, *Revolutions*, p. 4; author's emphasis.
37. Ibid. p. 4.
38. Ibid. p. 6.
39. Of course, it could be argued that the accession of William of Orange ultimately represented the victory of parliament over the monarchy, and therefore a dilution of monarchical power – a power already threatened by the regicide of the Civil War and the excesses of the Restoration period.
40. Marshall, *Demanding*, pp. 306–7.
41. Ibid. pp. 307–8.
42. Arendt, 'Totalitarian Imperialism: Reflections on the Hungarian Revolution', p. 26.
43. Gordon, '"The Perplexities of Beginning": Hannah Arendt's Theory of Revolution', p. 114.
44. Hunt, 'The World We Have Gained: The Future of the French Revolution', pp. 8, 18.

45. Ibid. p. 12.
46. Ibid. p. 11.
47. Marx, 'The Eighteenth Brumaire of Louis Bonaparte', p. 22.
48. Starr, *Logics*, p. 2.
49. Baker and Edelstein, 'Introduction', p. 4.
50. Ibid. p. 4.
51. Ibid. pp. 2, 3.
52. Guy Debord used the idea of the 'spectacle', an updated version of Marx's concept of alienation but with theatrical overtones, to analyse the repressions of late capitalism.
53. Cited in Starr, *Logics*, p. 3.
54. For a detailed discussion of the global protest movements of 1968, see Carole Fink, Philipp Gassert, Detlef Junker and Daniel S. Mattern, *1968: The World Transformed* (Washington, DC: German Historical Institute, 1998). See also Jameson (1985).
55. Kurlansky, *1968*, p. xv.
56. Hobsbawm, '1968', p. 130.
57. Bourg, 'Writing on the Wall: 1968 as Event and Representation', p. 287.
58. Gitlin, *The Sixties*, p. 84.
59. Contrary to these claims, Kraus writes that Acker did not interact with Marcuse but chose to associate herself with the philosopher, possibly 'to position her work within an intellectual history where it rightly belonged'. Kraus, *After Kathy Acker*, p. 47.
60. Katsiaficas, 'Marcuse as Activist: Reminiscences on His Theory and Practice', pp. 192–3.
61. Acker, *My Death My Life by Pier Paolo Pasolini*, in *Blood and Guts in High School Plus Two*, p. 339.
62. Ibid.
63. Marcuse, 'Reflections on the French Revolution', p. 44.
64. Marcuse, *An Essay*, p. 16.
65. Harvey, *The Condition*, p. 38.
66. Barber, *A Hard Rain*, 5.
67. Acker, 'Devoured by Myths', in *Hannibal Lecter, My Father*, p. 4.
68. Gair, *The American Counterculture*, pp. 4–5.
69. Harvey, *A Brief History*, 41.
70. Ibid. p. 41.
71. Heath and Potter, *The Rebel Sell*, p. 6.
72. For an analysis of punk's relationship with postmodernity, see Ryan Moore, 'Postmodernism and Punk Subculture: Cultures of Authenticity and Deconstruction', *The Communication Review* 7 (2004), pp. 305–27.
73. Henderson, 'From Counterculture to Punk Culture p. 277.
74. Ibid. p. 286.
75. Acker, 'New York City in 1978', in *Hannibal Lecter, My Father*, p. 39.

76. Ibid. p.42.

77. Henderson, 'From Counterculture to Punk Culture', p. 289.

78. Hell, p. 137.

79. Stosuy, 'Introduction', p. 20.

80. Siegle, 'Downtown Writing', p. 138.

81. Ibid. p. 3.

82. Siegle, *Suburban Ambush*, p. 3.

83. Lee Konstantinou, *Cool Characters: Irony and American Fiction* (Cambridge, MA: Harvard University Press, 2016), p. 115.

84. Ibid. p. 16.

85. For different responses to the May 1968 events and their reception, see Ross, *May '68 and Its Afterlives*.

86. Starr, *Logics*, p. 2.

87. Ibid.

88. Bourg, *From Revolution*, p. 4; author's emphasis.

89. Hewlett, *Democracy*, p. 135.

90. Hewlett, *Badiou*, p. 17.

91. MacKenzie, 'What is a Political Event?', p. 1.

92. Massumi, 'Translator's Foreword', p. xi.

93. Badiou, *Polemics*, 85.

94. The event is a central concept of Deleuze and Guattari's collaborative work. See their *Anti-Oedipus*, *A Thousand Plateaus* and *What is Philosophy?* Prior to collaborating with Guattari, Deleuze had dealt extensively and most explicitly with the event in his *Difference and Repetition*, *The Logic of Sense* and *The Fold: Leibniz and the Baroque*, trans. T. Conley (Minneapolis: University of Minnesota Press, 1993).

95. Alain Badiou's major contribution to evental theory is *Being and Event* and its sequel *Logics of Worlds*. There has been a growing interest in Badiou's anti-postmodern approach among English-speaking audiences, who were introduced to his thought in his *Ethics: An Essay on the Understanding of Evil*.

96. Badiou, *Deleuze*, p. 90.

97. Badiou elaborated on his disagreement with Deleuze's notion of event on several occasions. See especially *Deleuze*, and 'The Event in Deleuze', trans. Jon Roffe, *Parrhesia* 2 (2007), pp. 37–44.

98. Badiou and Deleuze both place the event at the heart of their philosophical systems, yet their understanding of how events are produced and what qualifies as an event differ. At the same time, this divergence is not as dramatic as is sometimes claimed, and there has been increased interest reconciling their approaches. For example, Hollis Philips argues that Badiou's 'absolute beginnings' are in fact relative to the situation and a certain creative repetition does take place in his ontology. See Phelps, 'Absolute Beginnings', pp. 48–64.

99. Deleuze and Guattari, *What is Philosophy?*, pp. 96, 110.

100. Deleuze, 'Control and Becoming: in Conversation with Toni Negri', in *Negotiations*, p. 171.
101. Deleuze, *The Logic*, p. 80.
102. Ibid. p. 170.
103. Deleuze, *Difference*, p. 136.
104. Slavoj Žižek, *Organs*, p. 12.
105. Deleuze, 'May '68 Didn't Happen', p. 233.
106. Phelps, 'Absolute Beginnings . . . Almost: Badiou and Deleuze on the Event', p. 56.
107. Badiou's ontology is theorised as a mathematical equation, as in *Being and Event*. For a detailed treatment of his application of set theory, see Ed Pluth, *Alain Badiou* (Cambridge: Polity Press, 2010), pp. 29–66; Christopher Norris, *Badiou's Being and Event*; Peter Hallward, *Badiou*; Jason Baker, *Alain Badiou: A Critical Introduction* (London: Pluto Press, 2002), esp. pp. 39–58, 149–55; and Oliver Feltham, 'Set-theory Ontology and the Modelling of Change', in *Alain Badiou: Live Theory* (London: Continuum, 2008), pp. 84–135.
108. Cited in Hallward, *Badiou*, p. 81.
109. Badiou claims that natural situations do not contain evental sites, because they do not have any excrescences. A historical situation, however, is one in which there is an evental site and therefore it possesses capacity for events. Badiou defines an evental site as 'an entirely abnormal multiple; that is, a multiple such that none of its elements are presented in the situation. The site, itself, is presented, but "beneath" it nothing from which it is composed is presented. As such, the site is not a part of the situation. I will also say of such a multiple that it is *on the edge of the void*, or *foundational*' (*BE*, 175; author's emphasis).
110. Cited in Hallward, *Badiou*, p. 116.
111. As will be discussed in Chapter 4, in the second volume of *Being and Event* – *Logics of Worlds* – Badiou maintains the notion of a faithful subject as primary to his project, but also adds three other types of subjects formed in response to the call of the event: reactionary, obscure and resurrection subject.
112. Hallward, *Badiou*, p. 123.
113. Cited in Hallward, *Badiou*, p. 123; author's emphasis.
114. Badiou, *Saint Paul*, p. 111.
115. Žižek, *Organs*, p. 15.
116. Badiou, *The Century*, p. 132.
117. Bürger, *Theory*, pp. 27, 28.
118. As Hal Foster has noted, Bürger's pessimistic conclusions recall Marx's famous charge in *The Eighteenth Brumaire of Louis Bonaparte* (1852) that history occurs twice: first as tragedy, the second time as farce. Foster, *The Return*, p. 14.
119. Kuspit, *The Cult*, p. 107.

120. Ibid. p. 107.
121. Ibid. p. 102.
122. Maerhofer, *Rethinking*, p. 7.
123. Foster, *Return*, p. 8; author's emphasis.
124. Ibid. p. 11.
125. Ibid. p. 13; author's emphasis.
126. Acker's collaboration with The Mekons resulted in the release of their album *Pussy, King of the Pirates* in 1996.
127. Foster, 'This Funeral is for the Wrong Corpse', in *Design and Crime (And Other Diatribes)*, pp. 128–9.
128. Ibid. p. 129.
129. Ibid. p. 130.
130. I am indebted for this ghost/seed duality to Geoff Waite, who paraphrases the poet Linton Kwesi Johnson's comment on socialism thus: 'even if most people (still) regard socialism as a "ghost," this need not prevent others from seeing it (again) as a "seed."' Waite also discusses The Mekons in this context. Waite, *Nietzsche's Corps/e*, p. 3.
131. Rickels, 'Body Bildung', p. 103.
132. During her time in England, Acker was accused of lifting a four-page scene from Robbins's *The Pirate* into her novel *The Adult Life of Toulouse Lautrec by Henri Toulouse Lautrec* (1978). Acker's publisher Pandora requested a public apology, which she initially refused to sign, explaining how her appropriation of texts should be viewed as a postmodern collage, but eventually relented under pressure, later labelling the incident 'a horrendous experience that completely disrupted my life. [. . .] I felt very threatened as a writer'. McCaffery, 'An Interview with Kathy Acker', p. 84.
133. Acker, 'Dead Doll Prophecy', pp. 28–9. An earlier version of the essay was published under the title 'Humility' in Allison Fell (ed.), *The Seven Cardinal Virtues* (London: Serpent's Tail, 1990).
134. Acker, 'Dead Doll Prophecy', p. 29.
135. Ibid. p. 22.
136. Ibid.
137. Ibid. p. 27.
138. Acker's position on the role of art in society echoes Herbert Marcuse's. For a discussion, see Dew, pp. 28–32. See also Carol Becker, 'Herbert Marcuse and the Subversive Potential of Art', in Carol Becker (ed.), *The Subversive Imagination: Artists, Society, and Social Responsibility* (New York: Routledge, 1994), pp. 113–29.
139. Acker, 'Dead Doll Prophecy', p. 28.
140. Ibid. p. 34.
141. Ibid. p. 28.
142. Acker, 'Diary: At the Edge of the New', p. 44.
143. Ibid.
144. Ibid. p. 45.

145. Marcuse, *The Aesthetic Dimension*, pp. 32–3.
146. Acker, 'A Few Notes on Two of My Books', in *Bodies of Work*, p. 8; author's emphasis.
147. Zurbrugg, 'Introduction', p. 6.
148. Acker, 'After the End of the Art World', p. 7.
149. Ibid. p. 9.
150. Breedlove, 'lynnee breedlove on kathy acker – an interview', available at <http://remember-who-u-are.blogspot.co.uk/2010/08/lynnee-breedlove-on-kathy-acker.html> (last accessed 10 January 2019).
151. Ibid.
152. Ibid.
153. Acker, 'Proposition One', 40.
154. Cited in Acker, 'Proposition One', p. 39.
155. Cited in Acker, 'Proposition One', p. 40.
156. Cited in Acker, 'Proposition One', pp. 41–2.
157. Acker, 'Proposition One', p. 42.
158. Mark Seem, 'Introduction', p. xxi; author's emphasis.
159. Acker, 'Proposition One', p. 42.
160. Ibid. p. 43.
161. Ibid.
162. Friedman, 'A Conversation with Kathy Acker', pp. 20–1.
163. Dew, *Learning*, p. 22.

Chapter 1

'The Revolution Glitters': Revolutionary Terrorism in the 1970s Works

One defining aspect of Acker's work in the early seventies was her use of terrorism as a contribution to world revolt. Revolutionary terrorism is one of the recurring themes in this volume, but it receives its most literal treatment in this chapter. Here, I relate the turbulent and violent moments of late American counterculture in Acker's early works to two revolutionary movements: twentieth-century militant Maoism and nineteenth-century Russian terrorism. *The Burning Bombing of America: The Destruction of the US* (1972) and *I Dreamt I Was a Nymphomaniac: Imagining* (1974)[1] are two works which will be my lodestars. They both document the employment of images of violence and destruction for political purpose; both relate religious patterning to radical politics; both establish transhistorical and transnational political links; and both relate libidinal desire to revolutionary ends. These two works will allow me to track the development of Acker's early literary configurations of radical politics from the aesthetics of an exploding bomb and the politics of dissolution in *Burning Bombing* towards sacrifice-based models of political subjectivity in *Nymphomaniac*.

The terrorist turn

The 1962 Port Huron Statement may have diagnosed the ills of American society and, in doing so, communicated a mildly idealistic set of demands, but it was not a call for radical action. The first years of the SDS were relatively violence-free. The students mostly engaged in intellectual discussions working towards a peaceful resolution of the issues of inequality, racism, poverty and unemployment. But the 1960s saw violence erupt at the Democratic National Convention in Chicago, the assassinations of Martin Luther King and John F. Kennedy and the failure to stop the Vietnam War through peaceful protest. The rebellious spirit of the age was inflamed by race riots in numerous American cities, while multiple liberation and workers' struggles in the developing world furthered the mandate for militarism. It was only a matter of time before radical movements would emerge from these crises, and the SDS would transform itself into a radical revolutionary force. *Burning Bombing* explores that transition.

The terrorist bomb pervades *Burning Bombing*. It not only constitutes a means of destroying the urban landscape, but also subtends the novella's fragmentary structure. The explosion of the terrorist bomb motivates the dissolution of form, the following passage shows:

> the moon clashes against the light. you touch me O nymphomania!
>   China. the revolution   a beginning that makes sense   the peasants tortured   without food   turn over   a new life   a(wo)man wants to control his/her life   I will sacrifice all happiness for the sake of self-control. I will do anything to maintain my ability to make decisions. throw the bomb. we plant bombs in the edges of the rubble   fire escapes below SoHo   we kill everyone! (*BB*, 164)

The bomb's explosive force generates extra spacing between phrases, and opens up opportunities for new, insurrectionary references. It allows for an interchange and cross-inspiration between texts, space and time. Here, the revolutionary struggles of Chinese peasants and the rebels of New York's artistic neighbourhood intertwine. The bigger explosive upheaval is one where militancy is thrown together with sexual liberation. This sexual, burning desire for another way of living sees Acker in *Burning Bombing* speaking to Herbert Marcuse and Wilhelm Reich's sexual theories about the revolutionary possibilities of Eros.

In this way, the novella absorbs numerous ideological commitments of an evolving radical counterculture. From anarchism to communism to Maoism, *Burning Bombing* opens up to alternative political radicalisms and sometimes fusions. Maoism at the time was one of the most extreme forms of political inspirations. The novella's celebration of 'communist–anarchist revolution' (*BB*, 179) integrates such Maoist lessons with a more anarchist outlook; the way they call for the disintegration of the old world and the breaking of the chains of obedience; their collective, impatient desire for a new world; their emphasis on militarism, anti-elitism, direct democracy; the power of the masses, and the individual spiritual conversion. Fredric Jameson considers Maoism to be 'the richest of all the great new ideologies of the 60s' and points out they all suffered the same fate. The efforts of the reactionary campaigns of the 1980s to 'Stalinize and discredit Maoism and the experience of the Chinese cultural revolution', Jameson concludes, are 'part and parcel of the larger attempt to trash the 60s generally'.[2]

Burning Bombing evokes the Weathermen group (later known as the Weather Underground),[3] the most militant SDS movement, which adopted Maoist tactics and turned to terrorism. While originally the SDS did not have any partisan affiliations, its increasing militarisation and pro-Communist stance made it attractive to Communist applicants, and soon young Maoists became a numerous and influential group within its ranks.[4] The 'armed struggle'[5] and militant Maoist ideologies of such groups emerged from the need to correct ineffective, traditional forms of protest with drastic measures. The move to violence was a way of expressing personal rage; it was a moral mission, demonstrated through the willingness to sacrifice.[6]

The Weathermen group was formed during the split of the SDS in the summer of 1969. A call for immediate action was articulated in their founding document; 'You Don't Need a Weatherman to Know Which Way the Wind Blows'. The Weatherman name came from Bob Dylan's 1965 song 'Subterranean Homesick Blues', a tune which urged people to take liberation into their own hands. That founding document opens with a passage from Lin Piao (Lin Biao), Chairman Mao's militant supporter, and its pages are adorned with images of Marx, Lenin and Mao, and silhouettes of armed guerrilla fighters. The manifesto defined their programme as 'akin to the Red Guard in China, based on the full participation and involvement of masses of people in the practice of making revolution; a movement with a full willingness to participate in the violent and illegal struggle'.[7]

They turned that call to action into action. The Weathermen planted bombs in military and governmental buildings, and targeted banks and corporations. Their members carried English translations of Mao's Little Red Book (1964) and Sergey Nechayev's *Catechism of a Revolutionary* (1869) on them like talismans. One faction of the Weathermen called themselves the Narodniki, taking inspiration from a group of Russian radicals who formed the nihilist revolutionary movement called The People's Will, active between the 1870s and 1880s. The young nihilists believed that, as with their assassination of Tsar Alexander II, a better system could arise from their violent acts, there to replace the unjust political order.

The Western Left's attraction to Maoism had been ignited by a split between the Soviet and Chinese Communist Parties. In the light of Stalin's excesses, Mao became convinced that the Soviet Union had abandoned its revolutionary project and had entered instead a phase of revisionism, which he considered the betrayal of socialist ideals. Mao openly criticised the hierarchic ways of Soviet communism, and castigated the corruption of bureaucratic elites. Stalin, he was to say, had underestimated the revolutionary capacity of the peasants.

With the Soviet model discredited, and disillusioned by American Cold War policies, rampant consumerism and profound socio-economic injustices, Western protesters turned to Chinese peasant communism for inspiration. Groups from the New Left, including factions of the SDS, the Black Panther and Black Nationalism movements, alongside anti-Vietnam groups, boasted of imagined emotional or intellectual connections with the Chinese rebels. *Quotations from Chairman Mao Tse-tung*, less formally known as the Little Red Book, was read widely. And, as the SDS began to radicalise itself, it splintered into various Maoist factions.

Maoism's permeation of French political culture was to be even more profound. France experienced a short-lived but intense Sinophilia to the bitter arrival of the Chinese Thermidor. Acker drew on the French theoretical tradition for philosophical and aesthetic bases of radical politics. Many prominent figures of the 1960s and 1970s cultural avant-garde she read were pulled into Maoist organisations, such as the rebellious Gauche prolétarienne, and were associated with a literary journal *Tel Quel* (1960–82), which at its peak activity acquired an overtly Maoist revolutionary orientation.

In the events leading up to May in France, Maoism merged with the ethos of May, representing to many an authentic break with the social order. According to the Maoist Rolan Castro, the French students were drawn to China because, firstly, it offered '*a revolution within a revolution*': it rewrote previous revolutionary scripts narrowly occupied with the seizure of power to prioritise cultural and ideological transformation. Secondly, its '*revolution in civilisation*' replaced emphasis on central planning with qualitative change in everyday life (which in the post-Maoist period fused with the Situationist credo of revolution of everyday life), and thirdly, the slogan 'Seven hundred million Chinese people is not a kibbutz' promoted the message that China was able to inspire and harness the power of the masses.[8]

Maoist impact was remarkable, because the peasant movement captured the minds also of the intellectual elite. One of the most culturally influential Maoist organisations in France, the Gauche prolétarienne, originated from a small group of ultraleft student activists, students of communist philosopher Louis Althusser at the prestigious École normale supérieure (ENT). Greatly influenced by his theoretical Marxism, they took on the identities of China's Red Guards to cultivate aspects of Maoism (real or imagined), a model they considered well suited to anticolonial and anticapitalist critique. As Paul Berman has described them, they embodied a familiar twentieth-century archetype of a romantic revolutionary, adopting 'a posture of extremism and violence, slightly dandified'.[9] Alain Badiou's political activity started with a deep commitment to Maoism that he discovered in the wake of May 1968. The early Badiou, under Althusser's influence, affirmed Mao as the 'one great philosopher of our time', and anticipated a victory of anti-imperialist struggle, led by China, 'the steady rear guard of the global revolution'.[10] Although Simone de Beauvoir (another ENT graduate) did not succumb to such blind faith in victorious China, she remained a devoted Maoist sympathiser, holding the opinion that Maoists were 'a genuine form of contestation', who in the atmosphere of political withdrawal were able to 'stir things up and arouse public opinion', engage '"fresh forces" in the proletariat – youth, women, foreigners, workers in the small provincial factories' and apply new types of revolutionary activity such as 'wildcat strikes and sequestrations'.[11]

Tel Quel's main proponents included Foucault, Julia Kristeva, Roland Barthes and Philippe Sollers. At the height of the journal's influence, at the same time as it celebrated the elsewhere banned experimental work of Pierre Guyotat (whose *Eden Eden Eden* Amy Scholder singles out as an influence on *Burning Bombing*),[12] it devoted articles to and published translations of Mao's thought, and even organised a conference which aligned the work of Artaud and Bataille with the spirit of Maoism.[13] Special issues of *Tel Quel* on the Cultural Revolution were followed by Kristeva, Barthes and Soller's revolutionary tourism to China. As is now well known, during their visit, the Chinese officials hid many empirical failings of the Cultural Revolution from their view. It must be noted that Western radical intellectuals treated it as a 'trope'[14] rather than a geopolitical reference point, and were initially largely oblivious to authoritarian tendencies or the suppression of the arts under Mao. They became aware of the signs of failure of the Maoist promise around the time of Mao's death. 'Becoming Chinese' opened for many a way towards 'a radiant utopian future'.[15] It injected meaning to otherwise immobile revolutionary prospects.[16]

Burning Bombing is a perfect example of the cross-cultural transposition of ideas. In the mix are Reichmann and Marcusian libidinal politics and Maoist militancy, united in the desire for a new world. The titles Acker gave to chapters and sections of the novella, including 'The Betrayal of Friends', 'Communist Aesthetics', 'Communist Story I', 'Diary', 'Revolution II', 'Information Sexual Ecstasy Revolution III', 'The New Life' and 'VIOLET WOMEN', read like abstract rubrics from Mao's Little Red Book – a revolutionary pocket-sized catechism of take-away citations. First published in 1964, Mao's book 'rapidly became the must-have accessory for Red Guards and revolutionaries from Berkeley to Bamako'.[17] Under punchy headlines, such as 'People's War', 'War and Peace', 'Socialism and Communism', 'Correcting Mistaken Ideas', 'Youth', 'Women' or 'Study', the book cited Mao's key passages from his previous works. As observed by Andrew Cook, the quotation genre made it easy for the ideas to be removed from their original context and applied in new political settings. 'It is right to rebel'; 'Revolution is not a dinner party'; 'All reactionaries are paper tigers'; 'Political power grows out of the barrel of a gun' are some of the catchiest slogans which were extracted from the book and circulated the world.[18]

Lin Biao, Mao's militant supporter and promoter of the Little Red Book, is credited with having written the foreword, which recognises the power of the written word to effect material change. Coining powerful metaphors derived from the looming atomic threat of the Cold War, he elevated Mao's ideas to the 'spiritual atom bomb', putting forward the daring message that a spiritual conversion on a mass scale is more influential than the impact of the physical atom bomb.[19] The prognosis was that: 'Once Mao Tse-tung's thought is grasped by the broad masses, it becomes an inexhaustible source of strength and a spiritual atom bomb of infinite power.'[20] In Mao's propagandist imagination, the atom bomb is dismissed as a 'paper tiger', while his political thought disseminated through the Little Red Book becomes the ideal tool to capture the hearts and minds of the people and thereby propel the arrival of the new world.

The Violet Women of the apocalypse

The emblematic exploding bomb in *Burning Bombing* constitutes the crucial expression of urban terrorism of the late counterculture and its affiliations with militant ideology. But it also points us to Acker's related adoption of the biblical myth of the apocalypse as a matrix for the novella's structure, imagery and the articulation of revolutionary hopes. Seeing that the hippie utopia of the early counterculture has failed to establish paradise on earth, Acker resorts to apocalyptic means.

Burning Bombing draws on the tradition of apocalyptic writing, whose founding texts in the Judeo-Christian canon include the Book of Daniel and the Revelation of John, often called the Apocalypse. In an apocalyptic narrative, the narrator reflects on the injustices of a corrupt society and the impossibility of changing it without divine intervention.[21] The narrator is a subversive figure presenting views outside of the dominant society. Following God's intervention, the forces of evil will be destroyed and replaced by a new transcendental realm. In John's revelation, the glorious end is preceded by a series of fights between angels and demons as well as the reign of the Antichrist, the Second Coming of Christ, the world-shaking battle of Armageddon, a thousand-year earthly reign of Christ and the final lost battle of Satan, before the final emergence of 'the holy city, the new Jerusalem, coming down from God out of heaven, prepared as a bride for her husband'.[22] Thus, as Lois Parkinson Zamora points out, the apocalypse is not only a vision of chaos and gloom as it is commonly perceived, but it comes with an expectation of a communal happy end for the faithful ones. Apocalypse means 'revelation', envisioning 'a millennial order which represents the potential antithesis to the undeniable abuses of human history'.[23]

Apocalypticism is not limited to religious experiences, and various revolutionary movements have utilised it, consciously or less consciously.[24] As Todd Gitlin has observed, the American 60-ers espoused 'millennial, all-or nothing moods'.[25] The apocalyptic spirit affirmed many of the positive energies of the early counterculture, animated by the utopian promise of a New Jerusalem. But the later disillusionment with the hippie utopia and the rejection of its shortcomings by many, as well as the omnipresent climate of violence, sparked the movement's darker side. As pointed out by Jedediah Sklower, 'The radicalisation of left-wing students who resorted to terrorism (the Weathermen Underground) can [. . .] be interpreted as an apocalyptic reaction to the failure of the counterculture to overthrow capitalism and the technocracy. Lost utopia leaves one with so many options.'²⁶ Rock music readily registered this change of mood of the late 1960s in bands such as The Doors and The Velvet Underground, which now seemed to be more 'obsessed with destruction than with the hopeful outcome of transfiguration' – the mood picked up by punk bands in the 1970s and 1980s.²⁷

Burning Bombing's direct reference to Marguerite Duras's 1969 book *Destroy, She Said* (*BB*, 153) incubates female violence within the narrative. Here, Acker not only aligns herself with the contemporary French avant-garde writer and filmmaker's impulse to apocalypse, but also relates the destructive act to female instruction. With a hybrid form that moves between a novel, play and a film script, *Destroy, She Said* was profoundly influenced by the events of May '68 in France. Leslie Hill tells us in her *Marguerite Duras: Apocalyptic Desires* (1993) that at that time Duras was involved in the revolutionary organisation of students and writers, whose members included Maurice Blanchot. Their task was to formulate a new understanding of politics in response to the events, and they took the pursuit of 'a radical communism of thought' as one of their aims. This, in turn, lead to the articulation by its members of the politics of absolute refusal, an uncompromised radicalism and rejection of any political structure.²⁸ '[T]he task of theory', Blanchot proposed, 'does not consist in devising a programme or platform', but rather 'in maintaining an *affirmative refusal*, in articulating or maintaining an affirmation that does not make compromises, but challenges and is challenged, and has to do with worklessness, confusion, or the unstructurable'.²⁹ As Hill writes, such conceived, May was seen as an 'apocalyptic event', dissolving the traditional humanistic notions of identity and progress.³⁰ Blanchot framed the expected imminent international communism in apocalyptic terms: 'The theoretical hiatus is absolute; and the historical break decisive. The liberal-capitalist world, our world, and the present [without presence] of the demand of communism are separated only by disaster, and a change in the heavens.'³¹

Burning Bombing takes seriously the apocalyptic direction of the communist-anarchist idea that the world needs to be first destroyed in order to be rebuilt with a new set of values. The choice is either 'we are part of a decaying world or we are a new society' (*BB*, 140), and hence the call for destruction: 'O beautiful blowing up of the US! happen! happen!' (*BB*, 152), and the anticipation that the violence will be reconfigured into something beautiful: 'when the world turns communist   totally in spirit the opening of paradise   beginning trees and water come back   birds   huge red feathers blue jays mynah birds maggots of purple silk' (*BB*, 140). In this Manichean framing, the revolutionaries are elevated to the spiritual realm while the enemies are debased to the lowly material world: 'the communists are angels against the rich men' (*BB*, 143). The text is loaded with scenes of extreme apocalyptic violence against the enemy and related structures performed by the repressed revolutionary agent, women:

> underneath the women wait they've waited 3,000,000,000 years   to blow up the cities   slowly cut off each of Nizon's balls   each piece of cement flies off into the blackness forever gone each department store splintered into a thousand golden pieces (*BB*, 141)

As in Hebrew and Christian scriptures of apocalypse, the narrator conveys the desire for vengeance on her oppressors, but here these are women who are now endowed with divine powers of retributive justice. The proliferation of images of destruction correlates to the exploding narrative into myriads of textual fragments, phrases and scenes, shifting kaleidoscopically and removing hierarchical grammar structures and logical sequences that would traditionally hold them together. Multitudes; vast numbers bursting off into bits and pieces; loss of structure and cohesion; collisions and juxtapositions: they constitute the aesthetics of an exploding bomb that underpins Acker's apocalyptic vision.

Manichean dramatisation also applies to gender relations. Acker does not offer a rationalised discourse that will coherently outline the shortcomings of the counterculture with its neglect of women's liberation. Instead, we are presented with a highly polarised view of men and women:

> Men are humans who are bred trained they can do anything they are almighty they must not be concerned with daily life. Their essence is rape. Their desire is murder. They are forced to destroy (*BB*, 190)

By contrast, Acker's imaginary terrorist groups of Cat-Women and Violet Women

> are all-powerful and have no power over anyone else   they take care of themselves   they are not teachers-analysts-doctors of all kinds-lawyers   their arm hair curls around their ankles   gold cunt hair runs up their legs   grows out of fertile star navels (*BB*, 193)

It would be easy to accuse Acker of essentialism, but what Acker is doing here is employing an apocalyptic rhetoric which is meant to provoke a radical resolution of ongoing conflict. The Violet Women take on the role of a divine messiah in response to historical necessity. The present injustice and oppression call for a godly intervention. Male and female are juxtaposed as contrasting forces of good and evil, and the effect is the destruction of gender difference, and nascent hybridity: 'O communists O Silver Women-Men' (*BB*, 143). Rather than wishing to replace patriarchy with matriarchal power, the Violet Women are driven by the desire to eliminate present society whose values are based on domination, and replace it with alternative values and social forms. Hence Violet Women do not aspire to state power; instead they are 'all-powerful and have no power over anyone else'. The idea provoked here is that for the communist-anarchist project to be successful there must be a drastic dissolution of power-structured relationships and the associated sexual psychic structures, that is, a complete overhaul of social order, without which the revolutionaries would merely repeat the Saturnian–Oedipal refrain.

The group names denoting human-animal and human-plant hybridity such as Cat-Women and Violet Women are charged with multiple meanings and allusions. At the literal level, apocalyptic animals and the whole physical world participate in the historical drama. The boundaries between human and non-human are dissolved. The Violet Women permeate the sky and the earth. Consider the opening image in 'The Narration of the New World':

> Flowers: dandelions large small carnations pussy willows milk buds roses tulips lilies of the valley daisies daffodils hyacinths arise. Cats become people roam the countries sniff nose stare at running river. This is the new world. [. . .] green cats lions ten-feet-long whiskers frighten away the Evil Ones [. . .] the Violet Women are now animals cats glowing   burning panthers prowl on the tops of your bodies (*BB*, 187)

But the evocation of the cat family, here and throughout *Burning Bombing*, also implies Acker's improvisation with the reservoir of revolutionary imagery which often utilised the dramatic appeal of big cats, such as fierce and untameable tigers and panthers, to intensify its message. Moreover, a storming army of Violet Women is an antithesis of the quiet, passive, delicate and decorative status that women have shared with flowers in patriarchal societies. As Henderson has noted, Acker modelled her Violet Women on the 1970s lesbian feminist group The Lavender Menace,[32] a name which similarly connects awakened feminism with apocalypticism. The Violet Women are violent, and violet is the reddish-blue colour of the 'end-of-the-world-weather' (*BB*, 166). There is also an intense and often obvious effort throughout the novella to relate animals and plant imagery with the female body, eroticism and revolutionary energy, as in this vivid description:

> each cancer cosmetic transformed by the stone into pure cunt juice
> nectar we have cultivated the flower opens each velvet petal one at
> a time black and purple and yellow each part of each petal atom by
> atom smell starts appearing (*BB*, 141)

The Violet Women are part of the loosely networked alliterative assemblages which spread rhizomatically through *Burning Bombing* and its revolutionary contexts. Take the recurring word 'velvet', for example: in addition to its physical, feminine attributes ('is velvet soft? [*BB*,159]), it might be taken for an allusion to the name of rock band The Velvet Underground. The 'v' alliteration is also strikingly reminiscent of Guyotat's descriptions of the turbulent landscapes of the Algerian War in *Eden Eden Eden*, which end with the scene of a vortex: 'Venus veiled in violet vapours' and 'Vortex veering back to Venus';[33] we will return to the theme of turbulence and revolution in Chapter 4.

With the Cat-Women, the Violet Women and the Weather(wo)men, Acker improvises on imagery from the revolutionary past and present. As we have seen in the Introduction, the French Revolution introduced a whole new metaphorical content to the idea of revolution, and since then modern revolutions tend to abound in metaphors describing the untameable forces of nature capable of overcoming any obstacle. The self-fashioning of such Mao-inspired groups as the Weathermen, described by Gitlin as 'the gathering cyclone',[34] or of the militant Black Panthers, points to their continuation of the modern revolutionary model which associates revolution with nature and stormy weather.

Mao famously considered the 'third world' the 'storm zone' of world revolution.[35] Lowell Dittmer tells us that Mao subscribed to a 'storming' approach, a minority position that grew within the Chinese communist movement. In contrast to 'engineers' who espoused reserved calculation, Mao increasingly relied on storming, and was theoretically attracted to spontaneous, bottom-up, non-hierarchical models of change common to anarchism.[36] What separated him from the dominant communist school in particular was an emphasis on the mobilisation of the masses, and especially the peasantry. Mao conjured up vivid imagery to promote the countryside insurgence, as in this hydraulic metaphor: 'Our Chinese people possess great intrinsic energy. [. . .] The more profound the oppression, the greater the resistance; that which has accumulated over time will surely burst forth quickly.'[37] At the outset of his career, Mao prophesied: 'In a short time [. . .] several million peasants will rise like a mighty storm, like a hurricane, a force so swift and violent that no power, however great, will be able to hold it back.'[38]

Burning Bombing is a variation on the modern storming narrative, but it actively transforms it. Mao's nature metaphors, such as comparing the peasant army to a storm or dismissing the enemy as 'paper tigers', are part of his rich and varied persuasive rhetoric to captivate and mobilise his audience. The quotations make up a conventional, efficiently designed propagandist text grounded in a dualistic universe. By contrast, *Burning Bombing*, rather than merely inciting and describing revolution, *is* a revolution in writing.

The hierarchical language structure and traditional metaphor are not conducive to the revolutionised literary form. Acker therefore abandons hierarchical syntax, and discards metaphor and dualistic universe to offer us a disjunctive, antidualist and deeply anarchic text. Here, revolution is not like a storm: it is a storm; the revolutionaries do not simply behave like wild cats: they morph into Cat-Women. The Violet Women do not merely reflect the colour of a purple-blue sky: they become it.

Deleuze and Guattari cite Kafka as saying that 'Metaphors are one of the things that make me despair of literature,' adding that metamorphosis and metaphor are opposed, because in metamorphosis

> There is no longer any proper sense or figurative sense, but only a distribution of states that is part of the range of the word. The thing and other things are no longer anything but intensities overrun by deterritorialized sound or words that are following their line of escape. [. . .] There is no longer man or animal, since each deterritorializes the other, in a conjunction of flux, in a continuum of reversible intensities. [. . .] Rather, there is a circuit of states that forms a mutual becoming, in the heart of a necessarily multiple or collective assemblage.[39]

The hybrid formations of seemingly incommensurable elements transform the relationships between humans and the organic and inorganic world, freeing the world from the torture of binary divisions and repetitions of the Saturnian–Oedipal structure. The apocalyptic uprising results in 'TOTAL CHAOS' (*BB*, 197), where even the differentiation between lower and upper case disappears. The new Jerusalem is an undifferentiated mass of desire, an 'ENDLESS MIND-BODY PLEASURE ORGA (NI) SM' (*BB*, 196) which disallows re-Oedipalisation. A resolution such conceived is a radical break with the other apocalyptically structured revolutionary movements which merely reconstitute the Saturnian–Oedipal scenario in replacing one power regime with another. Nevertheless, we are left with a purely imaginary and deeply anti-humanist resolution of the conflicts of history. Not only that, the newly established universe of perpetual anarchy and 'UNINTERRUPTED GAYETY' (*BB*, 200) is located not on earth but in the secular heaven of 'OUTER SPACE' (*BB*, 197), from where the Violet Women send us messages, promising that they will 'DESCEND INTO THE EARTH' (*BB*, 201).

Prison revolts in *I Dreamt I Was a Nymphomaniac: Imagining*

The trio of novels reprinted in the *Portrait of an Eye* collection – *The Childlike Life of the Black Tarantula*, *The Adult Life of Toulouse Lautrec*[40] and *I Dreamt I Was a Nymphomaniac: Imagining* – takes us from the mythical space of *Burning Bombing* into a new political terrain. If *Burning Bombing* articulates apocalyptic expectations of a transformed future cosmos, the writing that follows looks to history as a source for political potentiality. It also departs from the explosive fragmentation of individual sentences and instead collages larger textual blocks. In *Black Tarantula*, the fictional 'I' acquires the identities of historical murderesses.[41] In *Nymphomaniac*, as we will see below, Blaise Cendrars's anarcho-surrealist novel *Moravagine* (1926) directly inspires Acker's hallucinatory narrative in which sexual obsession morphs into a mixture of historical and fictional rebellions and an array of shifting identities. In *Toulouse Lautrec*, the nineteenth century's artistic and revolutionary scene precedes commentaries on contemporary America's foreign policy.

'The revolution glitters' (*N*, 169), a phrase Acker translates from Blaise Cendrars, captures vividly the scattered trajectory of *Nymphomaniac*, a novel blazing with revolt. In it, Acker incorporates a

Cendrarian literary universe which puts the boundaries between fact and fiction, hallucination and reality, self and other, here and elsewhere, now and then, in crisis. From Cendrars and Louis-Ferdinand Céline, its innovative European forebears, *Nymphomaniac* takes its disjointed episodic structure, in which narratives cut into each other, and so 'nothing follows anything else'.[42] In modelling her nymphomaniac narrator on Cendrars's Moravagine – a wild, unruly character governed by excessive passion in both personal life and politics – Acker explores the climate of defiance she witnessed in the late counterculture and its reversal by conservative authorities.

In Cendrars's *Moravagine*, two comrades, almost opposites – a psychiatric doctor, Raymond, and the titular monster, Moravagine – are engaged in a journey around the globe. Prior to his travels, Moravagine spends the first hundred days of his life in an incubator and leads a sedentary indoor existence. The voyage starts off with Raymond assisting him in his escape from the hospital in Switzerland, and takes them from Europe to America and back. On meeting Moravagine, Raymond, who is the narrator of the story, foregoes his scientific career for a life of perpetual vagabondage. Moravagine is described as 'amoral' and 'an outcast', marked by an excess of passion and primal instinct. His over-lust eventually turns him into a serial killer of women (as signalled in the novel's title *Moravagine*). His childhood ends with his incarceration following the murder of the Austrian princess Rita:

> And here is the result. They lock me up. I go to prison. I'm eighteen. That was in 1884. They put me in the fortress of Pressburg. Ten years later they transfer me secretly to Waldensee, among the madmen. Have they quite given up all thought of me, then? I am a madman. And have been for six years.[43]

Acker's narrator follows a similar path, but the year is 1965, the prison is not Pressburg (German name for Bratislava) but Alcatraz, and the mental hospital is in San Francisco (*N*, 160). Both can be taken as allusions to America's increasingly prisonised landscape.

The narrator lusts after Peter, a transvestite 'who wants to get rid of leaders and money' (*N*, 164). Although she admires Peter's radical activism, initially, the sexual despair is in conflict with political conviction: 'I know about women's liberation, but I'm still pining away from desire' (*N*, 164). Equally, the rebellious lifestyle of Cendrars's Moravagine could also be explained as motivated by sexual frustration, supported by the fact that Raymond first sees him masturbating. Acker's narrator is pressed to choose 'between my desire to find Peter and my duty as a revolutionary soldier. I can't possibly do both. For the moment I pick up the ammunition box' (N, 166). But at the peak of revolutionary upheaval, once they are united, the erotic coupling and the political rebellion prove compatible and coincide. This can be seen as Acker's comment that the liberation of Eros alone, much as it stimulated the revolutionary energies of the sixties, if divorced from direct action, is insufficient in instigating a political transformation. At the same time, the coordination of the seemingly incompatible political and sexual motivations – of animalistic instinct and bold utopian schemes – casts a blow to those critical voices which downgraded the youth's revolutionary activity to mere hedonistic urges.

Acker's earlier novella, *Rip-off Red, Girl Detective* (1973), follows a similar pattern. A sexual liaison, little by little, mingles with a direct intervention in the social and political world. The narrator announces to her lover Peter: 'I want to do something better than fuck,'[44] and they subsequently become detectives and join the New York anarchist underground. Rip-off Red has an affair with a woman and declares 'she's my sister';[45] the narrator of *Nymphomaniac* follows Peter, who is now a transvestite: both of which are attempts at evading heterosexual matrices and Oedipal scripts. But here, too, the template of sexual desire is inseparable from political design, and their interconnectedness increases the potential for freedom. For the task is to reinspire passion, resensitise perception and reactivate thought: 'By thinking, dreaming, following sexual and other desires, and by inflaming you with sensuous images, we can get rid of the universities, the crowded towns, the bureaucracies. [. . .] I know we are all connected. Fucking is a religious ceremony.'[46] When social existence is full of fabricated emotion and fake connection, 'the nymphomaniac moments' offer glimpses of freedom.[47] Hence the narrator decides to both 'work harder and worship my passions'.[48]

But, as Houen points out, Acker complicates straightforward access to authentic feeling and dreaming. The narrator of *Nymphomaniac* admits that 'If everything is drag, there is no such thing as real love, or friendship. I am drag too' (N, 67). Dreams also seem unreliable reservoirs of unmediated desire. Because dreaming is susceptive to internal censorship, in the way that emotion is open to fabrication, Houen asserts that Acker's writing shows that 'One cannot simply rely on unadulterated accounts of dreams as guaranteeing escape from libidinal regulation,' and therefore Acker transforms dreams when transcribing them into her works.[49]

Textual transformation thus permits her to provoke potentials of revolutionary desire. Like personal dreams, historical scripts undergo various transformations in Acker's prose, in which the boundary between dreaming and history is blurred, thereby creating the effect of a hallucinatory history. Acker is less interested in a factual account – that 'as it happened' official history of causes and effects – but in the revolutionary potentials that an unlocked and unanchored history might offer. Hence *Nymphomaniac*'s entry into history is not through history textbooks but through Cendrars's deviated, mad, surreal account of revolutionary Russia.

Nymphomaniac revisits history by transforming Cendrars's dazzling depictions of Moravagine's wild anarchist activity in Russia in 1904, which involved numerous acts of violence and popular uprisings intended to ignite a full-scale revolution. Acker recognised that the America of the early 1970s shared its political perplexities with the Tsarist Russian Empire, where the unjust socio-political system created an environment for nihilism and terrorism. The proposed solution is the destruction of the current order, which necessitates a complete overturning of the ordinary world of morality and law and social hierarchy, with the hope of replacing it with a better one – though neither Acker nor Cendrars offers a vision of what a transformed polity might look like. Again, Acker substitutes the Russian and Polish epicentres of anarchist activity with American ones: Moravagine and Raymond's Moscow[50] is now New York City (*N*, 168); the first riots break out not near Smolensk but below the West Village; the wounded students are carried away not by the Cossacks but by the New York police; where Moravagine and Raymond pledge allegiance to Kropotkin and join up with the Russian and international radical movements, Acker's narrator, Peter and their revolutionary group connect with the New York and global anarchist network; and their ammunition reservoirs are now not Finland but Arkansas (*N*, 169).

As is now clear, it is typical for Acker to carry Cendrars's descriptions into an American setting, and she moves quickly back and forth between a Cendrarian universe and her own, expanding the terror into an atmosphere that transcends and relativises the borders of space, time and identity. In the following passage, Russian revolutionary history is filled with American content:

> I'm sure you all know the history of the US revolutionary movement. Runaway servants escaped Virginia tobacco slaves worn-out prostitutes religious dissenters helped the American Indians fight for

their lives. Attica Folsom etc. prisoners fight against the lobotomy-mongers, the men who want to plant dogs' brains in prisoners' heads and prisoners' brains in dogs' heads to see what'll happen. The most ardent adepts of the pure Maria Spiridonowa or the heroic lieutenant Schmitt lost their revolutionary ideals to commit crimes. (*N*, 170)

The passage represents a deterritorialised version of American history, bringing to the fore the relatively obscure events – the anti-slavery and anti-segregation movements of African Americans; the Native American revolts; the participation of the socially excluded – whose existence has been mostly sidelined or completely hidden from the standard textbook history. As Howard Zinn has pointed out, official American history is told through 'important' white male figures, while the American people appear to be passive. But 'under the surface', writes Zinn: 'Whenever injustices have been remedied, wars halted, women and blacks and Native Americans given their due, it has been because "unimportant" people spoke up, organized, protested, and brought democracy alive.'[51]

The passage is also deeply responsive to ongoing political events. *Nymphomaniac* grapples with the contemporary issues of race and violence that resurfaced in the wave of prison riots of the sixties and early seventies, including the 1971 riots at Attica prison, the bloodiest incident in US penal history. Over one thousand inmates, predominantly African American and Puerto Rican, protested against the terrible conditions in the Attica State Penitentiary, New York by taking prison officials hostage. Governor Nelson Rockefeller's order to retake the prison by force resulted in carnage, leaving forty-three Attica prisoners and eleven guards and civilians dead.

Following the massacre, the African American artist Faith Ringgold paid homage to the thirty-nine prisoners in her widely circulated poster entitled 'United States of Attica', which, similarly to Acker, places the Attica events in a wider historical context. It features a transformed map of the United States in which geographical names are replaced with dozens of historical examples of brutality and genocide committed by the American system at home and abroad on oppressed groups including Native Americans, witches, blacks and Asians since the days of colonisation, and their resistance to that oppression. Painted in vibrant red and green, the symbolic colours of the Black Liberation movement, the poster invites others to contribute events that have been hidden from American consciousness.

Placing the fight of prisoners in Attica and Folsom for their rights within the context of dissident tradition in America, Acker manifests their political content and ongoing significance. We are urged to consider them as an integral element of the collective movements for social change occurring in various sections of American society at the time, ranging from Black Power and Black Nationalism to a resurgence of anarchist, socialist and communist doctrines; to feminism, queer movements, and opposition to Vietnam War. The Attica rioters' demands of improved living conditions were not different from what had motivated many revolts throughout history. Moreover, as Foucault was determined to demonstrate, the disciplinary system in prisons extends itself to society as a whole, operating in educational institutions, asylums, hospitals and industries, thereby ensuring the docility of citizens in all areas of social life.[52] For Acker, a prison revolt that challenges that docility is thus a crucial element in the broad movement for change. The architectural and social design of prisons alone, as widely illustrated by Foucault, might be seen as arising from the authorities' fear of prison riots. As recounted by Acker, the Adjustment Center at Folsom Prison 'is a prison within a prison. It has maximum physical control and is segregated from the rest of the prison in a separate building' (N, 174). The physical architecture is supported by a social architecture imposed upon prisoners by classifying them into categories depending on the estimated risk they pose within the prison: militants, prison artists, weakies, prison rats, escape risks, druggies and the mentally ill (N, 175).

Ascribing a political character to prison riots challenges the traditional reception of them as unrelated to society, unsophisticated explosions of violence that are to be expected of imprisoned criminals. As Robert Adams writes, prison riots have tended to be viewed as mindless and purposeless eruptions of disorder, confirming to unsympathetic bystanders and authorities the broad indiscipline and aggressive 'macho' masculinity of the prisoners, many of them black and Latino.[53] It has also been noted that the term 'riot' depoliticises prison violence and consigns it to the realm of criminal rage. The *American College Dictionary* defines a riot as 'the execution of a violent and unlawful purpose by three or more persons acting together, to the terror of the people', usually accompanied by 'unbridled outbreaks of passion or emotion'.[54]

The political upsurge of the 1960s and the early 1970s had a profoundly destabilising effect on the existing systems of authority, upsetting political and moral standards and threatening the comfortable existence of the white middle-class population. Acker suggests that the rebellious movements, including the multiplying prison riots, had the potential to push the government and conformist society to the limit in the hope of a major transformation in the way that the populist riots on Russian soil were driven to do in the lead-up to the long-awaited first Russian Revolution of 1905. This prompts Acker to plug into Cendrarian prose for some of the wildest scenes of Moravagine's experience of the Russian rebellion, presented in a carnivalesque mode:

> There're daily scenes of madness and suicide: Hookers believe other workers should respect them. Workers turn against their bosses. Soldiers refuse to fight.
>
> A man drinks menses blood to make another man love him. A musician coats her hands with dog shit to massage a poet's aura. Men are fags. Women dykes. All couples practice [*sic*] platonic love. [. . .] In the Plaza, the Papillon, ministers covered with spit mingle with bald revolutionaries and long-hair students who vomit champagne into the debris of dishes and raped women. (*N*, 170)

Moravagine is now cast as 'Bob Ashley', an avant-garde composer whose experimental composition technique influenced the shifting moods in *Nymphomaniac*. Like Moravagine wearing drag and impersonating various revolutionaries, Ashley is believed to be 'the famous terrorist Samuel Simbirsky who killed the Russian Alexander II' (*N*, 171). The subversive use of drag in *Nymphomaniac* points to the mutability of identity, here challenging not only traditional gender distinctions, but also becoming a means of dedication to political subjectivity through giving up on one's ordinary identity.

Revolutionary hero-martyrs

By the end of the novel, a familiar pattern emerges where rebellion is followed by the ugly monster of reaction. Cendrars evokes the terrifying and murderous punishment of revolutionaries after the defeat of the Russian Revolution of 1905,[55] which gave birth to a dark period of melancholy, as will be discussed in Chapter 3. While Cendrars allows his protagonists to leave post-revolutionary Russia to continue their travels through the American continent, *Nymphomaniac* ends with the government's backlash and images of confinement. The final sentence brings the novel full circle to incarceration, from the escape from prison, to vagabondage and participation in revolutionary fervour, to being locked up again: 'The Black Tarantula, like Peter Gordon, is sentenced to a lifetime punishment in a small cell' (*N*, 184). And yet, I argue, Acker's revolutionary project, rather than ceasing, brings to the forefront the notion of revolutionary martyrdom. The martyr figure will establish a contrast between the temporal, closed and linear history, and the atemporal dimension of evental truth.

The novel's final section, 'Dykes', first focuses on the passionate lesbian relationship of Katty and Patty, which permits Acker to maximise the mix of libidinal and historical potential when the novel then moves to a profoundly sympathetic but formal catalogue of fictionalised outlines of disenfranchised inmates. They are contemporary experimental artists and radical intellectuals, people from the artistic environment Acker knew, including Robert Sheff, Peter Gordon, Melvyn Freilicher, David and Blaise Antin, and even Acker's persona as 'the Black Tarantula'. Acker details racial and class-based biases of the American prison system which led to their criminalisation and incarceration. We learn about the subsequent grossly unfair treatment, abuse, indeterminate sentences and unjustified segregation of the inmates by prison officials. The locked-away artists take on the identities of imprisoned Black, Chicano and Native American citizens. The case of Peter Gordon, for example, 'a Black citizen, 46 years of age' (*N*, 180), contains a brief account of his original arrest as an ordinary lawbreaker, and the circumstances of the disproportionately long sentences and unjustified solitary confinement at Folsom Prison. As we learn from Gordon's and other examples, 'Prison officials are here magnifying minor incidents in order to warehouse Peter Gordon whom they view as a Black leader who might conceivably influence younger Blacks' (*N*, 180). Similarly, David and Blaise Antin's petitions to improve the conditions at Folsom get them put in jail 'because of suspicion of agitation, not because of the charges filed against them' (*N*, 183).

In this way, Acker expresses the artistic community's solidarity with incarcerated activists, and in particular Black, Chicano and Puerto Rican prisoners, who now constituted the majority of the population of American prisons. Acker and the Left see the increase in the non-white prison population as directly related to the unconcealed racism of the American judiciary and the government's repression of the Black Nationalism and civil right movements. Indeed, as Bert Useem and Peter Kimball have pointed out, the rise of Black and Latino prisoners coincided with the outburst of multi-ethnic struggles in the 1960s.[56] A number of anti-war and Black Panther and other leftist activists were imprisoned at the time, and when they came into contact with everyday law offenders, they gave their grievances public visibility, fostering an interaction between prisoners and the politically engaged groups on the outside.[57]

Acker's David and Blaise Antin's petitions in the cause of prison reform, and their subsequent incarceration, echo the activism of Angela Davis – a radical feminist and anti-prison campaigner, communist with ties to the Black Panther Party, and author of influential works challenging racism, poverty, patriarchy and the abuses of human rights by the American judiciary system. Acker and Davis once lived together, and Acker felt there was a kinship between her own work and Black writing and militancy. Black narratives taught her 'how to be surprised, how to write something that's not dogmatic, how to be political'.[58]

Davis's activism extended to supporting the Soledad Brothers, three African American inmates (George Jackson among them, discussed below) accused of killing a prison guard. Her advocacy for political prisoners led to three capital charges followed by incarceration, and subsequent acquittal thanks to a powerful international campaign of support. In her essay 'Political Prisoners, Prisons, and Black Liberation' (1970), Davis makes a connection between crime and an unequal distribution of wealth and employment in capitalist social organisation. She also considers the overrepresentation of people of ethnic backgrounds in prison as a direct effect of racism, insisting on their status as '*political* prisoners [. . .] in the sense that they are largely the victims of an oppressive politico-economic order, swiftly becoming conscious of the causes underlying their victimization'.[59] Prisons, in Davis's estimation, have come to be seen as 'an inevitable fact of life, like birth and death'.[60] Davis has continually challenged the supposed naturalness of prisons within the American landscape, questioning the democratic spirit of the country whose major social programme in advancing security and freedom is mass incarceration.

In modelling her heroic prisoners on zoomorphic Moravagine, an archetype criminal, Acker elevates to the level of absurdity the stereotyped identity of a captive supposedly naturally prone to uncontrolled lust and greed and excesses of primitive passion and monstrous violence, who like a wild animal released from a cage is ready to burn, rape, kill and loot. The narrator of *Nymphomaniac* 'was born evil and became more evil and more evil by chance' and is possessed by 'proud desires' and 'ungovernable passions' (*N*, 126). Through this outrageously amplified portrayal, and the mocking inversion of cause and effect, Acker satirises the widespread stigmatisation of criminals as inhuman animal beings, while repeatedly demonstrating that it is the political system that is ugly and bestial and produces its own monsters. Indeed: 'In this city which is based on money', the narrator reasons, 'lust oversexuality poverty false anthropomorphism suffering' are the consequences (*N*, 126). The statement of demands of the participants of the 1971 Attica Prison uprising, read out by Elliott James ('L. D.') Barkley, contained a desperate plea to be recognised as human beings: 'We are men! We are not beasts and we do not intend to be beaten or driven as such. The entire prison populace – that means each and every one of us here – has set forth to change forever the ruthless brutalization and disregard for the lives of the prisoners here and throughout the United States.'[61] Similarly reflecting on the dehumanising experience of her imprisonment, Davis has observed that the prison officials establish a racist regime to turn prisoners against each other in order to prevent them from reflecting on their wretched condition: 'Jails and prisons are designed to break human beings, to convert the population into specimens in a zoo – obedient to our keepers, but dangerous to each other.'[62]

The prisoner profiles catalogued by Acker evoke the incarceration of such political prisoners as George Jackson, an African American who for a petty crime was given a sentence of 'one year to life'. He spent ten years in Soledad Prison – including over seven years in solitary confinement[63] – before being moved to San Quentin, where he was shot and killed by a prison guard for purportedly attempting an escape. To Jackson's sympathisers on the left, there is no doubt that he was kept behind bars because of his 'political consciousness'.[64] Like Malcolm X and many others, Jackson converted his incarceration into an individual evolution to political militancy. He affiliated himself with the Black Panther Party and stimulated intense revolutionary organising from within prison walls while developing a radical vision of class-based revolution followed by a future beyond capital, tracking his lineage to Marx, Lenin, Mao and others.[65] The letters from Soledad Prison document his transition into a revolutionary. Introduced by Jean Genet, who also spent much time in prison, they were the most widely read literature on Black militancy within and outside of prison walls. There, Jackson expressed his raging fury:

This monster – the monster they've engendered in me will return to torment its maker, from the grave, the pit, the profoundest pit. Hurl me into the next existence, the descent into hell won't turn me. [. . .] I'm going to charge them reparations in blood. I'm going to charge them like a maddened, wounded, rogue male elephant, ears flared, trunk raised, trumpet blaring. [. . .] War without terms.[66]

In this dramatised passage, Jackson desires to be resurrected as a monster that would revenge itself on the system that brought it into being. There is a clear correlation here between Jackson and Acker's narrator's diagnosis, namely that America's oppressive capitalist system produces criminal behaviour and employs mass incarceration as a way of dealing with the problem. Both express impatience with improvement through reform in the current shape of American democracy, whose ideals have been highly compromised by the demands of the capitalist economy, and recognise the necessity of violent means of change. The opening of the section detailing the uprising in *Nymphomaniac* contains the verses: 'Today's society makes us / Murderers liars assassins. / If I trust you / A revolution will happen.' (*N*, 161). When the revolution happens,

We scientifically demonstrate the legality of individual expropriation under all forms: theft, assassination, extortion, sabotage of factories, pillage of public welfare, destruction of paved roads, destruction of underwear. We scientifically demonstrate that a corrupt society forces us to do these things in order to stay alive. (*N*, 169)

In this fairly closely cribbed passage from Cendrars, Acker highlights the common anarchist argument according to which the state machinery concentrates wealth and privilege in the hands of the few while effecting a series of negative consequences on individuals, such as crime and poverty. In underscoring the social rather than psychological causes of crime, this argument questioned the popular rehabilitation programmes that prevailed in American prison for decades, which were aimed at correcting criminals' mental deficiencies to bring them onto a lawful path.[67] 'I was born knowing nothing and am a product of my total surroundings' – Jackson compellingly denies any psychological basis for his unlawful behaviour, blaming instead 'the capitalistic dog, the imperialistic, cave-dwelling brute that kidnapped us, pulled the rug from under us, made us a caste within his society with no vertical economic mobility'.[68]

A political prisoner of such a strong military stance and outreach did not last long. Each prisoner profile listed by Acker repeats the Jacksonian pattern of severe punishment for suspicious revolutionary activity. Together they form a catalogue resembling saints' legends, which in effect converts what the government deems to be monsters into martyrs. The recurring notions of subjective conversion into a revolutionary and selfless sacrifice for others further confirm the framework of religiosity in Acker's search for a new figure of political subjectivity. The assimilation of hagiographic profiling in *Nymphomaniac* is also strikingly reminiscent of the section of 'Revolutionary Profiles' of eight radicals from the seminal book on the Russian revolutionary movement, *Underground Russia* (1883), written by an active nihilist, Sergei Mikhailovich Kravchinsky, also known as Stepniak.[69] This work covers the emergence of the nihilists in the 1860s – a group of young radical propagandists who 'went to the people', inspired by the coterminous revolutionary aspirations of the Parisian Communards[70] – and, after the disillusionment with their pilgrimages to the people, their evolution into terrorists whose acts notably included the hunting down and assassination of Tsar Alexander II. The word 'nihilist' was popularised in Ivan Turgenev's novel *Fathers and Children* (1862). For Stepniak it signified 'absolute individualism' to be achieved through 'the negation in the name of individual liberty, of all the obligations imposed upon the individual by society, by family life and religion'.[71]

According to Stepniak, the figure of the terrorist possesses the following attributes: 'He is noble, terrible, irresistibly fascinating, for he combines in himself the two sublimities of human grandeur: the martyr and the hero.'[72] Unlike the propagandist, who uses 'Words', the terrorist proceeds with 'Acts'.[73] Moreover, as noted by Peter Scotto, Stepniak's figure of the terrorist replaces the propagandist's Christian ideal of loving one's enemy with hatred, while combining 'the martyr's readiness for self-sacrifice with the hero's drive to victorious action'.[74] His loyalties lie no longer only with the people and the nation as a whole, but also with those engaged in a similar struggle, his comrades 'who languish in the horrid cells of the central prisons'.[75] Like Acker's hagiographic portraits of befriended artists turned radicals, Stepniak wrote about revolutionaries he knew personally (except for Gesia Gelfman, also known as Gesya Gelfman and Jessy, Hesse or Hessy Helfman) and considered his friends.[76] They all received severe punishment for their revolutionary activity, from imprisonment to death: Yakov Stefanovich was incarcerated; Dmitry Klements sent to Siberia; Valerican Ossinsky, Dmitry Lizogub and

Sofia Perovskaya executed; Gelfman died awaiting execution; Peter Kropotkin and Vera Zasulic were political refugees.[77]

While Stepniak is adamant about removing any 'religious feeling' from his portrait of the terrorist, the figure is steeped in metaphysics but of a different kind. As Houen has noted, the terrorist has qualities of a messiah, a 'spiritual militant', though one that is opposed to God.[78] Indeed, '[p]roud as Satan rebelling against God, he opposed his own will to that of the man who alone, amid a nation of slaves, claimed the right of having a will.'[79] Moreover, he is 'immortal', Stepniak insists, and: 'His limbs may fail him, but, as if by magic, they regain their rigour, and he stands erect, ready for battle after battle until he has laid low his enemy and liberated the country.'[80] This is not unlike Cendrars's virile Moravagine and Jackson's monster, a 'maddened, wounded, rogue male elephant' returning from hell with a vengeance. Houen relates the terrorist figure to Nietzsche's 'Overman', as both figures place emphasis on exceeding subjective possibilities. For Nietzsche, such a position is available only to men.[81] But Stepniak recognised that nihilism was closely tied with the movement of emancipation of women in Russia.[82]

Women were drawn to nihilism because it was the only available intellectual movement which in its programme of world transformation included the emancipation of women.[83] Moreover, with the invention of dynamite, physical strength became less important. Sofia Perovskaya, a member of The People's Will, participated in the assassination of Tsar Alexander II, for which she was executed, becoming the first woman in Russia to mount the scaffold for a political offence. In rejecting traditional gender roles, female nihilists were considered enemies of the state, as criminals. Nihilist women wanted both sexual and professional freedom, which the nihilist movement accommodated, but this invited a flurry of charges by the anti-nihilists of being 'a bunch of libertines, whores or nymphomaniacs'.[84] Hostile accounts of Perovskaya emphasised her unfeminine qualities, describing her as 'aloof, secretive, stubborn, rude, scornful of men, heartless, evil and cruel'.[85] It was not uncommon for radical women to defeminise themselves on entering the terrorist phase, then and now. Perovskaya swapped feminine dress for boyish outfits and plain hairstyles, and the Weather Underground leader Bernardine Dohrn covered her attractive figure in nondescript, worn-out clothes.[86]

Perovskaya and numerous other Russian radical women were a unique phenomenon of female dissidence at the time in Europe, setting an example for further generations of women of Tsarist Russia who joined the revolutions of 1905 and 1917, and inspiring Acker's female protagonists in *Toulouse Lautrec*, as I shall elaborate further. Previous outbursts of radical female activism had occurred during the French Revolution, and numerous revolutionary leaders proclaimed that any successful revolution requires the participation of women, but female revolutionary spirit died down with the suppression of the Paris Commune.[87]

Maria Spiridonova was a leading terrorist of the later generation of radicals of the 1905 uprising. Her name appears next to that of Pyotr Schmidt's, another revolutionary leader, within the context of America's dissident movements in *Nymphomaniac* (N, 170). Acker sees contemporary parallels for their martyrdom by relating their sacrifice to the political prisoners of the New Left. Spiridonova belonged to a terrorist group within the Social Revolutionary Party which employed similar tactics to their predecessors, The People's Will. She assassinated a police official, for which she suffered abuse by the Cossacks during her arrest, and was sent to Siberia. She soon became recognised as a hero by the socialists, becoming an incarnation of what Sally Boniece has called 'the myth of the revolutionary martyr-heroine'. She was admired across Russia, by educated people and working and illiterate classes, for her heroism, her suffering and the sacrifices she made for the liberation of others.[88] She spent over thirty years in prison, and after years in exile from the communist dictatorship she was executed in 1941.[89]

We are reminded of Badiou's truth procedures, those experiences of love, political struggle, scientific discovery and artistic creation which allow access to the 'inhuman': that which is in excess of our life. For Badiou, such a connection with the infinite is realised in the heroic figure:

> We must create a symbolic representation of this humanity which exists beyond itself, in the fearsome and fertile element of the inhuman. I call that sort of representation an heroic figure. 'Figure', because the action of a figure is a symbolic one. 'Heroic', because heroism is properly the act of the infinite in human actions. 'Heroism' is the clear appearance, in a concrete situation, of something which assumes its humanity beyond the natural limits of the human animal.[90]

In his book on St Paul, Badiou is little concerned with the historicity of the apostle and his religiosity. It was more important, Badiou insists, to establish him as a 'poet-thinker of the event',[91] a universal figure seized by truth which emerged in response to the event of the resurrection of Christ. The interest in St Paul sprang from the need for 'a new militant figure', and so Badiou sees him as a model ready for appropriation for contemporary political ends.

The 'human animal' Badiou refers to above is a critical term describing the tendency of 'contemporary "democracies"' to reduce people to a mere species (C, 175). So conceived, people are incapable of political projects, courage or revolutionary collectivity. It is a 'project-less humanism', subtended by 'domestication', where 'man only exists as worthy of pity. Man is a *pitiable animal*' (C, 175; author's emphasis). It is thus a different conceptualisation of people's animality from Acker's human–animal hybrid. Both Acker and Badiou affirm 'the fearsome and fertile element of the inhuman',[92] and in Acker becoming-animal constitutes one of the figures of revolutionary force that exceeds the limits of ordinary identity. Yet whereas Badiou distances himself from sacrifice, Acker's early political subjects are steeped in animality, sacrificing themselves and thereby returning themselves to the infinity of the natural world.

Acker makes the point that political subversion and artistic creativity, such as her writing and the artistic works of her friends, are part of the same revolutionary endeavour. The epigraph of *Nymphomaniac* contains the charge: 'This is very nonpolitical, therefore reactionary.' It suggests that the literary universe that follows is devoid of any political significance. Yet Acker authorises the aesthetic and political fusion with a rebuttal: 'But what would the world have to be like for these events to exist?' (*N*, 94).

Acker's next work, *Toulouse Lautrec*, is another compelling articulation of a political subjectivity figured through martyrdom and sacrifice. As elsewhere, Acker's preference is for some of the most tormented and tragic historical figures. Her 'Christs' of 1870s and 1880s Europe and America include the political actors Sofia Perovskaya, Charles Gallo, the martyrs of the Chicago Haymarket Affair and the Parisian Communards, as well as Vincent Van Gogh as an exemplary artist-martyr. Acker associates the self-sacrificial dynamic with both committed revolutionaries and artists, demonstrating the different ways in which people can intervene in the world and exceed their subjective limits.

The antithesis of a docile citizen in *Toulouse Lautrec* is the figure of a hero-martyr who sacrifices personal identity and wordly existence to become a revolutionary. The verbal exchange between the prostitutes of Montmartre, Berthe and Giannina, becomes an arena for Acker to offer some extreme examples of political commitment from French, Russian and American history.

Berthe recalls the case of Charles Gallo, who in 1886 threw a bottle of vitriol and fired three shots in the Paris Stock Exchange. Gallo, formerly a notary clerk, developed anarchist beliefs after being convicted for counterfeiting. No one was hurt during the attack, but during his trial (which resulted in a sentence of twenty years of hard labour in a penal colony, where he soon died) Gallo took the opportunity to effectively communicate his anarchist views and hatred of social injustice.[93] As Acker's protagonist Berthe relates to her friend Giannina, Gallo exclaimed, 'Long live revolution! Long live anarchism! Death to the bourgeois judiciary! Long live dynamite! Bunch of idiots!' (*TL*, 201).

To provide examples of female heroism, Berthe then admires the Russian nihilist Perovskaya: 'Five years ago March first The People's Will, a group she was part of, murdered Tsar Alexander II. As she died, she rejoiced, for she realised her death would deal a fatal blow to autocracy.' She adds, 'I'd like to have the guts to follow that woman' (*TL*, 201). Acker summons Perovskaya as a model of female radicalism. In Ebbessen's words, 'by referring to the female Russian revolutionary Perovskaya [Acker] puts women back into history and gives our poor Montmartre prostitutes an active and powerful model, even in her failure'.[94]

In another historical reference, Acker recalls the tragically large number of dead Communards of the Paris Commune, which I discuss at length in Chapter 4. Although unnamed, they represent the workers' revolutionary spirit and drastic moments in the history of revolutionary sacrifice and martyrdom. The following passage describes the violent suppression:

> On Sunday May 21 the first detachment of Versailles troops entered the capital. This entrance caught the Commune unawares. Thiers' army made up of prisoners of war and provincial recruits shot everyone in sight. They killed 25,000 people. The Communards, retreating from Paris, burned as much as they could. Marshal MacMahon of the Versailles army declared order was restored. The death of the Paris Commune was the death of the workers' revolutionary power. (*TL*, 202)

The passage about the Parisian martyrs ends with the confirmation of the necessity of sacrifice: 'Now we have to give up our lives to cause any destruction of this society' (*TL*, 202).

The historical section ends with the drama of the 1886 Chicago Haymarket affair, considered the pivotal moment in American anarchism. A bomb was thrown during a meeting of Chicago workers peacefully protesting against the killing of four strikers at the McCormick Harvester works, leaving 'demonstrators policemen wounded killed' (*TL*, 205).[95] Although there was no evidence to identify the bomb thrower, nine Chicago anarchists were arrested; one disappeared; four were sentenced to death by execution; the fifth took his life in his cell and the rest were sent to prison.[96] Witness the court hearing drama as retold by Acker:

THE D.A.: The defendants are to remain seated!
(All the anarchists stand up and scream.)
JUDGE: The court will not permit itself to be intimidated by this uproar. I declare that, if the slightest disturbance is injected into the trial, I shall bring in a verdict of guilt against the defendants.
SEVERAL ANARCHISTS: Cut it short! Judge us now, without letting us be heard! That won't take so long!
THE ANARCHISTS (EN MASSE): Condemn all of us! All! All!
The court sentences four of the anarchists to death.
The court sentences four of the anarchists to long prison terms.
(*TL*, 206)

Acker's framing of the hearing of the Chicago anarchists as a Greek tragedy in which the anarchists are never allowed to be heard highlights the cruel unfairness of the proceedings. Indeed, as Acker writes, the authorities' savage response to the incident is the effect of the fear of anarchy: 'The city panics! Bomber terrorists're going to take over!' (*TL*, 205). One of the executed, August Spies, speaking in his own defence in court, questioned the Christian values of the country which punishes the innocent, while emphasising that the spirit of worker liberation would not die out:

if you think that by hanging us, you can stamp out the labor movement – the movement from which the downtrodden millions, who toil and live in want and misery – the wage slaves – expect salvation – if this is your opinion, then hang us! Here you will tread upon a spark, but here, and there, and behind you and in front of you, and everywhere, flames will blaze up. It is a subterranean fire. You cannot put it out.[97]

Their widely reported trial sparked interest in anarchists and their ideas, and the Haymarket anarchists have since been considered the martyrs of the labour movement. Amongst those immediately influenced by the trial was the American anarchist Emma Goldman, who said that the death of the Chicago labour leaders 'brought me to life and helped to make me what I am'.[98]

The later section entitled 'the desperation of the poor' recounts the biographical details of Vincent Van Gogh, who, beyond sacrificing his ear, made multiple sacrifices for his art and to improve the lives of poor people. We are made to see the parallels between the automutilation and autodestruction of an artist and the sacrificial acts of the terrorist revolutionaries. 'Such are myself, Gaugin, and Van Gogh', the narrator chips in, 'sufferers who make others suffer' (*TL*, 216).

From Acker's biographical sketches we learn that Vincent Van Gogh came from a typical middle-class family espousing Christian values. Such families

> often dread the emergence in their midst of some rebellious member likely at any moment to shatter the rigid framework of the home and destroy its unity, an adventurer destined to carve an empire from the ends of the earth, a scientist who may later revolutionize the laws of physics, a thinker who breaks new ground, or an artist whose turbulent genius will scandalize his native land before it comes to idolize him. (*TL*, 216)

Thus Acker frames Vincent's entry into the world in a profoundly status-quo-shattering evental sense. What follows is a collection of episodes from Vincent's life dedicated to artistic and social labour that make up a hagiographic composition: young Vincent is 'intent on revealing the light of the gospel to those who most needed it: miners living in extreme poverty and engaged in the hardest possible work' (*TL*, 219); his 'apostolic career' then extends to 'selfless generosity: teaching the children, tending the sick, distributing his scanty possessions, money, clothing, and furniture' (*TL*, 219). His love is 'less for God' and more 'for humanity'. He 'stripped himself of everything he had and made himself the poorest of the poor' (*TL*, 219), yet despite his best efforts to help and be accepted by the mining community, the workers never treat him as their own. 'Whatever advance and sacrifices he made, the Borain proletariat misunderstood him as had his own family' (*TL*, 219). This echoes the failed project of the Russian propagandists to convince the peasants to support their cause.

Taken together, the multitude of examples in Acker's early works – the locked-away New Left activists; Charles Gallo; the Parisian Communards; the Chicago anarchists; the Russian nihilists and the tormented Vincent Van Gogh – point to the inherent failure of sacrificial acts to achieve their goal. The assassination of the Tsar not only failed to abolish autocracy but led to a long period of repression and reaction by his successor, Nicolas II. The number of executed nihilists exceeded the number of authorities they assassinated. In the aftermath of the repressed Paris Commune, France returned to a conservative government. Van Gogh's efforts to be accepted as a people's missionary and a path-breaking artist during his time were in vain. The brief existence of the Weathermen and the Black Panthers was speedily and brutally suppressed. The attacks on symbols of power, such as the Russian Tsar or the French stock exchange, escape rational discourse. The sometimes obvious futility of revolutionary terrorism has invited charges of both the short-sightedness of such acts and 'an addiction to destruction for its own sake'.[99] In the light of the 2001 terrorist attacks on the American homeland, the ongoing 'war on terror' and the rise of fundamentalism, the use of violence for political purpose is met with revulsion. The contemporary re-evaluations of nineteenth-century Russian terrorism increasingly criminalise and pathologise the phenomenon.[100]

But through the notion of repeated failure of revolutionary acts Acker nevertheless underscores their seriality[101] and their connection to the infinite. By creating connections between political movements across time and geographical zones, Acker underscores the endless replaying of the revolutionary script and the ongoing rebirth of its defeated heroes, reincarnated as the Black Tarantula, Moravagine, Henri Toulouse Lautrec, Pier Paolo Pasolini,[102] Rimbaud, Colette Peignot and numerous other subversive messiahs who populate her works. As Acker's dollmaker asserts in Dead-Doll prophecy: 'THEY CAN'T KILL THE SPIRIT'. In this essay Acker inscribes herself as a martyred writer, misunderstood and penalised for her faith in her method of expression and allegiance with the artistic community, represented through her incorporation of other people's writing into her own, which law and society took for the crime of plagiarism.

Finally, we should note that Acker's religious patterning entails not only spiritual rebirth but also the materiality of the earthly human struggle and human suffering. Her martyred heroes are wounded, tortured, starved, filled with love and desire, bleeding, confined to a cell, executed in front of the baying mob. So conceived, Acker's political subject evokes a suffering Christ. In 'Only a Suffering God Can Save Us' (2012), Žižek stresses the relatability of the suffering Christ to the human experience:

> a God who – like the suffering Christ on the Cross – is agonized, who assumes the burden of suffering, in solidarity with the human misery. [. . .] It was already Schelling who wrote: 'God is a life, not merely a being. But all life has a fate and is subject to suffering and becoming. [. . .] Without the concept of a humanly suffering God [. . .] all of history remains incomprehensible.' [. . .] Why? Because God's suffering implies that he is involved in history, affected by it, not just a transcendent Master pulling the strings from above: God's suffering means that human history is not just a theater of shadows, but the place of a real struggle, the struggle in which the Absolute itself is involved and its fate is decided.[103]

Conclusion

Passion, desire, zoomorphism, apocalypticism, self-sacrifice, martyrdom, solidarity, militant feminism, community, the interconnectivity of revolutionary movements: they constitute some of the fundamental themes which characterise Acker's works of the late counterculture, and which will become matrices for formulations of the political in her later works. Nihilistic passion for destruction marks this early phase, which is followed by Acker grappling with the politically barren cynical area of the eighties, but Acker will continue writing her 'subversive hagiographies',[104] and among them is the life of a suffering saviour and outcast Don Quixote from her 1986 work *Don Quixote: Which Was a Dream*, to which we now turn.

Notes

1. Hereafter referred to in the text as *Burning Bombing* and *Nymphomaniac*.
2. Jameson, 'Periodizing the 60s', p. 189.
3. To meet the demands of the women's liberation movement, the Weathermen were later renamed to Weatherpeople, Weatherforce and Weather Underground, but the original name remained most popular in use.
4. Parry, *Terrorism*, p. 324.

5. See Varon, *Bringing*, pp. 1–19.
6. Varon, *Bringing*, p. 8.
7. Asbley et al., 'You Don't Need a Weatherman to Know Which Way the Wind Blows' (June 1969). Available at <https://archive.org/stream/YouDontNeedAWeathermanToKnowWhichWayTheWindBlows_925#page/n7/mode/2up> (last accessed 10 January 2019).
8. Roland Castro, cited in Wolin, *The Wind*, p. 123.
9. Berman, *A Tale of Two Utopias*, p. 267.
10. Badiou, cited in Hallward, *Badiou*, p. 31.
11. Simone de Beauvoir, cited in Wolin, *The Wind*, p. 140.
12. Amy Scholder, ed., *Rip-off Red, Girl Detective* and *The Burning Bombing of America*. For an analysis of Guyotat's influence on *Burning Bombing*, see Georgina Colby, *Kathy Acker: Writing the Impossible* (Edinburgh: Edinburgh University Press, 2016), pp. 58–64.
13. For an overview of themes, see Patrick French and Roland-François Lack (eds), *The Tel Quel Reader* (London: Routledge, 2004).
14. Wolin, *The Wind*, p. 20.
15. Ibid. p. 3.
16. Ibid. p. 124.
17. Cook, 'Mao's Little Red Book', p. i.
18. Jones, Andrew F., 'Quotation Songs: Portable Media and the Maoist Pop Song', in Alexander C. Cook, p. 46.
19. Lin Biao, 'Foreword to the Second Chinese Edition' (December 16, 1966). Official English translation is available at <www.marxists.org/reference/archive/lin-biao/1966/12/16.htm> (last accessed 10 January 2019).
20. Ibid.
21. I base my brief outline of apocalyptic narrative on Zamora, *Writing*, pp. 1–24.
22. John, cited in Zamora, *Writing*, p. 2.
23. Zamora, *Writing*, p. 10.
24. Norman Cohn's *The Pursuit of the Millennium* (London: Secker and Warburg, 1957; completely revised edition, London: Paladin, 1970) was one of the first studies to argue that the medieval millennial movements found an expression in many violent political movements of past and present, including communism, Nazism, and later the third world liberation struggles and youth protests of the 1960s, a position that many critics contested. John Gray's *Black Mass* (London: Penguin, 2008) is a more recent uncovering of the apocalyptic patterning of secular revolutionary movements.
25. Gitlin, *The Sixties*, p. 422.
26. Sklower, 'Preface: Dissent within Dissent', pp. xviii–xix.
27. Den Tandt, 'The Rock Counterculture from Modernist Utopianism to the Development of an Alternative Music Scene', p. 84.
28. Hill, *Marguerite Duras*, pp. 8–9.

29. Maurice Blanchot, cited in Hill, *Marguerite Duras*, pp. 8–9.
30. Hill, *Marguerite Duras*, p. 9.
31. Blanchot, cited in Hill, *Marguerite Duras*, p. 9.
32. Henderson, 'From Counterculture to Punk Culture: The Emergence of Kathy Acker's Punk Poetics', p. 286.
33. Guyotat, *Eden*, p. 163.
34. Gitlin, *The Sixties*, p. 350.
35. Zedong, cited in Ross, *May '68*, p. 92.
36. Dittmer, *China's Continuous Revolution*, p. 6.
37. Mao Zedong, cited in Meisner, *Mao's China and After*, p. 199.
38. Zedong, 'Report on an investigation of the peasant movement in Hunan', p. 286.
39. Deleuze and Guattari, *Kafka*, p. 22.
40. Hereafter referred to in the text as *Toulouse Lautrec*.
41. For a discussion of *Black Tarantula* as 'full blown Punk', see Henderson, 'From Counterculture to Punk Culture: The Emergence of Kathy Acker's Punk Poetics', pp. 286–94.
42. Acker, 'An Informal Interview with Kathy Acker on the 23rd April, 1986', p. 2.
43. Cendrars, *Moravagine*, p. 46.
44. Acker, *Rip-Off Red, Girl Detective*, in *Rip-Off Red, Girl Detective and The Burning Bombing of America* (New York: Grove, 2002), p. 8.
45. Ibid. p. 18.
46. Ibid. p. 67.
47. Ibid. p. 68.
48. Ibid. p. 69.
49. Houen, *Powers*, p. 156.
50. Cendrars, *Morevagine*, p. 64.
51. Zinn, 'Introduction', p. 24.
52. See Michael Foucault, *Discipline and Punish: The Birth of the Prison*, trans. Alan Sheridan (New York: Vintage Books, 1995).
53. Adams, *Prison Riots*, p. 11.
54. Ibid. p. 10.
55. Cendrars, *Moravagine*, 66.
56. Useem and Kimball, *States*, p. 23.
57. Ibid. pp. 17–18.
58. Acker, 'An informal interview with Kathy Acker on the 23rd April, 1986', p. 3.
59. Angela Davis, 'Political Prisoners, Prisons, and Black Liberation', in Zinn, *Voices*, p. 496; author's emphasis.
60. Angela Davis, *Are Prisons Obsolete?*, p. 15.
61. Barkley, p. 498.
62. Angela Davis, *An Autobiography*, p. 52.
63. George Jackson, *Soledad Brother*, p. ix.
64. Jonathan Jackson Jr, 'Foreword', p. xix.
65. George Jackson, *Soledad Brother*, p. 16.

66. Ibid. p. 222.
67. Useem and Kimball, *States*, p. 16.
68. George Jackson, *Soledad Brother*, p. 111.
69. I owe this analogy to Peter Scotto, who has identified similarities between Stepniak's profiles of revolutionaries with tales of saints and martyrs in *Paterikon* in the Russian Orthodox literature. See Peter Scotto, 'The Terrorist as Novelist: Sergei Stepniak-Kravchinsky', p. 112.
70. Stepniak, *Underground Russia*, p. 17.
71. Ibid. p. 4.
72. Ibid. pp. 39–40.
73. Ibid. pp. 30–1.
74. Scotto, 'The Terrorist as Novelist', p. 110.
75. Stepniak, *Underground Russia*, p. 111.
76. Ibid. p. 46.
77. Scotto, 'The Terrorist as Novelist: Sergei Stepniak-Kravchinsky', p. 107.
78. Houen, *Terrorism*, p. 57.
79. Stepniak, *Underground Russia*, p. 44.
80. Ibid. p. 41.
81. Houen, *Terrorism*, p. 57.
82. Stepniak, *Underground Russia*, p. 18.
83. Stites, *The Women's Liberation*, p. 100.
84. Hingley, *Nihilists*, p. 32.
85. Stites, *The Women's Liberation*, p. 147.
86. Parry, *Terrorism*, p. 328.
87. Stites, *The Women's Liberation*, p. 153.
88. Ibid.
89. Boniece, 'The Spiridonova Case, 1906: Terror, Myth and Martyrdom', p. 151.
90. Badiou, *Philosophy for Militants*, p. 42.
91. Badiou, *Saint Paul*, p. 2.
92. Badiou, *Philosophy for Militants*, p. 42.
93. Hubac-Occhipinti, 'Anarchist Terrorists of the Nineteenth Century', pp. 125–6.
94. Ebbessen, *Postmodernism*, p. 111. For a discussion of historical female dissidence in *The Black Tarantula*, see Henderson, 'From Counterculture to Punk Culture: The Emergence of Kathy Acker's Punk Poetics', pp. 286–94. See Diane Fare, 'A Spectacle of Pain: Confronting Horror in Kathy Acker's *My Mother: Demonology*', *European Journal of American Culture*, 21: 2 (1 July 2002), pp. 98–111, for an analysis of Acker's incorporation of the work and biography of Colette Peignot (also known as Laure), a French revolutionary activist and author.
95. To commemorate the police casualties during the 1886 riot, the Chicago Weathermen, Bill Ayers and Terry Robbins, planted a bomb that blew up a statue in Chicago. See Varon, *Bringing*, p. 76.

96. Avrich, *Anarchist Voices*, p. 46.
97. Spies, 'Address of August Spies' (7 October 1886), p. 221.
98. Emma Goldman, cited in Avrich, *Anarchist Voices*, p. 46.
99. Hingley, *Nihilists*, p. 97.
100. Anemone, 'Introduction: Just Assassins?', p. 6.
101. After all, the brutal repression of Nicolas II gave birth to another generation of terrorists, leading to the revolution of 1905, whose suppression, in turn, fuelled the revolution of 1917.
102. Another important avant-garde influence on Acker, Pasolini adopted Christological themes to his radical politics, as explicated in Stefania Benini's study, *Pasolini: The Sacred Flesh* (2015). Also see Sam Rhodie's *The Passion of Pier Paolo Pasolini* (1995) for an account of Pasolini's commitment to revolution.
103. Žižek, 'Only a Suffering God Can Save Us', pp. 156–7.
104. I borrow this term from Stefania Benini. See Benini, *Pasolini: The Sacred Flesh* (2015).

Chapter 2

(K)night Time: Cynicism in *Don Quixote*

Published in London in 1986, two years after Acker had left New York, and nearly two decades after the worldwide countercultural protests of 1968, *Don Quixote* documents her anxiety over the triumphant conservatism of the Reagan and Thatcher years. With the decline of the American Left and the abatement of social movements, there was a pained feeling of lack of alternatives, and Acker saw a disenchanted American and British society retreating from political life. Cynicism flourished in a climate where utopian belief was in crisis, and Acker wanted to instil revolutionary spirit into politically barren times. In what follows, I argue that she did this by launching a saviour figure, Don Quixote, who is equipped with a set of practical tools derived from the subversive tradition of ancient Cynicism to fight the complacency and self-interest associated with the modern cynical rationality. I aim to show how *Don Quixote* reveals the many faces of modern cynicism, challenging its claims to realism and uncovering its unsettling affinities with totalitarianism. As an alternative to the pervasive realpolitik, Acker turns to a dreampolitik that she locates in the historical example of Spanish anarchism.

'What of the night?' – cynical 'remainder'

'[T]here's no world for idealism', asserts Acker's protagonist in the opening page of *Don Quixote*. The novel offers one of the most compelling confrontations between a bleak realist outlook on society and the dream of a society transformed. It concerns a single questing knight, here a 'female-male or a night-knight', who sets out on a mission to find love and change the world for the better. The knight wants to become a saviour, declaring herself ready 'to right all wrongs' (*DQ*, 14), a mission completely incompatible with the cynicism of a society which has given up on hope. Yet the novel simultaneously projects a more pessimistic view of devoting oneself to bettering the world. The 'knight''s homophonic double 'night' threatens to reverse the noble quest and thereby render it futile.

Like the author of the original *Don Quixote*, Miguel de Cervantes, Acker inserts her narrative within the frame of a chivalric romance to subvert it. Whereas traditional chivalric literature starts with the parentage and the birth of the hero, who then either pursues a secular goal such as the platonic love of a lady or embarks on a mission with a religious purpose such as the Holy Grail, the dispatch of Acker's female-male 'hero' into the world of adventures begins with the scene not of birth, but of abortion. Even in the novel's subtitle – *Which Was a Dream* – the dreams that in a political context would contain visions of emancipation are lost, consigned to the past tense.

Don Quixote repeatedly states the failure of revolution and draws attention to the impossibility of political creativity and progress. Reversing the Enlightenment's solar myth of revolution, where the energy of the dawn is put into the service of rebirth and a new beginning, *Don Quixote* lingers in darkness. From another Spanish influence, the artist Francisco Goya, Acker inherits grim realism: 'the earth is dead: The soil is barren. The hills behind are barren. The sky is barren. The sky is always nighttime' (*DQ*, 76). What are *Don Quixote*'s resources for revolutionary transformation and happiness in this night?

Badiou asks the postmodern philosopher Jean-François Lyotard a similar question, derived from the Latin Vulgate Bible, with regards to Lyotard's progressing melancholy: '*Custos, quid noctis?*', 'Watchman, what of the night?'[1] For Badiou, Lyotard is a thinker of the 'night' which has become an insistent 'genre' of the late twentieth-century politics.[2] But Badiou looks for traces of possibility in Lyotard's nocturnal order. 'Watchman, what of the night?' headlines Badiou's inquiry into what possibilities Lyotard can discern in this darkness brought on by the triumph of 'the Kapital' and the death of the politics of serious hope. With regards to this question, Andrew Gibson points out that Lyotard and Badiou conceive the same reality very differently: whereas Lyotard is lodged in the world eclipsed by the capital and the end of emancipatory politics, Badiou is captivated by rare revolutionary events.[3] Badiou's politics affirms mornings and begins in events unexpectedly erupting with a flash, a burst of colour on the border between night and day. The nocturnal eventlessness that characterises Lyotard's world ('There are no things, there are no people, there are no frontiers, there is no knowledge, there are no beliefs, there are no reasons to live/die'[4]) retains nothing from the vital intensity of revolutionaries meeting at the break of day. Gibson considers Badiou's account of events incomplete, because it rarely confronts what is left after the event, that 'other history'.[5] In response to this, Gibson develops the concept of 'the remainder' and proposes that writers of modern melancholy, notably Gustav Flaubert, are better equipped to attend to the post-evental. In order to uncover revolutionary value in *Don Quixote* we must also put Badiou's familiar emphasis into reverse. The novel attends primarily to the remainder, where events are few and far between, and revolutionary belief has been replaced by deep cynicism, but it nevertheless sustains the possibility of a better world.

There was much to be cynical about in the 1980s United States and Britain. The countercultural movements had died down; their more radical members came out from the underground and were given prison sentences; some looked for alternatives while others reintegrated into mainstream society. David Harvey has diagnosed the progressing neoliberalism under Reagan and Thatcher as 'a regime of endless capital accumulation and economic growth' with little regard for ecological, political and social responsibility.[6] The neoliberal ideology co-opted countercultural protest, channelling the ethos of personal freedom espoused by the counterculture into commercial and entrepreneurial freedom.

For William Chaloupka and other social theorists, the Cold War period marked a high tide in American cynicism. American leaders practised 'the ultimate cynicism' when they applied violence and incited paranoid fear in the service of peace and democracy.[7] Richard Nixon used the fear of communists to get elected as a senator in California and became president in 1968 on the promise that he would end the Vietnam War, which went on for nearly another decade. The director of the FBI, J. Edgar Hoover, fuelled the cynical culture from the first day of his appointment by seeking out conspiracies, convincing Nixon and Lyndon Johnson of the secret forces at the heart of social and political matters. Cynicism in American politics displays a circular logic, where, Chaloupka writes, 'Cynical leaders generate citizens who are cynical about politicians, who then respond with yet more cynical ploys.'[8] Vietnam demonstrated to the American public that politicians employ Machiavellian tactics and violence under the cover of peace, and that corporations profit from the war economy. The evolving impact of the media, television in particular, further complicated citizens' trust in government. Investigative journalism exposed the mismatch between politicians' stated intentions and their actions. The public tuned into the news coverage of Vietnam and the Watergate scandal, and began to reassess their opinions on the conduct of domestic and foreign affairs. Acker draws extensively on muckraking journalism and repackages it as fiction.

The remainder in *Don Quixote* is primarily made up of the culture of cynicism in 1980s American and Western Europe. But in this post-revolutionary disenchanted world, the questions Acker poses are not cynical: how could anyone expect a welcoming life to emerge in these dark times? Are love, community and a better world possible? Rather than asking whether one should be cynical, or how to avoid cynicism, Acker uncovers forms of cynicism which can contribute to revolutionary politics. The alternative forms of cynicism revealed by *Don Quixote* are evocative of an ancient Cynical tradition (conventionally spelt by scholars with a capital 'C' to distinguish it from modern cynicism, which has a pejorative meaning).

It is no coincidence that Peter Sloterdijk and Michel Foucault undertook a serious study of ancient Cynicism around that time, also searching for more engaged models of citizenship. Sloterdijk's monumental *Critique of Cynical Reason* appeared in Germany in 1983, and Foucault, who had not read Sloterdijk, the following year delivered five lectures at the Collège de France on the theme of ancient Cynicism. Both sought to revive the spirit of ancient Cynicism embodied by Diogenes of Sinope, seeing it as a potentially transformative mode of existence for contemporary dark times. Although Acker never explicitly claims allegiance to Greek Cynics, the strategies of resistance against the powerful present in her work are traceable to those practised by Diogenes and his followers. Many of these strategies she inherits through the twentieth century's social and artistic revivals of the Cynical tradition, notably Dada, elements of the culture of protest and provocation of the 1960s, and later punks, as well as the anarchist tradition generally. Acker applies ancient modes of critique in a contemporary context while developing her unique Cynical language and addressing classical Cynicism's shortcomings and limitations. She replaces a primarily male and solitary, sometimes misanthropic, lifestyle with a feminist ethos and search for community, feeling and love.

From the shrewd diplomacy of selfish, power-obsessed political leaders to melancholy intellectuals and a disaffected public, modern cynicism in *Don Quixote* assumes many forms. It permeates the social and political reality in a variety of ways, often standing in direct opposition to the ideals of ancient Cynicism. Neglecting to differentiate between different configurations of cynicism in *Don Quixote* invites the charges of nihilism, namely the idea that Acker merely perpetuates disenchantment with revolutionary politics. Instead, this chapter argues that Acker combats modern cynicism with its ancient predecessor. Parrhesia (truth-telling), the grotesque body, and satire are the three classically Cynical tools that she employs repeatedly to advance a potent critique of a modern cynical rationality, which she identifies as both harmful and non-revolutionary.

Ancient and modern cynicism

In its popular, modern use, the word 'cynic' has negative and unpleasant connotations. A cynic revels in depreciating any trace of idealism; in wrecking noble initiatives and lofty aspirations; in rejecting ethical and social values, and in dismissing the concepts of truthfulness and honesty. Yet cynicism did not always connote a disillusioned, contemptuous and self-absorbed individual. Ancient Cynics believed that human nature is good, but has been corrupted by institutions which entrap individuals and manufacture superfluous needs. It was their optimistic belief that it was possible to strip away layers of false desires and hypocritical conventions and live a more authentic and ascetic life.[9] Sloterdijk, Foucault and other scholars of cynicism reveal a fundamental distinction between the modern and ancient variety that will be of particular use to us: while modern cynics are focused on *thinking* – they know about omnipresent deception in the world, but are too disillusioned to act – the classical Cynics use the knowledge to *live* differently, with the aim of transforming the world and the self.

Ancient Cynicism was a critique of the Platonic philosophical tradition which idealised the world and regarded humans as rational and sophisticated beings while devaluing humanity's bodily and sensory existence. It was a performance of social critique based on an alternative lifestyle, dedicated to nature and simplicity. It has survived in the popular imagination as a set of stock images, personalities and anecdotes. One of the best known Cynical philosophers is

Diogenes of Sinope (c. 412–323 BC), who is said to have lived in a barrel, surrounded by dogs, and who wandered the streets of Athens in broad daylight with a lit lantern searching in vain for an honest man.[10] His philosophical career began with his exile from Sinope, which, in one version of the story, was caused by him allegedly taking part in his father's scandalous practice of defacing the city's currency, thereby excluding it from circulation. To 'deface the currency' became a motto for his philosophical vocation, which he adopted in the non-literal sense of the debunking of custom, convention and hierarchy.[11] Diogenes then moved to Athens, where he lived in utter poverty. As reported by the literary gossip Diogenes Laertius, he had a profound antipathy towards employment, marriage and procreation, refusing any occupation other than critiquing and mocking the inhabitants of the city. Devoted to his mission of adulterating currency, he exposed the artifice, imposture and hypocrisy of Athenian life. It was for his 'barking' at the fellow citizens, as well his homelessness, shamelessness and outrageous humour and street theatre, that Diogenes won the nickname 'dog' – the Greek *kyon* from which Cynicism takes its name. For both modern users of English and ancient Greeks the nickname 'dog' is a term of abuse, implying shameless, marginal and antisocial behaviour. Indeed, the so-called 'dog-philosophers' were known for various shocking acts, including incest or fulfilling a bodily need in public, and it was not uncommon for them to receive insults or be physically attacked by their contemporaries. For a few, however, as William Desmond puts the point, they were like 'kings' – admired and respected for having the courage to despise their rulers, and for their complete abandonment of what most people deem life's necessities, such as having a home.[12]

The philosophy of ancient Cynicism lacked official doctrines and systematic presentation, operating more as a movement than a school, which deemed it unworthy of study to Hegel, who removed it from academic histories of philosophy. Nevertheless, based on the fragmentary and partial information available on Cynics, scholars have been able to reconstruct a set of fundamental qualities and philosophical convictions which animated and guided them. They include, amongst others, the notion of (i) self-sufficiency, intimately linked with the idea of (ii) freedom, and the activity of (iii) parrhesia, freedom of speech.

According to another legend, when Alexander the Great heard about Diogenes's popularity, he travelled to consult him. He found Diogenes in Corinth, basking in the sun. The sovereign stood over him, casting shade over Diogenes, and offered to fulfil any request that the philosopher wished. To the young emperor's surprise, Diogenes's only response was: 'Stand out of my light'. This archetypal anecdote offers the ultimate example of what the Cynics believed to be the fundamental task of philosophy, and what a genuine philosopher should be: a parrhesiast, that is, the one who uses parrhesia, ordinarily translated into English as 'free speech'. By instructing Alexander to move aside, Diogenes displays his courageous commitment to frankness in all circumstances. The Alexander anecdote also comes with the message that for the Cynics, the main condition of human happiness is self-sufficiency and freedom. The all-powerful emperor had nothing to offer that was of use to Diogenes, who preferred a completely natural lifestyle, being dependent upon nothing other than himself, and only needing that which would sustain him in his journey: sunlight, water, healthy food, fresh air and somewhere to lie down. More importantly, as Louis Navia glosses, 'Diogenes does not need Alexander, and neither does he need that for which Alexander stood, namely, the state.'[13]

In their commitment to a virtuous life, and in rejecting hierarchy and celebrating instead individuals' freedom from the authority of the state and its coercive institutions, Cynics anticipated many anarchist ideals. It is thus not surprising that we will find Acker's commitment to many anarchist beliefs to be underpinned by the legacy of ancient Cynicism. The Greek culture not only provided anarchism with its name, but also with a rich repository of thought and models of living without rule(r)s. Peter Marshall notes that the later anarchists, such as Kropotkin and Godwin, were inspired by libertarian elements found in the philosophy of Socrates, and, after him, Epicureans, the Cynics and the Stoics. Thus Diogenes of Sinope is considered to be 'one of the great forerunners of anarchism'.[14]

Modern cynicism retained little from its classical predecessor. The commitment of ancient dogs to defacing the coinage and living a life without conforming to the established order mutated into a position of withdrawal and quiet critique. Scholars agree that cynicism acquired its modern meaning in the Enlightenment. Since then, it no longer denoted an ascetic philosopher but any contemporary cynical person who holds the belief that all humans' actions are ultimately motivated by self-interest and power. In her *The Cynic Enlightenment* (2010),[15] Louisa Shea tells us that the modern concept of cynicism began to emerge when the Encyclopaedists such as d'Alembert, Diderot and their contemporaries became interested in reviving Diogenes's Cynicism, albeit in a 'polished' version. Although the philosophers of the Enlightenment were largely attracted to Diogenes of Sinope's critique of power and directness, because of social pressures they rejected the indecent aspects of his language and his actions. In order to keep their respectable positions in society and maintain financial stability, d'Alembert and others chose to express their criticism of the government and society in a discreet, polite manner. The ancient Cynic's imperative to 'live differently' was replaced by the Encyclopaedists' imperative to 'think differently', as Diderot put it.[16]

Immanuel Kant's essay 'What is Enlightenment?' makes the modern split between thought and behaviour clear and glaring. In it, Kant famously defines Enlightenment as man's 'release from his self-incurred tutelage', which is a courageous commitment to use one's capacity to reason without direction from authority.[17] But the imperative to 'Have courage to use your own reason!' Kant supplants with a motto: 'Argue as much as you will, and about what you will, but obey!'[18] Here, Kant makes evident the distinction between the public and private use of reason. As Slavoj Žižek points out, Kant's 'Argue [. . .] but obey' dictum does not rehearse the familiar conformist stance whereby individuals are free to think whatever they want in private, but in public they must obey the authorities.[19] Rather, the opposite attitude appears: 'a scholar before the reading public' is to use his reason freely; but in private, for example in 'a particular civil post or office which is entrusted to him', he is to obey.[20] This dictum, as Žižek writes, underpins Kant's fundamental notion of a 'conflict of the faculties', where the realm of arguing, which encompasses philosophising, criticising, questioning and thinking independently, is kept strictly separate from the structures of ideology and power, such as law and theology, which regulate behaviour.[21] This is the territory of modern cynicism, where thinking differently or knowing better are unmatched by action.

Sloterdijk has much to say about cynicism of the modern kind. His *Critique of Cynical Reason*, which he wrote under the shadow of conservatism that swayed Germany in the 1970s and the general feeling of disaffection with the 1968 revolts, considers cynicism to be a major challenge to contemporary emancipatory politics. Sloteridjk relates modern cynicism to the Enlightenment's failure to produce a free and just society. As Louisa Shea remarks, Sloterdijk continues the critical tradition of Theodor Adorno and Max Horkheimer, who in *Dialectic of Enlightenment* (1947) saw how the Enlightenment's ideals of knowledge, progress and emancipation descended into a totalitarian nightmare. But Sloterdijk's additional concern, Shea comments, is that alongside the threat of 'instrumental reason', the pervasive ideology of cynicism is another dangerous legacy of the Enlightenment.[22] According to Sloterdijk, the Enlightenment's mission of disenchantment, rather than opening new avenues for emancipatory solutions free from naivety, myth and superstition, unleashed a new force of destruction in the form of complacency and resignation.[23] In Sloterdijk's words, 'Modern cynicism presents itself as that state of consciousness that follows after naive ideologies and their enlightenment. [. . .] Cynicism is *enlightened false consciousness*.'[24] Modern cynics are enlightened but apathetic,[25] as despite possessing knowledge about the status quo, they will 'go on as before'. With an attitude of sarcastic distain, and in spite of 'knowing better', a modern cynic rejects the classical Cynic's imperative to 'live differently', since life does not offer any prospects for meaningful change.

Modern cynicism as a form of ideology

For Sloterdijk, Badiou, Žižek and others, contemporary cynicism is a form of ideology. Drawing parallels between ideology and theatre, Badiou writes that 'ideology stages figures of representation that mask the primordial violence of social relations (exploitation, oppression, anti-egalitarian cynicism)'.[26] Those discourses, symbols and signs will organise consciousness in ways that are favourable to dominant relations of power. Evoking Louis Althusser's classic definition, Žižek writes that ideology is a subject's naive '"false consciousness", misrecognition of the social reality which is part of this reality itself'.[27] Žižek was one of the first theorists to engage directly with Sloterdijk's alarming diagnosis of the cynicism abroad in contemporary society. In *The Sublime Object of Ideology* (1989), Žižek asks whether cynical subjectivity can still be considered in this ideological sense, given that 'cynical reason is no longer naive': '[t]he cynical subject is quite aware of the distance between the ideological mask and the social reality, but he none the less still insists upon the mask', a phenomenon he calls 'a paradox of an enlightened false consciousness'.[28] In Žižek's depictions, cynics delude themselves by thinking they are beyond the structures of power, but by doing nothing to change them, they participate in and perpetuate the ideological reality. As he puts it: 'Cynical distance is just one way [. . .] to blind ourselves to the structuring power of ideological fantasy: even if we do not take things seriously, even if we keep an ironical distance, *we are still doing them*.'[29] As Adrian Johnston explains, 'The current strategy of capitalist liberal-democratic ideology encourages individuals to be as dismissive as they desire precisely so that they find their conformity bearable as something depersonalized, disavowed, and thereby held at arm's length.'[30]

Both Žižek and Badiou update, rather than discard, the classic concept of ideology, which presupposes that behind the mask of 'false' consciousness there is a 'true' consciousness of reality to be revealed. They claim that the real is beyond representation and as such can only be re-represented and misrecognised. Badiou refers to the concept of 'distancing' in the performing arts (coined by Bertolt Brecht), arguing that 'ideology organizes a consciousness separated from the real that it nevertheless expresses'.[31] Thus it is not that ideology is merely an illusory or false representation of reality, but rather that the reality itself is ideological: 'the real [can] operate only though fictions, montages and masks'.[32] Understanding modern cynicism as a form of ideology will allow us to comprehend it not as an attitude that can unmask all deception and have access to the 'true' reality, but rather as a default and pervasive rationality in contemporary society.

Needless to say, modern cynicism has a particularly corrosive relationship with politics. It prescribes failure to any emancipatory project, and produces docile, apathetic, embittered subjects incapable of imagining alternatives. *Don Quixote* radically challenges such a mindset. Adopting Cynicism allows Acker to re-inscribe agency within the otherwise overdetermined and impotent subjectivities populating the remainder. Her postmodern Cynic is socially constructed but remains open to subversion and re-fashioning. Don Quixote is well aware of the contingent status of her identity and that reality, rather than 'true', is structured by normative social discourses: 'There's no way out of any appearance because an appearance is only what it is' (*DQ*, 190). This is thus an update on the ancient Cynics' original belief that a more authentic existence lies beneath social masks, which motivated their commitment to defacing ideals and conventions. Because the real is always mediated and represented in social reality, and can only operate 'through fictions, montages and masks',[33] Don Quixote cannot simply shrug off identity in order to have direct access to experience. What she can do instead is refuse to let 'political leaders locate our identities in the social' (*DQ*, 18), by exposing the dominant ideological hold as a mere appearance and ridiculing its pretences to 'truth', while promoting alternative models of 'doing' identity.

Some critics prefer to read Cervantes's Don Quixote not as a madman who becomes a knight-errant, deluded that he is someone else, but as an actor who takes on and practises a new role, and in so doing parodies established normative identities. It is that performative aspect that makes Acker's Cynical hero distinctively postmodern. Acker creates a particularly intriguing example of self-fashioning modelled on Cervantes's protagonists. Sloteridjk writes that Cervantes's cowardly Sancho Panza and Don Quixote's pretended nobleness are representative of the Cynical military process at play, where the traditional notions of heroism are subverted.[34] Acker extends Cervantes's military Cynicism by creating a hero who further disrupts the contours of a male martial character. The process of Cynical self-fashioning also applies to choosing a name:

> Just as 'Kackneyed' is the glorification or change from non-existence into existence of 'Hack-kneed', so, she decided, 'catheter' is the glorification of 'Kathy'. By taking on such a name which, being long, is male, she would be able to become a female-male or a night-knight. (*DQ*, 10)

In this act of naming, Don Quixote plays with the cultural material creating a comic effect, and in assuming derivate, hyphenated identities, she highlights the shifting nature of things, thereby creating space for Cynical re-fashioning and re-inscription. In this way, Acker tells us that alternative existences in the remainder need to be fashioned rather than uncovered: it is an act of construction rather than revelation.

The idea of acting out an identity rather than having a stable essence is strongly reminiscent of Judith Butler's famous notion of performativity. In *Gender Trouble*, Butler argued that gender categories, rather than substantial and natural, are produced and stabilised by power structures through repeated citation of norms and their transgression.[35] According to Butler, 'Gender is the repeated stylisation of the body, a set of repeated acts within a highly rigid regulatory frame that congeal over time to produce the appearance of substance, of a natural sort of being.'[36] The repetitive, or 'citational' character of performative identity, Butler asserts, opens up the possibility for a marginal subversion of the reigning gender norms through 'resignification', namely the repetition of a signification in a different context, the effects being a parody of mainstream gender identity and exposure of it as fiction. The question for Acker concerning how to do cynicism echoes Butler asking 'not *whether* to repeat, but *how* to repeat and, through a radical proliferation of gender, to displace the very norms that enable repetition itself'.[37] If, as Sloterdijk said, cynicism is now our armour,[38] Acker seeks to do cynicism differently by wearing a Cynical drag, while exposing dominant cynicism's complicity with the capitalist rationality.

Against modern cynicism's schizophrenic split between theory and praxis, and between body and mind, Acker's aim is to restore, to borrow Shea's expression, ancient Cynicism's '"homophonic" relation between word and deed'. This is achieved through three interrelated Cynical strategies: parrhesia, which combines speaking and action, related to the elevation of satire as the most appropriate mode for effectively communicating social criticism, and the grotesque body as the privileged locus of resistance.

Political incorrectness: Acker as a parrhesiast

During his adventures, Cervantes's Don Quixote, unlike the people around him, considers an inn to be a castle, a lowly peasant girl a princess, a flock of sheep an enemy army and a barber's basin the legendary golden helmet of the king Mambrino. The knight declares a group of windmills to be an army of monstrous giants whom he wishes to attack, to the bewilderment of his squire, Sancho Panza, who corrects him: 'those you see yonder are no giants, but windmills; and what seem arms to you, are sails, which being turned with the wind, make the mill-stone work'.[39] But Don Quixote is sure of his perception, insisting that if the elements of the real world contradict his mental images, it means that they are ploys set by malicious enchanters who want to deceive people. He explains: 'those enchanters, by whom I am persecuted, take pleasure in presenting realities to my view, and then changing and metamorphosing them into such figures and forms as they choose to bestow'.[40]

Enchantment is one of the central concepts in Cervantes's novel that Acker translates to contemporary contexts. Like Cervantes's, Acker's world is populated by 'evil enchanters', whose deceptions are discussed at length in the section entitled 'Don Quixote in America, the land of freedom' (*DQ*, 101). This unforgiving label applies to all 'who control the nexuses of government and culture, 're persecuting and will continue to persecute us until they have buried and downed, drowned us in our own human forgetfulness' (*DQ*, 102). Richard Nixon, Henry Kissinger, Ronald Reagan, Andrea Dworkin and their entourage belong to this infamous group, and Acker's Cynical vanguard, Don Quixote, sets out on a mission to expose their misconduct and moral failings beneath amiable appearances. The radical feminist Dworkin stands out in this list of male leaders, but as Acker explains in an interview, this was aimed not as a personal attack, but a criticism of Dworkin's 'dualistic argument that men are responsible for all the evil in the world'.[41] This is part of Don Quixote's wider attack on the propagation of 'us against them' politics, which she sees as responsible for deep divisions within and outside of society.

Like Cervantes's Don Quixote, Acker's knight possesses the ability of dual cognition, one that is not limited to dream visions or gratuitous delusions. They can both perceive the world in both its non-enchanted and enchanted form; that is, as it appears to them and as it appears to others. Hence, they do not consider windmills to be just giants, but giants cleverly disguised to look like windmills. This ability to see through the acts of the evil enchanters enables them to challenge the reality accepted by the majority as the 'true' one. At the heart of this lies Don Quixote's Cynical debunking of the myth of America as the land of freedom. During her travels, the knight discovers that the American populace have been led to believe that they live in the freest and the most democratic country in the world, whereas in fact the American ideal of freedom is subjugation dressed up as freedom: 'America's the land of freedom. That is, America's the land of myth or belief of freedom' (*DQ*, 112).

The notion of American uniqueness goes back to the first Puritan settlers, who believed that they were separating themselves from the evils of the Old World and creating a New World. When in 1630, John Winthrop, the governor of Massachusetts Bay colony, used the words 'We shall be as a city upon a hill', he suggested that America provided a superior model that all humankind could look up to and emulate. The belief in exceptionalism translated into many forms, such as the doctrine of Manifest Destiny, which propelled Americans to consider themselves as divinely ordained to advance across the continent. It ideologically justified conquest and domination of the Native American nations, and throughout American history was embraced by strategically expansionist American leaders on their mission to spread American-style freedom and democracy into other parts of the world. Don Quixote learns that the myth of American freedom was solidified through the American Revolution, when Americans revolted against the motherland England to become the first nation to be born out of a revolution. Americans thus resisted the burdens and oppressions of Old Europe, where, as the narrator tells us, 'a dog's life had been (and is) determined by the class and history into which it was born' (*DQ*, 112). But being free from foreign rule does not translate into personal freedom. The class divisions remain under the veneer of national interest, where one class is privileged and the rest is ignored. As Marxist historian Howard Zinn has argued, Americans are continuously taught that they are one big family:

> It is pretended that, as in the Preamble to the Constitution, it is 'we the people' who wrote that document, rather than fifty-five privileged white males whose class interest required a strong central government. That use of government for class purposes, to serve the needs of the wealthy and powerful, has continued throughout American history, down to the present day. It is disguised by language that suggests all of us, rich and poor and middle class, have a common interest.[42]

Citizens are expected to support or even risk their lives for the decisions of the ruling elite to invade other countries in the name of democracy and freedom. Powerfully highlighting the fact that many Americans live a miserable existence – the hungry, jobless, homeless; those struggling to make ends meet – Acker literalises the familiar proverb of living a dog's life by turning them into dogs. A bitch approaches the evil enchanter Nixon to question him about American values: 'What was the American Revolution? What's this American freedom? Commerce's thriving in this country: the Heads of Commerce're getting wealthier' (*DQ*, 108). Rather than being liberated, ordinary American citizens are free to work, free to buy and free to turn themselves into a commodity, and free to starve. There appears to be no alternative other than following the rationality of cynical self-interest to ensure economic survival: 'The self-made American dog has only itself and it must make success, that is, survive. It isn't able to love, especially, another living dog' (*DQ*, 112).

Because Americans are continuously fed the myth of freedom, the need for revolution is eradicated in American society. Simply put, people who believe that they are free do not revolt. To keep revolution at bay, Nixon suppresses discontent and propagandises the myths of American optimism and freedom: 'Our country doesn't allow negativity'; 'there's no nihilism in this country' (*DQ*, 115). The bitch points out that Nixon's version of freedom is, in fact, freedom's opposite: 'In peace as now: freedom is starvation' (*DQ*, 108). She then asserts 'What if we, due to our freedom, revolt? When freedom revolts and wants to name itself, it leads people to the torture cells of the secret police's prisons' (*DQ*, 108).

There are significant Orwellian undertones in these passages. In the political reality of mid-eighties UK and America, Don Quixote detects the oppression and manipulation that characterised the totalitarian society in George Orwell's 1949 momentous *Nineteen Eighty-Four*. The three slogans that are listed on posters everywhere in Oceania (central location of *Nineteen Eighty-Four*), 'WAR IS PEACE', 'FREEDOM IS SLAVERY' and 'IGNORANCE IS STRENGTH',[43] are the fundamental examples of 'doublethink' – the ability to hold two contradictory beliefs as valid. Don Quixote recognises this kind of schizophrenic thinking in Cold War American society, where 'freedom is starvation', and where violence and nuclear weapons become the agents of peace.

For decades since it was published, *Nineteen Eighty-Four* was circulated as a cautionary tale against Soviet communism, thus serving the anti-socialist rhetoric of the Cold War era in the West. It suffered clichéd readings, interpreted, like its predecessor *Animal Farm*, as an unambiguous allegory of Stalin's terror in post-revolutionary Russia. But a more recent readership has come to see it as a criticism of any totalitarian system of power. Of course, Acker is not the only one to see parallels between Orwell's dystopia and the way the American government manipulates public opinion to achieve its ends. In his introduction to the 2003 Penguin reprint of *Nineteen Eighty-Four*, Thomas Pynchon identifies the widespread practice of Orwellian-style doublethink under George Bush Jr's presidency. The Department of Defence has become accepted as 'a war making apparatus', and the Department of Justice and the related institution of the FBI are responsible for a series of abuses of human rights and constitutional law.[44] The media, which pertain to be free, perpetuate further the logic of doublethink by neutralising each presented truth with its equal opposite in order to achieve objectivity.[45] The public are perpetually misled about events by various forms of 'spin', to which they respond with cognitive dissonance: 'We know better than what they tell us, yet hope otherwise. We believe and doubt at the same time.'[46] As a result of mixed, reductive messages from leaders and the media, people acquire a confused conscience, trusting and distrusting the government at the same time, while the role of those in power remains unthreatened. Unsurprisingly, by producing inaction, withdrawal and apathy, doublethink creates ideal opportunities for modern cynicism to thrive.

Don Quixote wants to put a stop to this. She declares: 'All political techniques, left or right, are the praxis and speech of the controllers. How can we get rid of these controllers, their praxis and speech or politics?' (*DQ*, 22). In her commitment to fight against hypocrisy, deceit or what Acker labels 'Superficialities' (*DQ*, 102), she takes on the role of the American Diogenes. The challenge is to overcome the numerous schizophrenic divisions that arose in the difficult context of an absence of clear moral positions. To make a contribution to radical politics, as Don Quixote's stance makes clear, it is necessary to follow ancient Cynics in their synthesis of thinking and living differently, and parrhesia provides such a productive union. As one of the dog characters exclaims: 'Freedom is nothing until it's used' (*DQ*, 108).

Don Quixote's mission to expose the truth about misconduct by the powerful is far from a solitary endeavour. Acker's parrhesia is a deeply collaborative project. She is keen to connect with 'textual friends',[47] as Spencer Dew calls them, in search of a community which shares her commitment to truth-telling. In *Don Quixote*, as elsewhere, Acker incorporates into her prose muckraking exposés from various cultural critics, investigative journalists and other politically engaged writers who are devoted to revealing truths that have been suppressed from the official narrative. 'I'm a sort of mad journalist, a journalist without a paid assignment,' she once wrote about herself.[48] *Don Quixote* contains extensive passages imported from Seymour M. Hersh's venomous 1983 book of investigative journalism, *The Price of Power: Kissinger in the Nixon White House*. This material informs Don Quixote's critique of the evil enchanters of America. Don Quixote resolves to 'find out how the American government works' (*DQ*, 102), and it is through Hersh's uncompromising reportage on Kissinger and Nixon that the knight learns about greed, hypocrisy and other moral failings of American leadership.

Hersh's journalism spans four decades, from coverage of the war in Vietnam and the CIA's domestic surveillance to wars in Iraq and Afghanistan and his more recent exposé on conditions at the Abu Ghraib prison in Iraq. At the time that Acker was working on *Don Quixote*, Hersh already had a reputation for being one of the most feared investigative journalists in America. His exposure of the My Lai massacre in Vietnam had won him worldwide recognition and the Pulitzer Prize for international reporting in 1970. Hersh was one of the first to challenge the initially complacent media reporting on Vietnam, before the media joined the side of the anti-war protesters. Although he often puts himself at considerable personal risk, he refuses the label of a 'courageous journalist', eager to point out that his reporting has been a lucrative activity and has won him awards.[49] However, Robert Miraldi writes that 'anger is what fuels Hersh',[50] emphasising the underlying sense of responsibility to the public and personal rage within Hersh's reporting. Indeed, Hersh has considered himself 'a mouthpiece for people on the inside', recognising that 'You get a sense I am a vehicle for a certain form of dissent.'[51]

A heavily documented book, *The Price of Power* solidified Hersh's position as one of President Nixon and the National Security Adviser and Secretary of State Henry Kissinger's foremost acerbic critics. Based on hundreds of interviews, *The Price of Power* re-examines their partnership, revealing the dark side of their foreign policy-making. Hirsh first saw the need to conduct a thorough investigation into their conduct of foreign affairs while scooping a series of revelations on domestic ground, when he worked for the *New York Times* investigating the Watergate Scandal, a turbulent time 'when the press – and the nation – became aware of the distance between the truth and what we were told had happened'.[52] In his trenchant critique, Hersh conveyed a message to the public that Nixon and Kissinger's commitment to the public good was a campaign based on deception. The ample evidence he gathered documents the two men's involvement in unethical conduct, abuses of power at home and abroad, their selfish motivations, personal antagonisms, secrecy and the political cost of their decisions and operations. Hersh burrowed into multiple controversies, including those surrounding the war in Vietnam and illegal bombing in Cambodia.

Observers have ascribed animal qualities to Hersh's style of reporting, comparing his determination to 'the single-minded ferocity of the wolverine'.[53] Hersh's ability to penetrate through obstacles and layers of deception makes him a contemporary defacer of America's official currencies: freedom, peace and democracy. In so doing, Hersh shares many qualities of the ancient Cynical dogs. His writing style is biting and dogged, and seems suitable for the dirty content he drags out of his interviewees and from the bowels of the Library of Congress. He concludes *The Price of Power* with the following assessment:

> In the end, as in the beginning, Nixon and Kissinger remained blind to the human costs of their actions – a further price of power. The dead and maimed in Vietnam and Cambodia – as in Chile, Bangladesh, Biafra, and the Middle East – seemed not to count as the President and his national security adviser battled the Soviet Union, their misconceptions, their political enemies, and each other.[54]

Over several pages, Acker creatively reworks a chapter from *The Price of Power* entitled 'A Greek Tragedy and a Civil War in Africa'. One of the instances of Nixon and Kissinger's misdeeds concerns the dangerous (and largely suppressed) information provided by a Greek journalist, Elias P. Demetracopoulos, about Nixon's support for the Greek military dictatorship. According to this journalist, in Acker's rewriting of Hersh, the Greek junta contributed 'hundreds of thousands of dollars from the Greek KYP' (*DQ*, 104), the Greek intelligence service, to sponsor Nixon's 1968 presidential campaign, using businessman Thomas A. Pappas as a conduit since it is illegal for US elections to be financed by foreign governments, and a number of steps were taken to disguise this clandestine collaboration.

Acker then recounts the tragic struggle for independence of the Biafrans during the Nigerian Civil War (1967–70), unpacking the ways in which the rhetoric deployed by Kissinger and Nixon (whom she singles out as evil enchanters) disingenuously presented them as the protectors of human life. After Hersh, she quotes one of Nixon's speeches from his 1968 presidential campaign: 'While America is not the world's policeman, let us act as the world's conscience in this matter of life and death for millions . . .' (*DQ*, 106, ellipsis in original). She then exposes a large gap between diplomatic niceties and the tragic reality, retelling from Hersh how the Nixon administration failed to intervene and, consequently, did not prevent mass famine in Biafra. She invokes Roger Morris, a member of the National Security Council, who said that Kissinger 'had no rational reason for letting those kids starve; it just did cause it was scared to alienate Richardson [the Under Secretary of State] cause it and Richardson have other fish to fry' (*DQ*, 106). As observed by Nicola Pitchford in her reading of the passage, as long as the good relations between Kissinger and Richardson are officially preserved and the politicians maintain the nation's appearance of power, the failure to prevent mass starvation is rationalised.[55]

Here, as throughout the novel, Kissinger is revealingly denied the subject position 'he/his' and is instead damningly referred to as 'it'. The narrator lays bare the inhumanity and crude self-interest that underpinned Kissinger's dealings with the Biafran cause:

> Although Kissinger according to Kissinger, cause it had emotions, wanted to help the Biafrans, the State Department was stopping it. So, in order to get the Nobel Peace Prize, Kissinger barked an order to Morris to woof negotiations secretly with the Foreign Minister of Biafra in the *SATURDAY REVIEW*'s editor's apartment. [. . .] Privately Kissinger and Morris found all of this a big joke. (*DQ*, 106)

It is not hard to discern that Acker's replication of Hersh is awash with cynicism, confirming Chaloupka's diagnosis that cynicism in American politics is on a loop, feeding from the cynical leaders to a cynical public and back. Both Acker and Hersh expose the deceit, hypocrisy and manipulation of America's commanders-in-chief. The world they describe is populated by Cervantesque evil enchanters and their helpless victims. Acker's writing is propelled by anger similar to that of Hersh, and like him she writes with a metaphorical cynical spasm.

There is more to Acker's cynicism than figurative foam in the mouth. Without doubt, Hersh's *The Price of Power*, by making visible the human cost of Nixon and Kissinger's foreign policy, provides a powerful anti-memoir to the view of Kissinger as one of the greatest American diplomats. Yet Hersh is likely to leave the reader enlightened and even more cynical, reaffirming the disillusioned views about the political system and leadership, and offering no alternative (though this is not to say he might not provoke meaningful political action in the form of a protest, for example). Moreover, Hersh's reportage can be consigned to history, and his linear argument contested by opponents' counter-arguments. By contrast, Acker writes with a revolutionary agenda in mind, and her strategies of critique steeped in ancient Cynicism directly serve military ends. Committed, radical muckrakers, Acker's narrators do not merely observe, but they interfere both verbally and physically.

What Don Quixote shares with the ancient Cynics and Christ (who has been associated with the movement) is her parrhesia. Foucault understands it as a practice of social critique which combines an uncompromised dedication to criticising the powerful with a rigorous commitment to self-fashioning in accordance with what one preaches. Thus he defines parrhesia as a 'verbal activity', where speaking is a kind of doing. His fundamental criteria for parrhesia are met when someone 'chooses frankness instead of persuasion, truth instead of falsehood or silence, the risk of death instead of life and security, criticism instead of flattery, and moral duty instead of self-interest and moral apathy'.[56] In this, parrhesia is clearly distinguished from modern cynicism, where 'self-interest and moral apathy' flourish. As opposed to a rhetorician who may not even believe the convictions they disseminate but has the skill to flatter and manipulate the public opinion, a parrhesiast cultivates a bond between their beliefs, their conduct and their discourse, and speaks out of moral duty to help themselves as well as others while taking considerable risk.

It might be perplexing, at first, to see Foucault, who carefully documented how different regimes of power produce different knowledges, prescribe truth-telling as a source of ethical empowerment in our historical present. Whereas the ancient Cynics sought to reveal things as they really were and to penetrate to the truth of human experience, poststructuralists are aware that everything is appearance and discount truths as mere contingencies. Moreover, in the days when we are inundated with contradictory messages, how can we distinguish truth from rhetoric, spin and marketing tricks that have dominated contemporary political discourse? What happens to the truths exposed? Do we become more cynical and desensitised? How exposure and knowledge may translate to collective action, rather than feeding cynical detachment, is precisely Acker's concern. '[E]specially after Watergate', she told Lotringer, '[e]verybody now knows what's happening. They might not want to see it, but certainly all the information is out in the open. [. . .] [P]eople sort of know. They just don't give a damn.'[57] Finally, how can parrhesiastic values of truth-telling be transmitted in a work of fiction and be potentially transformative?

Here we should note that Foucault is unconcerned with the empirical definition of truth, namely, whether what we say is accurate and factually verifiable. According to Foucault, parrhesia has to do with the courage to step up, criticise the powerful and act on what we consider to be true. In his lectures he concluded: 'My intention was not to deal with the problem of truth, but with the problem of the truth-teller, or of truth-telling as an activity.'[58] Nancy Luxon tells us that in practising parrhesia people become an 'expressive subject' rather than just a knowing subject focused on facts; the 'dare to know' is transformed into 'dare to act'.[59] Acker's satire shatters the illusions Nixon and Kissinger created to propagate their power. Thus, paradoxically, the distorted reality that satire achieves through hyperbole, caricature, lampoon and the grotesque can be considered more truthful than their official speeches.

But the status of satire became contentious. Following the decision of the committee in 1973 to award Kissinger the Nobel Peace Prize, the American satirist and song-writer Tom Lehrer declared satire dead: 'Political satire became obsolete when Henry Kissinger was awarded the Nobel Peace Prize.'[60] The reality became too serious to deliver criticism through humour, he insisted. In turn, the *New York Times* snidely labelled it 'the Nobel War Prize'. However, these can be argued to be satirically exaggerated statements in themselves, and Acker, like her fellow Juvenalian satirist William

Burroughs, cultivates a satiric spirit and elevates satire as a privileged mode of social criticism, perhaps rendering Lehrer's statement premature.

The disliked political leaders are addressed as 'it' in her novel to show her contempt for their dehumanising actions, and nearly all characters, including the knight, her squire and political figures, are transformed into dogs (not to be confused with dogs/Cynics). Through the use of animal metaphors and caricature, Acker creates a hyperbolised picture of the politicians' corruption and primitive egoism. She combats cynicism with its classical predecessor:

> An old friend and operative of Nixon's, Murray Chotiner, barked to Demetracopoulos to '. . . lay off Pappas. It's not smart politics. You know Tom Pappas's a friend of the President.' In 1976, Henry J. Tasca, a career Foreign Service officer who had been Nixon's Ambassador to Greece, woofed on oath to the house Intelligence Committee that Pappas had been a conduit. Tasca died in an automobile accident in 1978. After the junta's seizure of power, the Pentagon began to sell defence materials as 'surplus goods' to the junta. They couldn't sell them as defence materials cause the American dogs disapproved of the junta. Hypocrisy's greed's tool. With every year, the total worth of these military goods climbed by ten million dollars. The USA government is run by greed. (*DQ*, 104)

Don Quixote's satirical scorn is achieved through a mixture of examples rather than linear argumentation and ordering of facts. The saturation of content with a variety of styles and examples is typical of the ancient satires of Juvental and Menippus, which were sometimes referred to as 'hodge-podge' and 'mish-mash'.[61] Acker's attraction to Cervantes's *Don Quixote*, widely identified as a Menippean satire, can be seen in part as propelled by the desire to put to use *Don Quixote*'s subversive Menippean legacy, which is rooted in ancient Cynicism, in her own political agenda.

Menippean satire belongs to what Mikhail Bakhtin has labelled the 'dialogical' literary tradition, which subverts the 'monological' forms of writing he relates to the institutional forms of absolutism, dogmatism and repression.[62] In Acker, dialogism does not preclude the possibility of parrhesia. On the contrary, it is the inclusion of contesting voices that puts the monological 'praxis and speech or politics' of controllers into radical question. With the Menippean mode Acker's writing shares its commitment to subversion, manifested in its openness to a plurality of styles and forms, and the overarching presence of comedy, fantasy, utopianism and parody, as well as grotesque depictions of the body. Ackeresque blunt, satiri-cal tongue, with its characteristic bite, expressed through carica-ture, hyperbole, pun, dialogue and oxymoron, is also distinctively Menippean. These inherited literary strategies are Cynical in the classical sense because, in keeping with the premise of the Cynical ethos of homology between word and deed, the aim is not just to ridicule, criticise and distance oneself from the despised reality – which would amplify the feelings of impotence, negativity and frus-tration akin to a modern cynic – but to transform reality.

Critics have argued that because the relationship of Menippean satire with the empirical world is antithetical, or at least problematic, it requires a synthetic performative act of interpretation on the part of the reader, which mobilises a positive dialectical process of trans-formation. This is what Theodore Kharpertian has observed when he identified transformative potentials in Pynchon's Menippean satires:

> The criticism of Menippean satire involves the recognition of the dia-lectical nature of the genre's interrelation with experience, for it is from the complex, antithetical interaction between text and experience in the consciousness of the reader – already itself a plurality – that new syntheses become possible, even going as far perhaps as revolutions in the very assumptions upon which prevailing conceptions of text and experience are grounded.[63]

Anchored in the Menippean tradition, Acker's satirical mode is underpinned by a positive political programme, as although, to put it in Kharpertian's words, her satirical depictions induce an oppres-sive negativity, they destabilise familiar perception, 'opening the possibility of regarding the object or objects of attack – indeed all experiential objects and states of affairs anew'[64] – thereby making the reader an active participant in Acker's imagining the possibility of a different world.

'Body, talk'

Acker's novels' frequent focus on the biological body also returns us to the inherited Cynical legacy. On the one hand, the grotesque con-figurations of the body are a familiar satirist's weapon used to mock and degrade the powerful, as the following depiction of the presiden-tial couple examplifies: 'Mr Nixon completely stopped fucking Mrs Nixon. It touched its shrivelled red quivering cock. This is America, disgrace of the West, slave manufacturer in the void of two oceans' (*DQ*, 111). On the other hand, because the power of words to serve truth has been compromised in the Cold War era, Acker advances parrhesiastic frankness and honesty through prioritising the body. The refusal of traditional verbal communication is encapsulated in the imperative from *Pussy, King of the Pirates*: 'Body, talk.'

For Plato, the body was a mere decaying container imprisoning the soul. By contrast, the Cynics attacked abstract ideas and embraced the here and now, as well as the body with all it has to offer. In adopting an animal lifestyle, Don Quixote makes her body the principal manifestation of the Cynical ethos. Intensive labour on the mind as well as the body allows her to challenge the schizophrenia of modern cynicism, which hypocritically separates word and thought from embodied life: 'In my vision, those who're enchanted, since they're no longer in touch with their own bodies, have no ideas what their needs are. Therefore they don't need to eat, shit, or fuck, and they don't care who they elect as their political leaders' (*DQ*, 189). In *Don Quixote* the body becomes a crucial component of the parrhesiastic game. As Acker once commented, 'At the end of my version of *Don Quixote* I started turning to the body as a source for new models of writing.'[65] Acker's proposed re-education is centred on the body. It is not aimed at spreading abstract knowledge (which produces docility), but rather at fostering oneness between knowledge and action, and rendering absurd any knowledge acquired through oppressive education:

> All the accepted forms of education in this country, rather than teaching the child to know who she is or to know, dictate to the child who she is. Thus obfuscate any act of knowledge. Since these educators train the mind rather than the body, we can start with the physical body, the place of shitting, eating, etc., to break through our opinions or false education. (*DQ*, 165–6)

In keeping with Cynicism's radical demands of living differently, Acker celebrates socially abject corporeality. Acker and Sloterdijk both want to challenge modern cynicism with abjection, but with gender-specific nuances. While Sloterdijk puts emphasis on bodily functions culturally or biologically assigned to men, Acker discovers a specifically female language of the body. However, they both perceive the bodily and the sexual realms to be potential sites of resistance. Sloterdijk's Diogenes reminds us of Bakhtin's François Rabelais's carnival utopia where hierarchies are reversed, prohibitions broken and grotesque bodies celebrated. Sloterdijk finds a sense

of protestation against the established ways of speaking and thinking in the outrageous Cynical gestures such as urination in public.
But critics have identified conceptual and practical problems with
Sloterdijk's bold postulation of 'pissing as world-changing'.[66] Shea
points out, meanwhile, that Sloterdijk's uncomplicated portrait of
a Cynic's body is naively idealistic, vague and essentialising in that
it 'neglects the extent to which bodies are themselves historical constructs inscribed within dominant discourses'.[67]

Whereas Sloterdijk is very much preoccupied with the ecstatic,
wholesome body untainted by social and historical conditioning,
Acker's bodily grotesqueries are not always celebratory. With their
enslaved, ageing, starved, deteriorating and diseased bodies, rather
than being liberated, her characters are often hopelessly corporeal.
Janey, the protagonist of *Blood and Guts in High School*, states
'I'm tough, rotted, putrid beef. My cunt red ugh' (*BGHS*, 18). In
Eurydice in the Underworld (1997), the narrator's cancerous body
is objectified by the medical scrutiny of health professionals. When
Acker does register unbridled female carnal desire, it is usually
within the confines of the utopian space of a dream. The heroine
of *Rip-off Red, Girl Detective* records her lesbian encounter that
took place on an airplane, lifting above the daily reality of con-
straint and repression: 'I seem to be weightless; no, it's just the
atmosphere inside the airplane. My body floats in waves, an endless air ocean' (*RRGD*, 12); 'Now desire doesn't center in my clit
but turns around my body, my nerves swirl until my body shivers
and trembles to touch this stranger in every way and everywhere'
(*RRGD*, 15). Outside the erotic fantasy realm, however, Acker's
female heroines are often engulfed and limited by their biological
femaleness: their bodies are censored, veiled, in pain, with a sell-
by date, used for male pleasure and procreation and weaker than
men's. As Acker put it in an interview: 'This society tells me that a
woman after 30 doesn't have a body unless she has children. You
can't even be a whore after 30.'[68]

The body does retain some residue of authenticity. As the dog
character in *Don Quixote* asserts: 'The body cannot lie' (*DQ*, 176).
In pornographic writing, for example, Acker has recognised a certain
simplicity, concreteness and honesty which are lacking in standard
communication: 'you don't know how you're manipulated when
you read a newspaper, yet pornography is very direct, you know
exactly what the manipulation is. It's made for this very quick pleasure . . . it's almost like meaningless language . . . and that's interesting.'[69] Dreaming is yet another realm beyond rational control

that forms part of a Cynical routine. 'Sounds like you completely technologized yourself,'[70] was Rickels's reaction to Acker's sleep sessions deliberately interrupted for transcribing dream content. Moreover, the animalistic grotesque reductions which run across Acker's novels – humans transformed into dogs, cats and fish – are classically Cynical. Her affinity with the punk counterculture of the late 1970s and early 1980s (it is not a coincidence that punks wore dog collars) and other subversive communities further aligns her ethos with the Cynical lifestyle.

In addition to the multiple revelations taken from Hersh, in the documentary section of *Don Quixote* we are presented with a letter in which the knight pleads with Nixon to take action and put an end to the Biafran tragedy. But it is not an ordinary letter. It lacks the fancy rhetoric and calculated argument that characterises the official talk of politicians. The letter closes with the words:

> please accept my apology that my left hand isn't forming these letters correctly. I wasn't sent to Oxford or anywhere, so what I do write is cut crosses into the insides of my wrists. I write in fever. I hope these letters find you in good health. (*DQ*, 107)

Writing in skin, Don Quixote viscerally connects with the Biafran victims. Her letter conflates their suffering with the victims of AIDS and the poor Haitians (*DQ*, 107), sending a disturbing message about the American government's neglectful and abusive policies at home and abroad. It creates a powerful contrast in highlighting how Nixon and Kissinger's maximised focus on self-interest and personal well-being have had a direct effect on the bodies of the Biafrans: leaving them hungry and, subsequently, dead. Don Quixote's later declaration that 'Masochism is now rebellion' (*DQ*, 158)[71] overcomes cynical consciousness through compassion and suffering with and for another. A vulnerable embodied self engaged in thought and action: it emerges as an alternative to the cold, armoured subjectivity of a modern cynic. (In stark contrast, Acker's knight awaits an abortion and adopts 'pale or puke green paper' as her armour [*DQ*, 9].) Don Quixote's Christ-like, counter-intuitive masochism, asceticism and altruism are clearly at odds with the prevailing attitudes of self-preservation, competition and accumulation. For Acker, the body is 'that which is subject to change, chance, and death'.[72] Expressed not only through radical words or thoughts, Don Quixote's is an embodied protest. The crosses in the skin make the homophonic relationship between word and deed complete.

Don Quixote brings our attention not only to the abuses of power, but also to the dangers of dwelling in a disengaged cynical consciousness which takes these abuses, ulterior motives, self-interests and scandals for granted. Modern cynicism prevents the emergence of new imaginative horizons and, in its Hobbesian repercussions, Acker warns us, may also legitimise and foster political positions not far removed from totalitarianism.

In the shadow of Hobbes

In her depiction of the Nixon administration Acker invokes the forefather of realpolitik and moral relativism, Thomas Hobbes. Hobbes visits Nixon and his wife in their bedroom as the Angel of Death, claiming that Nixon has summoned him (*DQ*, 109). Interpretations of Hobbes's thought vary widely.[73] In her appropriation of the Hobbesian outlook, Acker brings to the fore the dangerous side of modern cynicism which has become associated with his name, Hobbes's 'state of nature' – a pathology that presents itself as political realism based on an assumption that humans are by nature motivated solely by self-interest. Grounded in the assumption that individuals are inherently greedy and competitive, this position has led some critics to associate Hobbesian governance with the logic of totalitarianism – a system which will uniformly dominate and impose prohibitions on subjects for their own good, promising protection, harmony and peace at the cost of their political freedom.[74] In *Don Quixote* we are pressed to make similarly unsettling connections between the Nixon administration and totalitarian leadership. Acker demonstrates how Hobbes's worldview has been utilised by American leaders practising realpolitik to legitimise untrammelled power politics and the violence that comes with it. This becomes an occasion to revisit the fundamental tensions and dilemmas concerning contemporary politics: 'Has evil always been part of human nature?' Don Quixote asks (*DQ*, 70). Is realism/cynicism or realpolitik the necessary evil? Is a moralistic idealpolitik naive, or even possible or desirable?

Acker's Hobbes is a cynic, but not in the spirit of Diogenes or even Rousseau. Rather, he bears clear hallmarks of modern cynicism, with selfishness, greed and indifference to others as its distinguishing qualities. Mazella tells us that it is Hobbes and not Rousseau who appears in the *OED*'s first recorded use of 'cynic' in its modern sense.[75] In *Leviathan* (1651), Hobbes forcefully argued that 'a general inclination of all mankind' was directed towards 'a perpetual and restless desire of power after power, that ceaseth only in death'.[76] In Hobbes's view, peace in the political commonwealth requires an absolute sovereign who creates laws that regulate all political, ethical and religious matters. Hobbes's cynical view of man's underlying inhumanity to man reduces people to self-preserving animals. The only way to ensure their collective security, in order that they try not to 'destroy, or subdue one another',[77] is by means of an absolute authority.

The dog vocabulary plays a lead role in Acker's depiction of human behaviour according to this Hobbesian pattern. As the president and Mrs Nixon 'started to copulate' (*DQ*, 109), 'The Angel Of Death Or Thomas Hobbes Barks Arguments To Itself On Whether Evil Is Necessary In The Canine World' (*DQ*, 111). In Acker's portrait, Hobbes concludes that the state of war is a natural condition of dogs (humans) because they cannot control the passions that lead to war, such as the desire for power and glory. It is a dog-eat-dog world, in which 'every man is Enemy to every man':[78]

> Doggish life depends on unequal power relations or the struggle of power. This is the society in which we live. The life of a dog, even if the dog's dead like me, is solitary, poor, nasty, brutish, short. The condition of a dog is a condition of war, of everyone against everyone: so every dog has a right to everything, even to another dog's body. This is freedom. (*DQ*, 114)

Hobbes's world operates as a machine composed of only material bodies which behave according to the scientific laws of cause and effect. Therefore, 'Canine worlds [. . .] are material (just are), dualistic, and conditional' (*DQ*, 111). In keeping with this mechanistic rational mechanism, dogs (people) are denied the capacity for disagreement, questioning, visions of change, contradiction, laughter and spontaneity. Don Quixote laments over an overwhelming 'Impossibility Of Dreaming' (*DQ*, 117). Thus, when the dogs cry out to Don Quixote, 'is it possible that all the enchantments – poverty, alienation, fear, inability to act on desire, inability to feel – have made you unable to see and feel visions?' she admits: 'Yes. I am a failure' (*DQ*, 190).

Modern cynicism and emancipatory politics are diametrically opposed in *Don Quixote*. In a Hobbesian universe, succumbing to the power of the absolute sovereign is of more benefit to the individual than the riskier participation in a doomed revolt. From the perspective of self-interest and preservation, non-participation in the revolt is a rational choice of individuals. Even in potentially revolutionary circumstances, where people can exercise their collective power to disobey and overthrow the unjust system, in line with a realist argument, individuals are too egoistically motivated to join a risky revolt. Participation would be considered a mere 'drop in the bucket' and presumably not worth the heavy cost and sacrifice.[79] In contrast to Diogenes the Cynic's subversion of authority, such as his instructing Alexander the Great not to obstruct his sunlight, the Hobbesian cynic is likely to accommodate themselves to the status quo rather than questioning it. In Acker's diagnosis, 'Americans don't even bother to bark anymore' (*DQ*, 109).

Furthermore, Western history is undergirded by the lesson that revolutions end in failure. As capitalism is now commonly believed to be triumphant, despite its multiple injustices the alternatives have frequently been seen to be worse: '"There's no such thing as revolution", Nixon barked to the bitch. "There's only big business. We dogs've seen enough butcheries. We know the canine anatomy inside out"' (*DQ*, 108). But, as Acker puts it: 'It's easier to talk about how a revolution must necessarily fail, as intellectuals talk, when your kids have food shelter. When bitches can actually have kids' (*DQ*, 108).

Nixon and Kissinger, in Acker's characterisation, subscribe to Hobbes's philosophy of absolutism and political realism, which assumes that democracy, understood as rule by the people, is inadequate, and that the existence of unlimited authority acting outside of ethical considerations is necessary to secure national interests. They believe that 'the Europeans're barking foreign (that is American) economic control which they think is their starvation. If they're starving, it's their starvation. England's starving cause it won't accept our teachings on how to use nuclear and computer technology and think tanks on democracy' (*DQ*, 110).

In Anglo-American consciousness, realpolitik, as championed by Kissinger at the White House, is a direct descendant of the political realist tradition. It can thus be traced back to the dark writings of Thucydides in the fifth century BC, Niccolò Machiavelli's uncompromising realism at the turn of the seventeenth century, and Hobbes's theoretical interventions in the mid-seventeenth century. Unlike idealism, which furthered a belief in human progress and betterment of human nature, realism presupposes a cyclical view of history and understands human nature as fixed. To realists, humans are naturally aggressive, fearful, distrustful, power-seeking and in need of a stable government to control their base impulses.

But in contrast to realism, realpolitik is a relatively modern term, originally unrelated to the Machiavellian-realist approach to international politics. The historian John Bew explains that realpolitik was coined in mid-nineteenth-century Germany, in response to the deep disillusionment that followed a series of failed 1848 republican revolts in Europe against monarchical powers.[80] In its original context of post-revolution Germany, realpolitik denoted a sobering of domestic politics. The intention was to bring order to the state recovering from upheaval: to end dreaming and to 'get real'.[81] The word was then associated with Otto von Bismarck, who famously embraced politics as an 'art of the possible', and subsequently entered the English language through English–German rivalry leading up to the First World War, acquiring a predominantly negative meaning, converging with a cold-blooded, cynical, greedy type of Machiavellian conduct of international politics.[82]

With his marked preference for 'real' over 'utopian', Kissinger is now considered to be the key modern practitioner of realpolitik. Kissinger has often been criticised for his dark vision of democracy, which was at odds with an American sensibility firmly rooted in democratic ideals. Jeremi Suri writes that this apprehension of democracy was anchored in Kissinger's early life, when he experienced the collapse of Weimar Germany before his exile to New York.[83] Following Nazism's rise to power, he was strongly sceptical of a democratic system which, although centred on humanistic values and individual freedom, failed to prevent the emergence of violent movements and economic catastrophes. Realpolitik for Kissinger, then, was an alternative to what he considered weak, ineffective and unstable mass politics. Historians note that the coincidence of humanistic democracy with the rise and legacy of fascist power is a complex issue, but it was not unusual for those who have witnessed the atrocities of the Second World War to associate the expansion of democracy with the expansion of violence.[84] Kissinger's was a realist turn away from democratic idealism in favour of a tough decision-making government, operating under a strong, authoritative leader.

Acker's Kissinger is an American Leviathan, and his realpolitik becomes interchangeable with ruthless realism and cynicism, Hobbes and Machiavelli style. In the context of international relations, realism assumes that states reflect the selfishness of humans in that they are primarily motivated by self-preservation and an insatiable passion for power. Realists hold the view that within states human nature is tamed by authority, but since there is no international government, a Hobbesian state of war presides on an international level, giving an outlet to the evil inclinations of human nature and thus, in the words of Frederick Schuman, 'the law of the jungle still prevails'.[85] The international world is therefore inherently anarchic (understood by realists as barbaric, or in a state of war). Without one ruling body above it, it achieves only a temporary and expedient balance based on pure power politics where states are like 'billiard balls' which 'all bang against each other and have hard, impenetrable shells'.[86] *In Don Quixote*, the character Nixon expresses his dissatisfaction with other nations' resistance to America's promotion of other nations to 'nuclear' status: 'Kissinger and I believe that it's good to spread nuclear weapons around the world. But we're constantly hampered in every way, shape, at every step: we can hardly do anything for the world. Everyone hampers us. Everyone's against us' (*DQ*, 110). Don Quixote discovers on her journey that American politicians of real-politik are primarily driven by greed and fear. 'The USA government is run out of fear' (*DQ*, 103) – particularly the fear of predation from both the outside and inside. Witnessing Nixon and Kissinger's amoral tactics leads Don Quixote to censure the United States as 'religiously intolerant, militaristic, greedy, and dependent on slavery as all democracies have been' (*DQ*, 124).

The novel alludes to another theorist of cynical/realist politics, Machiavelli. There are many interpretations of Machiavelli's work, some of which emphasise its non-realist elements, but his *The Prince* (1532) has been commonly regarded as 'the greatest testament of the cynical technique of power'[87] and adapted as a set of codifications of maxims for the thinkers of realpolitik and cynical rulers.[88] In the section entitled 'INSERT', the outraged narrator proposes that the Prince should be elected the next president because the American leaders share his amorality. However, in contrast to Machiavelli's 'honest writings', the American president is more likely to 'enchant' the world, manipulate appearances and project himself as moral: 'The Prince isn't moral: he doesn't give a shit about anybody but himself. The Prince wouldn't die for anyone, whereas Our President will always die for everybody while he's garnering in their cash' (*DQ*, 21).

'Realism for the Cause of Future Revolution'

Acker's engagement with a set of paintings by Goya' extends the Spanish connection in her *Don Quixote*. As critic Fred Licht notes, the works of Cervantes and Goya conjure up a 'sober refusal to be consoled and the loneliness of an anguished mankind surrounded by an alien universe'.[89] Acker and Goya tackle the Hobbesian theme of 'man's inhumanity to man', along with the complex legacy of the Enlightenment: the irresolvable tension between light and dark, reason and unreason, dreaming and waking, progress and barbarism. In Goya's depictions of monstrous violence in the service of progress (from the shattering effects of the French Revolution to its drastic conclusion in Spain's war against Napoleon's occupation), Acker sees parallel perversions of reason in the surrounding nuclear madness.

The question for us to explore here is: is Goya – and is Acker through Goya – convincing us of the essential futility of any progressive endeavour? Goya's nocturnal grotesques pervade her *Don Quixote*, and those familiar with Goya will recognise the descriptions of specific works woven into the narrative. Her essay 'Realism for the Cause of Future Revolution' (1984) presents her 'simple descriptions' of a series of Goya and Caravaggio's paintings. In addition, her 1984 article for *Artforum*, 'Models for Our Present', contains a description of Goya's 'Saturn Devouring His Children' (1819–23; also known as 'Saturn Devouring His Son', or just 'Saturn'). Finally, the section 'Text 3' of *Don Quixote*, entitled 'The texts of War', revisits four of the five paintings she writes about in her 'Realism' essay, but here she never reveals that her subject is Goya's art.[90] Acker's characters' metamorphosis into dogs can be also traced back to Goya, and *Don Quixote*'s subtitle *Which Was a Dream* evokes one of Goya's most famous etchings, which we shall discuss now.

Goya's growing distrust in reason is perhaps best summarised in his *Caprichos 43* (1799), a grotesque etching entitled 'The Sleep/ Dream of Reason Produces Monsters'. As critics have noted, the ambiguity of plate 43 resides in Goya's play on the double meaning of *sueño*, which can mean both dream and sleep. 'The Sleep of Reason' would support a reading of the print as an enlightened message, namely that when reason lies asleep, evil appears. But understood as 'The Dream of Reason', however, the opposite appears to be true. As Robert Snell asks: 'is it that Reason itself is a sort of dream? A dream that produces monsters, like the revolution of the intellectuals, which devours both its progenitors and its children?'[91]

Goya once asserted that rather than wild creatures of the imagination, it is the supposedly rational discourse that is dangerous. He disclosed to his brother that 'I'm not afraid of witches, hobgoblins, apparitions, boastful giants nor indeed any kind of being except human beings.'[92] The middle part of *Don Quixote* echoes this misanthropic sentiment: 'Wars are raging everywhere. Males dumber than nonhuman animals're running the economic and political world' (*DQ*, 69). This statement is soon followed by scenes of nuclear testing and the birth of prehistoric monsters (*DQ*, 69–70). Don Quixote notes with indignation: 'Why is society so sick. No reason. It's sick because there are monsters in it.' Goya's beasts mutate into monsters from *Godzilla* films, creatures that arise out of a nuclear holocaust, an indirect commentary on nuclear tensions. The monsters talk critical theory. Is it uncontrolled madness that takes over when reason sleeps – reason applied in the service of a free and just society? Or, as Goya's ambiguous title of *Caprichos 43* also implies, might it be reason itself which produces a monstrous reality, when it serves the subjugation of individuals and nature? Here is an exchange between 'two monsters, the future rulers of our world' (*DQ*, 72):

> In the modern period, exchange value has come to dominate society; all qualities have been and are reduced to quantitative equivalences. This process inheres in the concept of reason. For reason, on the one hand, signifies the idea of a free, human, social life. On the other hand, reason is the court of judgement of calculation, the instrument of domination, and the means for the greatest exploitation of nature. As in De Sade's novels, the mode of reason adjusts the world for the ends of self-preservation and recognizes no function other than the preparation of the object from mere sensory material in order to make it that material of subjugation. Instrumental or ossified reason takes two forms: technological reason developed for purposes of dominating nature and social reason directed at the means of domination aimed at exercising social and political power.
>
> This tendency, predetermined by the drive for self-preservation, now pervades all the spheres of human life: this exploitation or reduction of reality to self-preservation and the manipulative other has become the universal principle of a society which seeks to reduce all phenomena to this enlightenment, ideal of rationalism, or subjugation of the other. (*DQ*, 72)

The two monsters' tortured insights echo Adorno's and Horkheimer's conclusions from their *Dialectic of Enlightenment: Philosophical Fragments*, in which they proclaim the collapse of knowledge into power and link enlightenment with domination. Writing (like Kissinger), under the shadow of totalitarianism, Adorno and

Horkheimer offer an apocalyptic evaluation of the Enlightenment project. Their pessimism inches back to Machiavelli, Hobbes, Mandeville, Sade and Nietzsche – a cabinet of '[t]he dark writers of the bourgeoisie',[93] as they label them. But unlike Kissinger's realpolitik – arising out of a Hobbesian rationality (in Acker's presentation at least) – which legitimises a ruthless approach to politics and related moral failings, the thinkers from the Frankfurt School wanted to rescue morality from instrumental reasoning.

They begin with a problem that while the Enlightenment's project was 'aimed at liberating human beings from fear and installing them as masters [. . .] the wholly enlightened earth is radiant with triumphant calamity'.[94] They challenge the belief that reason and the disenchantment (or demystification) of the world led humanity onto the path of a better world free from fear and superstition. Enlightened rationality, they famously argue, has turned back on itself to become an instrument of self-destruction. But they do not suggest that all reason is complicit in totalitarianism. There is a substantial latent attachment to reason as the necessary pre-condition of their critique. Above all, however, their theory is not against reason as such, but against its perverted instrumental forms (which operate by means of language, weapons and machines), which modernity applied in the service of domination under the pressures of the socio-economic structures of late capitalism. Instead of progressing, individuals have been regressing into mere exchangeable quantities in the machinery of control. There is thus no illumination but a 'new form of blindness which supersedes that of vanquished myth'.[95]

Adorno and Horkheimer's critique of instrumental rationality's quest for domination and power is a fitting theoretical context for Acker's elaboration on how war becomes a welcome state of affairs in the progress of the capitalist economy. America saw the post-Second World War climate as an opportunity for economic expansion:

> Throughout the Second World War, the United States was planning, then actually preparing (for) its role in the future post-war world. If there is to be such a world. Emerging militarily and economically unrivalled from the Second World War, America was uniquely and fully able to impose its hatred of nonmaterialism – its main ideal – on the remainder of the world. This belief in total materialism is or intimately connects to economic hegemony, for the economic base of this new order is large export markets and unrestricted access to key materials. (*DQ*, 72–3)

The narrative then lists out the evidence of the United States collapsing financial boundaries across the world to create convenient conditions for economic investments, for example through the establishment of the Organization of American States, the World Bank and the International Monetary Fund. Again, we are in Hobbesian territory: 'International finance (that is, American finance) is a war strategy, a successful one, which the Japanese copied' (*DQ*, 73).

If the discussion were to end here, we could conclude that Acker merely cultivates Goya's ugly landscapes captioned with Adorno and Horkheimer's critical insights. This would, in turn, invite the suspicion that the Ackerian stance only furthers a cynical disillusionment, or 'melancholic stagnation', to refer to Sloterdijk's dismissal of the Frankfurt School's usefulness for contemporary society afflicted by cynicism.[96] Although Adorno and Horkheimer's philosophy was committed to the need for emancipating man from domination, for many its ultimate value resides in the compelling diagnosis of the illness of society rather than the cure. As Shea notes, they 'retreat into a critical pessimism' and 'find pockets of resistance only in the courage to refuse facile reconciliations and, for Adorno, in the aesthetic domain of high modernism'.[97]

However, the fact that Acker inserts their critique into the mouths of the two monsters – 'the future rulers of the world' – rather than the narrator, or Don Quixote herself, is suggestive of the hyperbolising effect of grotesquely satirical discourse. Two interpretations can follow from this. First, Acker induces in readers a sense of uneasiness and urgency, and thereby draws readers into the process of transforming reality, demanding that a political revolution should follow from its insights. Second, Acker satirically distances herself from the monsters' ultimately cynical diagnosis of society as unalterable, where widespread exploitation, domination, self-interest and the denial of value beyond the system of capitalist exchange are taken for granted.

The inevitable bleakness of the world is also challenged in her 'simple descriptions' of Goya's paintings from the *Black Paintings* cycle. Let us focus on two paintings, 'The Dog' and 'Saturn', to see how Acker transforms melancholy into protest. She seems to be performing a paradoxical act because, on the one hand, she selects for discussion some of Goya's darkest and most disturbing paintings, which have been said to communicate the purposelessness of existence. On the other, she puts forward the controversial claim that Goya's distinctive visual idiom, which she calls 'realism' – one akin to nihilism even – is not only far from reactionary, but can also be utilised in the service of a future revolution.

For Licht, whom Acker cites in her essay, 'The Dog' painting is the culminatory depiction of '[t]he anarchic emptiness and purposelessness of existence', and 'a tragic emblem of meaninglessness'.[98] In this nihilistic reading, the silent canine gaze is directed into undifferentiated, empty space: 'whatever the dog is waiting for will never materialize', writes Licht.[99] Goya's dog could also be perceived as saddened by the recurrent horrors resulting from the war and revolution, and thereby embodying the qualities of a Saturnian melancholic. In the Quinta, Goya's country house where he painted the murals, as Juan José Junquera points out, we would have witnessed the famous 'Saturn Devouring His Children' and proceeded towards the image of a miserable dog near the door as we left the salon.[100] The animal has long been considered to be an auxiliary motif in the depiction of melancholy because 'the dog, more gifted and sensitive than other beasts, has a very serious nature and can fall victim to madness, and like deep thinkers is inclined to be always on the hunt, smelling things out, and sticking to them'.[101] But Acker's description bypasses these readings entirely:

> A dog is sticking its head over a barricade you can't see what the barricade is. The only event that is seen and seeable is the dog's head.
> Woof. The only language which is heard and sayable is 'Woof.'[102]

In contrast to a nihilistic paralysis where Goya's canine emerges as timid, alienated and silent, Acker's dog is active. It is consciously 'sticking its head'[103] above the barrier and imposed limitations. Whereas Licht's dog sees and waits for nothing – Godot will not come – there is nothing but darkness – Acker's dog definitely anticipates something. And it woofs!

Similarly, Goya's 'Saturn' in Acker's description no longer refers us back to the well-rehearsed revolutionary tragedy. Instead:

> The louder the cry, the less it's heard. A face and several limbs appear out of blackness. The eyes're so huge they are their own world. White flaccid hair floats out of the head's left side. Black pit the mouth vomits out white cloud, some kind of gook, leading to huge monster hands clenched over buttocks. The killer enjoys killing because he's eating the sap. All the bodies are distorted. No reason given for anything.[104]

For critics such as Ronald Paulson, Goya's 'Saturn', which adorns the dust jacket of his *Representations of Revolution* (1983),[105] encapsulates Vergniaud's words before the National assembly in 1793, in the face of the increasing violence of the policies recommended by his Montagnard rivals: 'Citizens, we now have cause to fear that the Revolution, like Saturn successively devouring his children, has finally given way to despotism and all the calamities that despotism implies.'[106] Yet Acker is unconcerned with the interpretations that have become almost inseparable from the paintings. She insists, 'I have simply described them. They aren't or don't include judgements. I haven't judged them. [. . .] What is being communicated by this "realism"?'[107] Spencer Dew detects a didactic mode at play in Acker's realism, inherited from Goya. Such a method performs 'a practical pedagogical function within Acker's texts, exposing readers to the world *as it really is* and thus teaching them how to see reality and the means by which representation of this reality is mediated more clearly.' The effect of this strategy is 'forcing readers to feel some of the discomfort *they should be feeling already*'.[108] The dog barks and the monster cries. The withdrawn melancholic dog now barks in the Cynical tongue. The cry, the scream and the woof indicate signs of raging protest. The previously territorialised creatures, the domesticated human-like dog and the Oedipalised monster, re-enter their animality, unleashed by 'this language which describes yet refuses to be reactive'.[109]

Modern cynicism and revolutionary cycles

Don Quixote links the drama of repetition and cynical disillusionment very closely. There is a recurrent problem with revolutionary endeavours: like human relationships, they invariably fail and merely repeat what came before. Reflecting on this state of affairs, Don Quixote entitles two subsections about her mission to save America 'The Failure Of My Writing' and 'What Can We Do?: The Failure Of Revolution' (*DQ*, 107). The dog that accompanies her confirms a sense of futility: 'Everything's the same as it ever was' (*DQ*, 123). More broadly, the novel operates in a cynical mode that is also cyclical. The novel's first section, entitled 'the Beginning of the Night', anticipates progression. But it soon becomes apparent that it does not fulfil our expectations of the episodic but strongly end-orientated model of a chivalric quest: the various scenarios do not progress but are transfixed; the focus is spatial and not temporal. As Richard Walsh has observed, 'Acker's work in general is not predicated upon narrative, but upon tableaux; she does not offer events but positions.'[110] Instead of the foregrounded progression and resolution, the narrative is locked in circularity. There are numerous false endings and textual affirmations of a cyclical nature, as illustrated by the headings: 'Actuality Repeats The Dream' (*DQ*, 153), 'THE LAST ADVENTURE', followed by 'UNTIL THIS BOOK WILL BEGIN AGAIN' (*DQ*, 175).

The coincidence of repetition with cynicism is most extreme in Acker's extended appropriations of Sade's *Juliette* (1797) in the section entitled 'AN EXAMINATION OF WHAT KIND OF SCHOOLING WOMEN NEED'. In these passages, Juliette's violent sexual education takes the form of the triple and quadruple repetition of each paragraph, creating a tension between progression and stasis. Consider the following excerpt from the conversation with the teacher:

'This is something new.'
'This is something new.'
'This is something new.'
'This is something new.' (*DQ*, 167)

The repeated line ironically evokes the common argument that revolutions inevitably fail because, while promising novelty and change, they are either suppressed, heavily compromised or only reinstate the previous order in a new form. There are Hobbesian undertones here: little changes but the leaders' names, and their new revolutionary governments are likely to display a thirst for power, corruption, bureaucratic indifference, and a repressive use of violence, which is not dissimilar from the governments they have overthrown. Undoubtedly, the revolutionary scenarios which populate Acker's novels are haunted by the pre-modern meaning of revolt as repetition. As we have seen, the word 'revolution' entered the political vocabulary in seventeenth-century England to define the Cromwellian regicide, and in parallels between the planetary and the political during the Glorious Revolution and the usurpation of King James II.[111] This meaning of revolution as repetition affirms Hobbes's prognosis that the reign of the essential leader will interminably reassert itself:

I have seen in this Revolution a circular notion of the Sovereign Power, through two Usurpers, from the late King, to this Son; for [. . .] it moved from King Charles the First, to the Long-Parliament, from thence to the Rump, from the Rump to Oliver Cromwell, and then back again from Richard Cromwell to the Rump, thence to the Long-Parliament, and thence to King Charles the Second, where long may it remain.[112]

One of the four texts in the middle part of *Don Quixote*, in particular, entitled 'Text 2: The Leopard: Memory', explores cynical consciousness born out of the return of the same. In it, Acker rewrites fragments of Giuseppe Tomasi di Lampedusa's historical novel *The Leopard* (1958), which follows a Sicilian prince through to his death while tracing the decline of the aristocracy at the time of the Risorgimento and the unification of Italy in 1860.

Acker commences the story with a revolutionary event: 'It was the year 1860. The Garibaldis had just landed in Palermo' (*DQ*, 60). There are seeds of a new beginning when the revolutionaries bring to Sicily the prospect of change. Revolution in the modern sense, with its promises of progress, democratic future, freedom and justice, is in the air. However, in both Lampedusa and Acker's accounts, the revolution fails to bring about the desired progress. David Gilmour deems *The Leopard* to be an accurate portrayal of the gap between ideals and reality: 'In many respects the *Risorgimento* was a deception for the Sicilians, a revolution which achieved little beyond exchanging their Neapolitan rulers for more distant and perhaps less tolerant northerners.'[113] In Lampedusa, rather than being defeated, the aristocracy is sustained through the Prince's involvement in the establishment of the government that replaces him. The Prince's opportunistic nephew, whom Acker evokes, suggests that to ensure its survival the nobility should participate in the political overthrow: 'Unless we ourselves take a hand now, they'll foist a republic on us. If we want things to stay as they are, things will have to change.'[114] Ultimately, however, 'Nothing in the town had changed: The Prince still ruled Palermo' (*DQ*, 61), and the populace 'exulted in the return of the monarchy' (*DQ*, 62). The evental promise is reduced to the banal gesture of repetition of the same. Acker writes that, for the Prince, 'nothing matters', and 'every event is every other event' (*DQ*, 65). Devoid of hope for positive change and collective action, the people observe political uprisings with cynical detachment: 'I'm anonymous: I'm at this party just like I'm watching a movie. No event touches me' (*DQ*, 64).

The first chapter of *The Leopard* is emphatically subtitled 'May, 1860', arousing expectations that an important historical event is to be recounted, and Acker's version reflects this. Yet despite these expectations, the revolutionary battles and the successes of Garibaldi occur off-stage. The focus is instead on the description of the Salina family palace outside Palermo. The family are gathered in an opulently decorated rococo drawing-room and have just finished their 'daily recital of the Rosary'.[115] The fact that the Prince has a strong interest in astronomy contributes to the overall message that the old cannot be converted into the genuinely new. His telescope becomes an instrument of an ironically distant assertion of the predetermined planetary paths traced in the political sphere and an inability to think beyond familiar constellations. As Acker's Prince is nearing death, he begins to feel nauseous and is losing perception 'in this world of whirling' (*DQ*, 67).

Acker also works through such cyclical non-changes in her later works. The literary basis for *Pussy, King of the Pirates* (1996) is Robert Louis Stevenson's *Treasure Island* (1883), and it again presupposes the linear structure of a quest: a search for buried treasure. The spark of revolution is ignited in a church by the prostitutes who then join the punk boys styled as William Burroughs's 'wild boys'[116] and travel with a group of female pirates. While the novel fulfils the conventions of the genre of adventure fiction – the treasure has been found – the revolutionary ideal which is at the core of Acker's writing is again caught up in the circuit of recurrence. The discovered treasure, rather than providing the fulfilment of social change, merely affirms its capitalistic underpinnings. The pirate world does not bring about the freedom of anarchy, leaving the characters O and Ange untransformed by their pirate experience. The very type of organisation that the pirates assume, with Pussy as their leader, 'king of the pirates', signifies the insistence of hierarchical-monarchical forms. They are dependent on wealth, have pirate banners and standards and replicate the hierarchies of the states from which they steal. A female pirate rebel in the role of a 'king' appears to lead us towards a cynical conclusion that even Acker's most anarchic group is unable to wish the state away.

We have seen that the deadlock of revolution as repetition is a common feature in Acker's works. Furthermore, because her novels perpetuate revolutionary failure, it could be concluded they merely feed into the nihilistic cynicism rather than overcoming it. However, it is when we approach Acker's reconfiguring of revolution as event that we can comprehend her unceasing commitment to radical politics and perceive her working through failure as an ongoing project of beginning again and unravelling the event's unpredictable becomings. To adapt Žižek's explanation of the Cultural Revolution, it 'continues to lead the underground spectral life of the ghosts

of failed utopias which haunt future generations, patiently awaiting its next resurrection'.[117] He invokes Beckett's famous formula
by way of illustration: 'Try again. Fail again. Fail better.'[118] Thus,
Acker's revolutions survive their failures to begin again and again.
Her consistent return to revolution suggests that its final historical
outcome and the humdrum of repetition do not exhaust the egalitarian promise contained in many past events, including the event
of Spanish anarchism.

Dreampolitik: Spanish anarchism

Don Quixote's subtitle, *Which Was a Dream*, might suggest a triumph of cynicism: all the revolutionary prospects have been discredited. The game is over, and we should all become realists and
concentrate our energies on surviving in this dark and dangerous
world. Simply put, stereotypical Hobbesians have a fixed view of
human nature, which they believe to be basically fearful, distrusting and self-interested, and prone to the chaos of anarchy if left
unsupervised. From Acker's perspective, such a cynical standpoint
is antithetical to creativity, potentiality and dreaming. Modern
cynicism stifles change and visions of alternative worlds, and, at
best, works within the coordinates of what is considered possible, assuming that all is known about relations between humans.
But just as Goya's etchings and paintings can be received in multiple ways, *Don Quixote* depicts both the end of dreaming and
a call for alternative visions. The final section of *Don Quixote*,
entitled 'DON QUIXOTE'S DREAM', coordinates visionary politics (dreaming), thinking, feeling and doing. Don Quixote looks
for specific instances of their productive coincidence: 'How are the
mind and the heart being educated to think and to act? To dream?'
In this, Acker instructs us that dreaming is a prerequisite to action
and change. The task of a Cynic, therefore, is not only to 'deface
the coinage' but to courageously extract political imagination from
the pervading schemata of causality.

   For Acker, it is extremely urgent to replace cynical realpolitik with
what we may call dreampolitik, to go beyond the confining limits of
the present. Now, more than ever, Acker considers it important to
seek inspiring models from the past to feed our political imagination:
'Where and when have people gotten along together and allowed each
other to dream publicly? That is, to do art?' (*DQ*, 202). Don Quixote declares that 'The Spain of the Spanish Republic of 1931' is her

'dream or model' (*DQ*, 204). The knight draws our attention to the selected processes and movements that made up the fabric of society in the Second Spanish Republic – a hopeful moment in history which brought an end to the Spanish monarchy and inaugurated democratic and economically redistributive reforms, before the sweep of the fascist tide has swallowed it up in the bloody Civil War, followed by the thirty-five-year Franco dictatorship.

To tell us about Spain, within its uniquely complex situation of national discord and worldwide economic depression before the Civil War, Acker turns to Gabriel Jackson's 1965 study *The Spanish Republic and the Civil War: 1931–1939*.[119] She is particularly interested in the intellectual and political formations which contributed to the Civil War: Krausism, as well as the regional liberation and anarchism movements, which the narrator offers as transferable though idealistic models for remoulding society.

The Spain of the Second Republic is a polarised country, split between the nationalist Catholic Spain, and a Spain under the spell of the eclectic intellectual current known as Krausism, imported from Germany by Spanish promoters of the idealist philosopher Karl Krause. The Spanish Krausists applied the doctrine of 'harmonious rationalism' to Spain's context. In Jackson's original words:

> If the universe was fundamentally harmonious, or at least evolving in that direction, then the solution to Carlist wars, and to revolutionary agitation by landless labourers, was to seek in the human past the natural forms of *convivencia* [coexistence] and to revise the political-legal system so as to conform to that convivencia.[120]

Rewriting Jackson, Acker elaborates how 'harmonious rationalism' can form the basis for reshaping contemporary society:

> Since reality or the whole is fundamentally harmonious, poverty other forms of human degradation all forms of human brutality and undue suffering are humanly rectifiable. If we are badly hurting each other and we don't know how to stop badly hurting each other, we need to learn other intellectual emotive and behavioral models. Since we have to broaden our education, historical and imaginative, we must adopt temporal and geographical internationalism. (*DQ*, 203)

Unlike Germany's other export – realpolitik – where the hard lessons from history teach us about the inevitability of tensions and war and determine the limits of what is possible, Krausism affirms potentials to evolve towards supreme harmony between individuals and nations. These ideals are to be achieved through re-education which is both 'historical and imaginative': one which combines active reflection on what 'was' with dreaming on what 'could be', and one that thrives on cooperation across space and time to bring welfare for all. In contrast to self-enclosed nationalistic Catholicism, which Acker regards as similar to England's chauvinistic hold on language and culture, Krausism and internationalism promote the idea that humanity is enriched through openness.

The search for educational internationalism brings Acker to Thomas Jefferson. Acker's cites from Jefferson's letter to his mentor, in which he writes that 'the diffusion of knowledge among people' is crucial 'to freedom, and happiness' (*DQ*, 203). Jefferson's reputation continues to be debated by scholars, and many have commented on the discrepancies between his idealistic rhetoric and its execution in the real world. The omission of that complex history is at odds with Don Quixote's muckraking instincts that we have become accustomed to. However, the framing of a dream allows Don Quixote to disregard any ambiguities. Jefferson's notion of freedom and education for all still stands and can be influential across the globe, and Acker even considers it realised, to some extent, in a Krausist secondary school in Spain. She singles out the Institución Libre de Enseñanza as an exceptional educational model where, as Jackson put it, 'Education should form the whole man, and so manual labour and artistic skills were given equal dignity with purely intellectual accomplishment.'[121]

Through such wholesome education we can acquire new patterns of 'feeling, intellect and behaviour' (*DQ*, 203), replacing those which perpetuate inequality and suffering. This process involves the shedding of old habits of thought, such as those ingrained beliefs about the universal hostility of man to man. Neta C. Crawford maintains that realists' unhopeful assumptions about human nature and a pessimistic view of history validate their preferred models of social and international structure:

> Negative views of human nature support those practices and institutions that depend on those views. If we believe that the escalation of conflict into war is inevitable, then its occurrence is understood as natural. A view that humans strive for domination, that domination and hierarchy are natural and inevitable, supports those who benefit from domination and hierarchy.[122]

In contrast to realists' uniformly negative view, the double universe of *Don Quixote*, poignantly captured in the knight–night binary, acknowledges potentials in people to be both bad and good, and elevates enlightenment through wholesome education – a productive union of feeling, intellect and behaviour – indispensable in the pursuit of the common good.

This last section of *Don Quixote* celebrates communities which functioned successfully without external authority by prioritising self-organisation and cooperation. First, challenging conventional hierarchies in education, the Institución Libre de Enseñanza promoted intellectual internationalism and stimulated mutual learning through informal interactions between students and teachers. Second, Acker is full of praise for the activism of the Basques and Catalans, whose anarchist background and unique language and culture united people from various social backgrounds against the chauvinistic hold of Spanish nationalism. Third, Acker offers up an example of anarchy in action: the Spanish anarchists – the greatest anarchist revolutionary movement in history, which flourished in Spain between the 1860s and 1930s before being defeated by Franco.

As we have seen, the typical Hobbesian claim is that leadership and hierarchy are required to keep people's basic instincts in check in order to prevent anarchic chaos. Without a centralised government, realists insist, society would collapse into a state of nature where anarchy goes wild, making the lives of individuals 'nasty, brutish and short'. Popular notions associate anarchy with disorder, disorganisation and bloodthirsty bomb-throwers on the one hand, and, on the other, dismiss anarchy as an impossible utopia conceived by naive dreamers who neglect to take into account the darker side of human nature.[123] By evoking the authentic example of the Spanish anarchists, Acker challenges these cynical assertions about the unfeasibility of anarchism. Impressed with the programme of anarcho-syndicalists, Don Quixote describes its early representatives in the following way:

Many of the early anarchist leaders resembled the mendicant friars of former centuries: abstemious wanderers, proud to possess little and to be under-dogs, though physically not developed accustomed to the most strenuous physical battles and physically demanding situations: all to accomplish something or other. They were motivated by that inner certainty which by its very being denies human leadership and any hierarchy except for that of gentleness and kindness. The anarchists, being nights, were knights. (*DQ*, 204–5)

Acker leaves Jackson's description largely intact, except for two notable additions. She inserts the term 'under-dogs', which creates a link with other dog characters populating *Don Quixote*. But rather than being withdrawn and melancholy, these anarchist wanderers, unrooted to soil and property, are positively motivated by lofty ideals. The rural Spanish under-dogs have much in common with the ancient Cynics and Stoics, as well as with early Christians, who arrived at similar anarchist conclusions. The paragraph closes with her own words, 'The anarchists, being nights, were knights.' In this way, she communicates that the passage between reality and the world of dreams (and ideals and imagination) is fluid. For Acker, the Spanish anarchists embody the crossing of the boundary between reality and a utopian vision of freedom and benevolence. In referring us to this unique period, she stimulates an interchange between an inspiring historical precedent and contemporary dreaming. *Don Quixote* raises the spectre of this inspiring historical force in order to create its potential collisions with our contemporary world.

In a similar vein, Cristina Garrigós considers Don Quixote a perfect mediating character between the seemingly contradictory spaces of reality and the dream: 'If Acker's novel is indeed a dream [. . .], then this opens up the possibility of living a life outside normative reality, a parallel universe of dreams, which exists on its own, but may sometimes collide with the real world.'[124] While grounded in historical reality, Don Quixote's dream of Spain is a cynicism-free zone: there is no mention of the ultimate defeat of the Spanish anarchists in the Civil War; or of their internal problems and failings, such as unchallenged patriarchy;[125] or that the movement could only thrive in the context of national conflict that led up to the Civil War, or of capitalism's ability to snappily absorb anarchists' rhetoric of freedom, internationalism, self-management and decentralisation.

Don Quixote is a Christ-like figure, who, in Garrigós words, stands for 'the promise of renewal',[126] anticipating a new world to come. But the new world is not to be achieved through the means of a religious miracle. Rather, Don Quixote's ultimate calling is, to evoke the Situationist slogan, that we 'be realistic, demand the impossible'. By means of the collision of our identifiable, visible world with the world of dreams, ideals and inspiring hidden history, Acker's dreampolitik rewrites the coordinates of what is currently considered possible. To put it in the words of Žižek, again, 'The only realist option is to do what appears impossible within this system. This is how the impossible becomes possible. [. . .] One must blur the line between what is possible and what is impossible'.[127]

Conclusion

Don Quixote is often presented as a caesura in the linear movement of Acker's writing. It marks what she and her critics identified as her final work of deconstruction, before the more constructive gestures of *Empire of the Senseless* (1988). As Acker was working on this novel she realised that, for her, 'deconstruction was used up as a writing technique', and hoped that 'there had to be something more than taking apart constructions. I was coming out of a funny kind of nihilism.'[128] As Christopher Robinson notes, *Don Quixote*, rather than neatly exemplifying feminist deconstruction, 'puts deconstructive theory simultaneously into action and into question', as Acker becomes increasingly disenchanted with the capacity of deconstructive writing to offset radical change.[129] Recognising the danger of her writing falling into the impotence of modern cynicism, of its becoming pseudo-rebellious, Acker said:

> *Don Quixote* ended something for me . . . pure interest in certain postmodern techniques, such as deconstruction. Which are very reactionary techniques. . . . I mean they're always reactions to things. And I suddenly became interested in what techniques wouldn't be reactionary, that wouldn't be bourgeois.[130]

Her heroine's quest for a better world is simultaneously an act of authorial self-questioning, an ongoing revision of a wide variety of literary methods and strategies. Foucault writes about parrhesia not only as an act of truth-telling in the sense of critique and exposure of injustice, but also as 'being courageous enough to disclose the truth about *oneself*'.[131] When Acker's heroine realises 'The vision is: there's no joy' (*DQ*, 190), she articulates the blank horizons which await those who merely sneer at the world but no longer seek to transform it. This is not to say that Acker disengages from her strategies of critique and exposure, as they remain an invaluable part of the Cynical toolkit of her later works. Moreover, I would argue that reading *Don Quixote* only as a work of deconstruction (of the systems of power, of texts written by men) is limiting because this would be to ignore the already emergent points in which the novel turns towards affirmative visions, such as her Spanish anarchism-based dreampolitik. *Don Quixote* further isolates and clears the ground for an impassioned engagement with the revolutionary past through the Russian historical avant-gardes in its remarkable middle component, 'Russian Constructivism', the subject of the next chapter.

Notes

1. Cited in Badiou, *Pocket Pantheon*, p. 90.
2. Badiou, *Pocket Pantheon*, p. 90.
3. Gibson, *Intermittency*, p. 50.
4. Lyotard, cited in Badiou, *Pocket Pantheon*, p. 92.
5. Gibson, *Intermittency*, pp. 44, 45.
6. Harvey, *Brief History*, p. 181.
7. Chaloupka, *Everybody Knows*, p. 33.
8. Ibid. p. 39.
9. Desmond, *Cynics*, p. 3.
10. Navia, *Diogenes the Cynic*, p. 55.
11. Desmond, *Cynics*, p. 20.
12. Ibid. p. 4.
13. Navia, *Diogenes the Cynic*, p. 209.
14. Marshall, *Demanding*, p. 69.
15. My very light overview of modern cynicism is indebted to this excellent account.
16. Cited in Shea, *The Cynic Enlightenment*, p. 24.
17. Kant, 'Was ist Aufklärung?', p. 29.
18. Ibid. pp. 29, 31.
19. Žižek, *Enjoy Your Symptom*, pp. ix–x.
20. Kant, 'Was ist Aufklärung?', p. 31.
21. Žižek, *Enjoy Your Symptom*, p. x.
22. Shea, *The Cynic Enlightenment*, pp. 146–7.
23. Ibid. p. 146.
24. Sloterdijk, *Critique*, pp. 3, 5; author's emphasis.
25. Ibid. p. xxvi.
26. Badiou, *The Century*, p. 48.
27. Slavoj Žižek, *The Sublime Object*, p. 25.
28. Ibid. pp. 25–6.
29. Ibid. p. 30; author's emphasis.
30. Johnston, *Badiou*, p. 92.
31. Badiou, *The Century*, p. 49.
32. Ibid.
33. Ibid.
34. Sloterdijk, *Critique*, p. 223.
35. Butler, *Gender Trouble*, p. 172.
36. Ibid. pp. 43–4.
37. Ibid. p. 148.
38. Sloterdijk, *Critique*, p. 324, p. xviii.
39. de Cervantes Saavedra, *The History*, p. 49.
40. Ibid. p. 171.
41. Friedman, 'A Conversation with Kathy Acker', p. 13.
42. Zinn, *A People's History*, p. 658.

43. Orwell, *Nineteen Eighty-Four*, p. 6.
44. Pynchon, 'Introduction', p. xi. More recently, Donald Trump's presidency sparked similar comparisons with *Nineteen Eighty-Four*. See, for example, Jean Seaton, Tim Crook and D. J. Taylor, 'Welcome to dystopia – George Orwell experts on Donald Trump', *The Guardian* (25 January 2017). Available at <https://www.theguardian.com/commentisfree/2017/jan/25/george-orwell-donald-trump-kellyanne-conway-1984> (last accessed 10 January 2019).
45. Pynchon, 'Introduction', p. xi.
46. Ibid.
47. Dew, *Learning*, p. 23.
48. See Acker, 'A Few Notes on Two of My Books', in *Bodies of Work*, p. 13. Journalism is one of the major outlets for political cynicism. H. L. Mencken, the influential American journalist, is usually paired with Mark Twain as being responsible for the emergence of American public cynicism. Mencken followed Twain in ridiculing the absurdities of American culture and authority, revelling in the exposure of sham and hypocrisy. As William Chaloupka writes, 'Mencken was the first great national curmudgeon. He modeled the attitude that would flavor journalism's New World.' Chaloupka, *Everybody Knows*, p. 103.
49. Miraldi, *Seymour Hersh*, p. 339.
50. Ibid. p. 344.
51. Hersh, cited in Miraldi, p. 342.
52. Hersh, *The Price*, p. 9.
53. Thomas Powers, cited in Miraldi, p. 340.
54. Hersh, *The Price*, p. 640.
55. Pitchford, *Tactical Readings*, p. 88.
56. Foucault, *Fearless Speech*, p. 20.
57. Acker, cited in Kraus, *After Kathy Acker*, p. 226.
58. Foucault, *Fearless Speech*, p. 169.
59. Luxon, 'Ethics and Subjectivity', p. 379.
60. Tom Lehrer, cited in Winkler, 'Persius and Juvenal in the Media Age', p. 513.
61. See Winkler, 'Persius and Juvenal in the Media Age', p. 514.
62. Bakhtin, *Problems*, pp. 106–9, 112–37.
63. Kharpertian, *A Hand*, p. 41.
64. Ibid. p. 41.
65. Rickels, 'Body Bildung', p. 62.
66. Babich, 'Sloterdijk's Cynicism', p. 23.
67. Shea, *The Cynic Enlightenment*, p. 163.
68. Rickels, 'Body Bildung', p. 103.
69. Deaton, 'Kathy Acker', p. 279.
70. Rickels, 'Body Bildung', 63.
71. For a positive reading of masochism in Acker as 'the heterotopia of the body, a form of masquerade' (p. 300), see Redding, 'Bruises, Roses:

Masochism and the Writing of Kathy Acker'. See also Brande, 'Making yourself a Body Without Organs: The Cartography of Pain in Kathy Acker's *Don Quixote*'. Drawing on Deleuze and Guattari, Brande argues that *Don Quixote* effectuates a 'literally painstaking cultivation of a subjectivity through the use of masochism as a strategy to temporarily shed identity or "individuality" – an individuality that is constructed by and essential to the various operations of power' (p. 193).

72. Acker, 'Against Ordinary Language: The Language of the Body', in *Bodies of Work*, p. 150.

73. Hobbes's work is at the core of political theory, then as now. The more recent scholarship, including Susanne Sreedhar's *Hobbes on Resistance: Defying the Leviathan* (Cambridge: Cambridge University Press, 2010), attempts a recovery of aspects of resistance in Hobbes's writings.

74. See, for example, Peter Bloom, 'Capitalism's Cynical Leviathan: Cynicism, Totalitarianism, and Hobbes in Modern Capitalist Regulation', *International Journal of Žižek Studies* 2.1 (2008), pp. 1–30.

75. In *Quarrels of Authors* (1814), Isaac D'Israeli attacks Hobbes's cynicism thus: 'our cynical Hobbes had no respect for his species [. . .]. Hobbes considered men merely as animals of prey, living in a state of perpetual hostility, and his solitary principle of action was self-preservation at any price' (cited in Mazella, p. 171). For a discussion of the significance of D'Israeli on Hobbes within the genealogy of cynicism, see Mazella, pp. 170–5.

76. Hobbes, *Leviathan*, p. 61.

77. Ibid. p. 87.

78. Ibid. p. 89.

79. Kavka, *Hobbesian Moral and Political Theory*, pp. 266–78.

80. John Bew considers these revolts an equivalent of the more recent 2010 uprisings in the Arab world, dubbed 'Arab Spring', where, similarly, the dream of constitutional rights and freedom quickly fell prey to corruption and repression. Bew, *Realpolitik*, p. 18.

81. Ibid. p. 30.

82. Ibid. p. 260.

83. Suri, *Henry Kissinger*, p. 20.

84. Ibid. p. 17.

85. Frederick Lewis Schuman, cited in Donnelly, p. 10.

86. John Peterson, 'Realpolitik: C'mon, get real', p. 4.

87. Sloterdijk, *Critique*, p. 238.

88. Donnelly, *Realism*, pp. 24–6.

89. Licht, *Goya*, p. 18.

90. Spencer Dew considers Acker's choice not to openly acknowledge Goya in *Don Quixote* a 'misstep'. For Dew, Goya is an essential reference for an engaged reading of the section entitled 'Text 3: Texts of War for Those Who Live in Silence'. See Dew, *Learning*, pp. 83–4.

91. Snell, *Uncertainties, Mysteries, Doubts*, p. 81.
92. Francisco Goya, cited in Carr-Gomm, p. 130.
93. Horkheimer and Adorno, *Dialectic*, p. 92.
94. Ibid. p. 1.
95. Ibid. pp. 28–9.
96. Sloterdijk, *Critique*, p. xxxvii.
97. Shea, *The Cynic Enlightenment*, p. 139.
98. Licht, *Goya*, p. 179.
99. Ibid. pp. 178–9.
100. Junquera, *The Black Paintings of Goya*, p. 135.
101. Klibansky et al., *Saturn and Melancholy*, p. 323.
102. Acker, 'Realism for the Cause of Future Revolution', in *Bodies of Work*, p. 17.
103. Ibid.
104. Acker, 'Models of our Present', p. 64.
105. Paulson, *Representations*, p. 367.
106. Cited in Weber, *Terror*, p. 228.
107. Acker, 'Realism for the Cause of Future Revolution', in *Bodies of Work*, p. 18.
108. Dew, *Learning*, p. 80; author's emphasis.
109. Acker, 'Realism for the Cause of Future Revolution', in *Bodies of Work*, p. 19.
110. Walsh, 'The Quest for Love', p. 151.
111. Lasky, *Utopia*, p. 248.
112. Cited in Lasky, *Utopia*, p. 247.
113. Colquhoun, 'Introduction', p. 5.
114. di Lampedusa, *The Leopard*, p. 41.
115. Ibid. p. 25.
116. See William S. Burroughs, *The Wild Boys* (New York: Grove Press, 1971).
117. Žižek, 'How to Begin from the Beginning', p. 216.
118. Cited in Žižek, 'How to Begin from the Beginning', p. 217.
119. This award-winning study was reviewed by Noam Chomsky in his debut essay 'Objectivity and Liberal Scholarship' (1969). Chomsky argues that Jackson applied his own counter-revolutionary capitalist-democratic agenda in his framing of the events in Spain when he neglected to acknowledge that a genuine anarchist Spanish Revolution took place, not merely a Civil War. Rather than simply preserving the Republic against the fascist forces, Chomsky claims, the workers wanted to restructure society, spontaneously launching a predominantly anarchist revolution. Acker only borrows from Jackson's opening chapter, where anarchism is discussed as one of the movements leading up to the Civil War.
120. Gabriel Jackson, *The Spanish Republic*, p. 12.

121. Ibid. p. 13. For a discussion of the influence of Krausism on Spanish cultural revival, see Christian Rubio, *Krausism and the Spanish Avant-garde: The Impact of Philosophy on National Culture* (Amherst, NY: Cambria Press, 2017).
122. Crawford, 'Human Nature and World Politics: Rethinking "Man"', p. 284.
123. Marshall, *Demanding*, p. ix.
124. Garrigós, 'Kathy Acker's Spanish Connection', p. 126.
125. Wilson, *Rules without Rulers*, p. 32.
126. Garrigós, 'Kathy Acker's Spanish Connection', p. 126.
127. Žižek, *Demanding*, p. 144.
128. Rickels, 'Body Bildung', p. 62.
129. Robinson, 'In the Silence of the Knight: Kathy Acker's *Don Quixote* as a Work of Disenchantment', p. 119.
130. Deaton, 'Kathy Acker', p. 279.
131. Foucault, *Fearless Speech*, p. 143; author's emphasis.

Chapter 3

Politics, Passion and Abstraction in 'Russian Constructivism'

'Russian Constructivism' first appeared in the middle of *Don Quixote*, published in 1986. It was then reprinted with slight alterations in Brian Wallis's edited volume *Blasted Allegories: An Anthology of Writings by Contemporary Artists* in 1989, alongside writings on the visual arts by Sherrie Levine, Barbara Kruger and Richard Prince, among others. Subsequently, it formed part of Acker's collection of essays on the city in *Bodies of Work* (1997). That Acker continued to circulate 'Russian Constructivism' in different places, shifting its status from a fictional piece to an art-text and to an essay, is only one reason to consider it an important segment in her literary oeuvre. Yet while *Don Quixote* has received considerable critical discussion, strikingly little of that discussion focuses on what is arguably its most remarkable component. Unsurprisingly, given its explicit borrowings from the visual art of Sherrie Levine, critics have tended to relate 'Russian Constructivism' to the procedure of appropriation, whereby its meaning becomes inseparable from postmodernist concepts and canonical texts.[1] The copying and manipulating of texts by others has come to be seen as an evacuation of a fixed meaning, a critique of the traditional notions of originality and authorship and, when Acker and Levine borrow material made by men, a feminist subversion of the male-centred canon.

Acker commented that she wanted to do with words what Levine did with her artistic and photographic copies. Considered the culmination of Acker's appropriation technique, *Don Quixote*'s middle section, comprising 'Russian Constructivism' and three other texts, was written, Acker notes, 'out of a Sherrie Levine-type impulse'.[2] Levine made obvious reprises in variable sizes, numbers, mediums and colours of works by Courbet, Mondrian, Malevich, Schiele, Duchamp and others, sometimes with minimal discernible difference from the originals. Her methods became so fused with the aloof postmodern rhetoric that when she displayed her series of rephotographs *After Walker Evans* in 1981, as one critic recalls, 'few people even bothered to look inside the frames to consider what she was rephotographing. [. . .] [I]t did seem embarrassing to be caught looking at them too closely. As initiates had concluded, the meaning of Levine's curiously covert art had to lie elsewhere, beyond the frames of these pictures.'[3] For the same reason, the particularities of 'Russian Constructivism' – its intertextuality, engagement with revolutionary history and affiliation with the visual arts – have been largely overlooked. Acker scholarship of the 1980s and 1990s, tending to concentrate on a feminine and postmodern aesthetic, identified an inherently subversive streak behind her appropriations of male texts. Martina Sciolino proposed that '[b]y breaking the laws that govern textual legitimacy through plagiarism, Acker dissociates herself from patriarchal literary tradition,'[4] and Naomi Jacobs argued that plagiarism in the middle section of *Don Quixote* allows Acker to 'dismantle' the 'tyrannical structures of official culture'.[5] The *Blasted Allegories* anthology, where 'Russian Constructivism' appeared, applied the postmodern concept of allegory to the works included in the volume, characterised by a sense of '[f]ragmentation, transience, appropriation, deferral of meaning, impermanence'.[6] However, this approach prevents us from interpreting the writing to form contextually grounded meaning, and thus does not give full justice to Acker's political programme anchored in the concrete context of historical events.

Levine's statement, 'I appropriate these images to express my simultaneous longing for the passion of engagement and the sublimity of aloofness,' proclaims attachment and detachment as equally important to understanding her relationship with utopian modernism.[7] Levine and Acker often said that they felt affinity with the works they reproduced. As Ellen Friedman signalled, 'Acker's plagiarism, while intent on subverting the notion of the master text, is often allied with the political messages of particular texts.'[8] When considering Acker's textual collages it is important, I think, to follow Barbara Burton's refusal to explain Levine's reproductions as merely 'conquering images', and her counter-suggestion that they should be viewed as 'screens capable of reinvestment in different situations'.[9] In what follows, I rethink 'Russian Constructivism' outside of the context of postmodern discourse of appropriation: in looking closely into Acker's aesthetic methods and borrowed sources and in asking why they were chosen and how they were transformed by Acker, I explore her utopian vision of creating possibilities.

The path of abstraction

Russian Constructivism is divided into five parts: '1. Abstraction', '2. The Poems Of A City', '3. Scenes of Hope And Despair', '4. The Mystery', and '5. Deep Female Sexuality: Marriage or Time'. There is no logical progression between them, and each part is a collage of heterogeneous styles, quotations and allusions. 'Abstraction' fuses bleak landscapes of contemporary New York with descriptions of St Petersburg derived from the masterpiece of Russian modernism, Andrei Bely's *Petersburg* (first published in 1913–14, and again in 1922 after radical revision). Subsequent sections contain a mini-dialogue from Shakespeare's *Romeo and Juliet*; allusions to revolutionary Russia and Spain; and Acker's creative translation and grammatical analysis of one of Catullus's poems. Interwoven with these are first-person confessions of an abandoned female lover, in which are contained other textual allusions.

Acker is extremely responsive to the painterly qualities of Bely's *Petersburg*. Scholars described his writing as visual in the avant-garde sense, examining its affinities with cubism, expressionism, futurism, suprematism and abstract art more generally.[10] They suggested that the motor of the plot – the exploding bomb – generates spatial and temporal fragments, symbolically representing Bely's blowing up of traditional narrative forms. Preserving *Petersburg*'s cubist and abstract attitudes, in the *Don Quixote* version of 'Russian Constructivism' (unlike in its reprint in *Bodies of Work*) Acker inserts extra spaces to set apart textual blocks with an already enfeebled causality between them, thereby increasing the fragmentation of the textual space. The plurality of materials used, including fragments of poetry and drama, a grammatical analysis, descriptions of St Petersburg's topography, elements of melodrama and pornography, creative formatting as well as the incorporation of a scrap of newspaper, aligns her writing with the collage phase of cubism as typified by Pablo Picasso and Georges Braque's *papier collé*, and its subsequent reworking by the avant-gardes. Cubism combined concrete and abstract forms, and for many artists their own passage into abstraction usually entailed a passage through cubism.

In cubism, becomings, processes and interactions between elements triumph over a terminal image we find in traditional portraiture, as Acker writes in her earlier novel *Great Expectations* (1983):

> Cézanne allowed the question of there being simultaneous viewpoints, and thereby destroyed forever in art the possibility of a static representation of portrait. The Cubists went further. They found the means of making the forms of all objects similar. If everything was rendered in the same terms, it became possible to paint the interactions between them. These interactions became so much more interesting than that which was being portrayed that the concepts of portraiture and therefore of reality were undermined or transferred.[11]

Acker's adherence to the aesthetic transformations of cubism ties in with Badiou's postulation that scientific, artistic, political and amorous truths that emerge after an evental breakthrough require our fidelity towards them. The event for Badiou is rare and deeply historical, and is first of all an extraordinary break with a prior order, such as the popular uprising in politics, the advent of cubism in art, the Copernican event in science, or falling in love. It is an 'intervention' that 'consists in identifying that there has been some undecidability, and in deciding it belongs in the situation' (*BE*, 202). The subject such as the artist must be prepared to agitate on behalf of the new truth that thus far has not been allowed within representation. Such militant fidelity, Badiou maintains, 'designates equally the feverish exploration of the effects of a new theorem, the cubist precipitation of the Braque–Picasso tandem (the effect of a retroactive intervention upon the Cézanne-event), the activity of Saint Paul, and that of the militants of an *Organization Politique*' (*BE*, 329).

Badiou's notion of the event resuscitates the radical potential that historical and cultural material holds for Acker, otherwise neutralised in the relativism, abstraction and imprecision that characterises postmodern approaches to her politics. There are parallels between the eruption of the feminine in the writing of female experimentalists and Badiou's account of an event which he envisions as a break with the prevailing order and the eruption of possibility. Friedman and Marianne Fuchs's *Breaking the Sequence: Women's Experimental Fiction* (1989), which did much to recover the tradition of experimental female writing, takes its title from Virginia Woolf's imperative for women to 'break the sequence' of patriarchal language and allow that which has been denied in the patriarchal construction of women to surface. Experimental women's writing and the event both disrupt dominant knowledge, and this disruption, through the militant labour of faithful subjects, makes possible the production of new knowledge. Thus, after the advent of cubism, it is not possible (or for Acker desirable) to return to the traditional modes of representation. Like the followers of Paul Cézanne who rejected imitation and academicism in art, Acker abandons the 'awful' rules of the nineteenth-century bourgeois novel, as they 'cut down possibilities',[12] embracing instead a plurality of materials, perspectives and unexpected interpretative outcomes. Acker's cubist writing reverses the reductive processes in traditional writing where 'The writer took a certain amount of language, verbal material, forced that language to stop radiating in multiple, even unnumerable directions, to radiate in only one direction so there could be his meaning.'[13]

Cézanne was also the original muse of Gertrude Stein's experimental writing, which influenced Acker. Notice how Stein subverts a hierarchical tree-like sentence structure, centred around a noun phrase and a verb phrase, in this excerpt from her prose poems collection, *Tender Buttons* (1914):

A CARAFE, THAT IS A BLIND GLASS
    A kind in glass and a cousin, a spectacle and nothing strange a single hurt color and an arrangement in a system to pointing. All this and not ordinary, not unordered in not resembling. The difference is spreading.[14]

Stein's democratisation of sentence elements is similar to Gilles Deleuze and Félix Guattari's non-hierarchical logic of rhizomatic connections created through the conjunction 'and . . . and . . . and . . .' (*TP*, 27, ellipsis in original), or through a simple listing, where phrases that suggest causality are discarded. For Stein, the concrete and the abstract exist on one plane, and a noun possesses no more importance – that is, meaning – than a preposition or a punctuation mark traditionally consigned to merely channel the meaning contained in a noun or a verb. As Kazimir Malevich writes, in cubist paintings there is no distinction between the background and foreground: 'a Cubist picture is equally valuable over its entire surface. [. . .] [O]ur attention is being moved away from the central point.'[15]

What cubism does to conventional optical perception is what Acker's experimental writing does to fixed meanings in language which communicate ideological constructs and historical closures that suppress alternatives, as Acker has one of her characters exclaim: 'What you call *history* and *culture* is the denial of our flowing blood' (*DQ*, 198, emphasis in original). Accordingly, Malevich writes that Cézanne's emerging cubist impulse 'draws us nearer to the plane, to the perception of the painterly body's structure' and in it 'we notice that which does not come within the optical field of an academic attitude or the optical interpretation of an artist's perception of space'.[16] Human vision has evolved so that we do not perceive the world in terms of intensities and interactions of line and colour. Rather, it organises lines and colours into terminate units. By contrast, abstract art and writing de-habitualise optical perception by challenging the synthesised totalities of image and thought. For Acker, conservative art merely reacts to societal expectations and gives in to the demands of the market and authority while suppressing other ways of making sense of the world, other narratives and histories. She writes: 'Art, since its very beginning in prehistoric caves, has been, in our present ways of speaking, conservative. [. . .] Roman art made dumb Roman politicians into gods. Christian art justified or rationalized the controller belief system' (*DQ*, 57). The phenomenon of cubism is thus one way of painting or writing in rupture with a given reality. Cubism's preoccupation with the materiality of the painting – the painting's 'as suchness', in Malevich's words[17] – enables Stein to intimate the tender texture of objects in *Tender Buttons* while displacing conceptual and linguistic certainties, and it enables Acker to extract political events from totalisations and preordained sequences in order to re-connect with their potentiality. Acker's aesthetic method is congruent with her political vision, whose utopianism involves creating possibilities radiating from events rather than imposing teleological schemas and blueprints for a perfect society. As she told *Bookworm*'s Michael Silverblatt in 1992, she aligns herself with those artists and writers who are 'looking for that deep, deep change that works through vision'.[18] Such a vision, rather than merely describing what is or prescribing what should be, shares with the audience the conviction that things could be otherwise.

Cubist painting and writing are not entirely analogous. Marianne DeKoven challenged the unproblematic alignment of Stein with a modern painting because 'unlike words, painted shapes are not necessarily signs', and words 'may or may not be used in an intentionally referential way – to say something coherent about a particular subject – but they always retain the lexical meanings they carry in the language'.[19] I want to suggest that Acker applies the tension inherent to abstract writing between pure abstraction and referential meaning to a specific political end. Let us look at the mini-prologue of 'Russian Constructivism':

> Petersburg, my city.
> Petersburg steeples triangles bums on the streets decrepit churches broken-down churches churches gone churches used as homes for bums for children forced away from the abandoned buildings they run.
> Son.
> 1.   (*DQ*, 41)

Acker's movement of words here is reminiscent of Bely's nervous repetitive style, his invention of rhythms and punctuations; and its spontaneity, with an end-rhyming sequence run-son-[one], is akin to the musical brushstrokes of Wassily Kandinsky or the emotional suggestiveness of Jackson Pollock's action painting. Although we can stop here and appreciate the passage on this abstract level, we cannot deny that it is charged with meaning, communicating an overwhelming sense of despair. And if we focus on the triple rhyme run-son-[one] and relate it to Bely's *Petersburg* and its revolutionary context, we can speculate that Acker alludes to the father–son conflict that forms a symbolic centre of Bely's work. The opening apostrophe, 'Petersburg, my city', can be read as a personification of the city as 'the father' and the son's impulse to run, to disobey. Bely's translators have commented that the city's name is tied with its founder-father Peter the Great, and 'as the "father of Russia" he [Peter] is the ultimate symbol of the paternal authority against which the "sons" rebel in various ways'.[20] This refers us the psychodrama of the Oedipal revolt against the father as well as the myth of Saturn, both underpinning Bely's story. Thus, on the one hand, abstraction in language allows Acker to create linguistic events that run shock-tremors though established meanings. This enables language to metamorphose and create unexpected configurations. On the other hand, abstraction in writing cannot erase referential meaning, but the meaning that Acker retains matters. The words and historical realities that circulate in the text, such as the Russian revolutions of 1905 and 1917, and the period of melancholy between them, Constructivism, Tatlin, passion and love, rather than becoming flattened, are firmly anchored in history, artistic legacy and raw feeling. As for Badiou, they will retain for Acker their historical specificity or affective strength and radiate with possibilities.

Popular definitions of 'abstraction' connote idealisation, distancing and withdrawal from material reality. The first entries in the *Oxford English Dictionary* favour the understanding of abstraction as withdrawal, separation or removal. The adjective 'abstract' means separated from matter, ideal, theoretical, and as a verb, to 'remove' and 'disengage'.[21] These definitions would have suited many modern artists who pursued ideal states but would have been complicated by Russian Constructivists, who privileged the materiality of objects and the worldliness of utilitarian design. To some, abstraction involved a considered pursuit of pure non-objectivity and of truthfulness to sensation rather than an imitation of an idea (the aim was to liberate art from the object and from the Renaissance humanist perspective, as in Malevich's suprematist compositions). To others, abstraction was an effect of the spontaneous expression of personal feeling discernible in abstract expressionism. Acker's attraction to the notion of abstraction lies in the characteristic definition of it in art history 'as a category that manages such contradictions', and as that to which 'tensions are integral'.[22]

When in 'Russian Constructivism' she writes 'Art criticism, unlike art,'s abstract' (*DQ*, 47), abstraction's polysemy is at play. In this instance, a critical analysis of a work of art is like abstraction that separates itself from matter, which is in contrast with art's immediacy. Yet for Acker abstract thinking that takes place in engaged theory and good art criticism need not annul art's immediacy, but can provide an important metalanguage through which to talk about art or even inspire artistic practice. Towards the end of 'Russian Constructivism', an unidentified filmmaker, in response to the question 'Does writing criticism stop you from making films?' says that 'They're just two different kinds of activities' (*DQ*, 54), adding that 'A critical way of talking about my work allowed me to go one step further in my work' (*DQ*, 55). Acker often commented on her affinity with politically engaged theoretical texts. Having been introduced to such theorists as Foucault, Deleuze and Guattari, Acker recalls that she 'suddenly had a theory for what

I was doing. Even more importantly, it was a theory that made sense to me because it wasn't just abstract theoretical garbage. It was grounded very much in the political and social world I saw around me'.[23] In 'Russian Constructivism' she denounces Jean Baudrillard's theory as reactionary and cynical because it abstracts any meaning from language and value (*DQ*, 55). In a different context, abstraction simply means that Bely's text, or Constructivist art, have been 'abstracted', or removed, from their original contexts, and made to work in a contemporary setting. Finally, as we can see in the contrasting questions Acker poses – 'What're the materials of this city?' (*DQ*, 46) and 'Is our city abstract?' (*DQ*, 47) – what Acker takes from Bely and his literary forebears is the corroboration of the myth of St Petersburg as abstract and premeditated, and yet sensual and unruly.

Acker and Bely meet in St Petersburg, 'the most abstract city in the whole world'

In 'Russian Constructivism' Acker creates visual and cultural parallels between present-day New York and early twentieth-century St Petersburg – a city famously described by Fyodor Dostoevsky as 'the most abstract and premeditated city in the whole world'.[24] If we place Acker's opening invocation side by side with Bely's 'Prologue', we will notice that whereas Bely uses deliberately grandiose language to achieve a mocking tone in the opening address –'Your Excellences, Your Worships, Your Honours, and Citizens'[25] – Acker's narrator, through a sombre tonality and shifting focus, hastens to expose the city's underlying ugliness. Yet we are struck by the underlying sense of stagnation, dread and despair in both. The imperial capital St Petersburg, and, implicitly, New York in the 1980s, is a city 'of no possible belief' (*DQ*, 42), with broken churches, lost passion and shattered political dreams. The loss of secular hopes within the political and social spheres the narrator sees as overlapping with the retreat of religious faith, which results in a purposelessness life: 'This new holy city is a reality not only without religion but also without anything to want or seek for: without anything' (*DQ*, 41). What is the effect of bringing two cities devoid of passion and belief into textual proximity? Is Acker merely cultivating the nihilistic ground she finds in both? And if not – as I am arguing throughout – how is the possibility of change imagined here?

In overlapping St Petersburg with New York Acker is performing a cubist collage. But rather than having a flattening effect, this unlikely pairing intimates manifold interactions. As Ebbesen has observed, Acker's ideological project exceeds the scope of postmodern art, which often lacks the depth and political conviction of modernism. Preserving the depth of historical reference, Acker, writes Ebbesen, 'wants to see history as alive, in process, and in the present'.[26] In 'Russian Constructivism', this is achieved through topological foldings of space and time which make manifest neighbourings which are invisible in traditional historical and geographical representations. What change can emerge from conflating two distinct but ultimately similarly lifeless worlds? Of key importance is the fact that Bely's city is *pre-revolutionary* (or more precisely inter-revolutionary: post-1905 and pre-1917). A revolution did happen in St Petersburg, as Acker told Melvyn Bragg in Alan Benson's 1984 documentary, commenting on 'Russian Constructivism', then a work in progress:

> I mean the whole nihilistic movement [in St Petersburg] . . . the idea I saw before the riots and despair. . . . I can see here [in New York] no possibility of revolution, no possibility of going against what's happening. . . . I also see the fact that the revolution happened in St Petersburg. . . . So in a way to put the two together is as if it could have happened. . . . Fiction should be useful and possible . . . and the impossible wonderful thing is that if I do make New York into Petersburg something would happen here.[27]

For Acker St Petersburg is a city of contradictions and opposing qualities: it is abstract and saturated in melancholy, and yet it is capable of sudden bursts of revolutionary passion that she wants to see happen in revolution-fearing America. By installing Tatlin's Tower – the symbol of Russian Revolution of 1917 – in mid-1980s New York, Acker wants to make it seem possible to our imagination that the world could be different.

Via Bely, Acker alerts us to a period in Russian history marked by a profound melancholy – the repressive decade-long aftermath of a failed revolution of 1905, which we saw in full fervour in *Nymphomaniac*. Bely's novel is set in St Petersburg during the revolution of October 1905, with the disastrous Russo-Japanese War, industrial strikes and anarchism in the background. Bely initially attached great significance to the upheaval, but his enthusiasm diminished after the Tsarist repression of 1906, with the government issuing political edicts in mid-1907 which brought the troublesome parliament to a close, officially shattering the promise of revolutionary change. He wrote *Petersburg* at that time, between the 1905 revolution and the outbreak of the First World War – a period remembered as an unprecedented climate of 'bad weather' and darkness, a peculiar 'epoch of moods' in which everything collapsed into melancholy. As Mark Steinberg writes, during this time Russian society felt 'no solid ground to stand on, no clear perspectives, no defined hopes and dreams', unable to 'find any "ideal" in life, to believe in the future'.[28]

St Petersburg cultivated melancholy more zealously than any other Russian city, which is captured by the literature about it, such as Bely's. The first Russian Revolution of 1905 was more a stimulus to express depressive moods in new narrative forms, rather than being the originator of them. As Steinberg notes, melancholy saturated the writings of Dostoevsky and his predecessor Nikolai Gogol.[29] 'The Petersburg text', as it came to be known, circulated the myth of the city which originated with Alexander Pushkin's poem 'The Bronze Horseman' (1833), about the city's creator, Peter the Great. The myth gave St Petersburg an identity based on the tension between the Western rationality of planned imperial order and dark Eastern sensibility. The Petersburg literature after Pushkin often problematised the city's dual nature. Acker's narrator also has an intimate knowledge of St Petersburg's unique qualities: 'Petersburg isn't Russian: it's a country on its own. Since it has no legal or financial national status; it's an impossibility, an impossible home; it's tenuous, paranoid. Its definitions and language're quantum theory, Zen, and the nihilism found before the Russian Revolution' (*DQ*, 42). Acker's cubist method makes it impossible to narrativise St Petersburg as following a linear abstract-passionate trajectory from first impulse to another. Rather, the two are always in tension, with deep emotion and yearnings for transformation dramatically undercutting abstract rationalisation and banality of repetition. The wilder coloration of St Petersburg manifests itself even when static forms appear most triumphant. In what Acker called 'pictures of hope and despair', a Dickensian phrase, she sustains the traces of possibility of the event of revolution and the event of love.

The city arose from Tsar Peter the Great's vision to create a modern city according to the Western Enlightenment's ideals of orderly, spacious and geometric urban planning, as opposed to Moscow's Eastern bend of its curved roads and narrow alleyways. Peter forced peasants to travel from across Russia to build it, and, in order to recreate the class system, he forced the social elite to relocate to St Petersburg. He became 'the great' because of executing many modernising reforms that increased Russia's imperial power, but many saw them as a forced experiment that further strengthened the traditional regime. The industrial expansion that followed in the nineteenth and twentieth centuries drew in incomers, most of them peasants, who lived in great poverty. Acker's New York is the St Petersburg of writers such as Dostoevsky and Bely in the way she draws attention to the oppression and poverty of the lower classes and areas unlikely to be frequented by wealthy citizens or tourists, as in her gruesome picture of poor areas with destitute immigrants:

> You, city, along one of whose streets a hundred bums're sitting standing and lying. Three quarters of these bums're black or Puerto Rican. The concrete stinks of piss much more than the surrounding streets smell. A few of the creeps smoke cigarettes. One half of the buildings lining the street're a red brick wall. Mostly the bums don't move or they move as little as they have to. (*DQ*, 41)

History, political creativity, decisions and feeling are all excluded from the scene. The city is saturated in hopelessness, lovelessness, despair, inertia. These are the characteristics of what Badiou has labelled *mondes atones* (atonal worlds), which are worlds defined by the absence of events (*LW*, 442–5). Certainly, there are facts that happen, but these are merely weak singularities of a passionless existence. Those lifeless atonal worlds Badiou contrasts with 'tense worlds' (Badiou's term) occasioned by an event. Unlike terrorist tensions in Bely's underground St Petersburg, New York appears completely atonal, and unalterable. For at least in Bely at the beginning a revolutionary organisation is plotting to assassinate the senator (which, as we find out, is futile). By contrast, New York's margins appear unthreatening, incapable of movement. A few lines later, as in a cubist painting which sustains a plurality of viewpoints, the narrator drops the perspective of the pedestrian to adopt a view from above by referencing official maps which impose an abstract order on unruly space: 'How is this City of Cities divided? As taught in school, Petersburg has five parts: its main part is the Nevsky Prospect' (*DQ*, 41). This formulaic, anonymous language, in being particularly resistant to modification, participates in the overwhelming stasis. But such intellectually dead descriptions Acker intersperses with a bleak socio-critique of the city 'whose first characteristic is it gives nothing' (*DQ*, 41). Even at such early moments Acker attempts to save the world from atony through brutal shifts of language and scene. For amidst the abstract descriptions of the city and pervading melancholy a sudden plea interrupts, reminding us of the martyred Don Quixote on her quest: 'Is there such a thing here as true love: that violence that's absolutely right?' (*DQ*, 42).

St Petersburg or New York's acute abstractions reflect the stratification of space in a Deleuzian sense: the city arises from the human transformation of the boggy islands; the territory is then further striated by empire-architecture, administrative divisions and summoned authorities, and controlled by state power. Deleuze and Guattari distinguish between striated and smooth space, defined respectively as 'nomad space and sedentary space – the space in which the war machine develops and the space instituted by the State apparatus' (*TP*, 474). In addition, they note that rather than excluding one another, the two spaces are in constant interchange. 'Smooth space', they specify, 'is filled by events of haecceities, far more than by formed and perceived things. It is a space of affects, more than one of properties' (*TP*, 478–9). While smooth space undergoes topological transformations which welcome constant variation and heterogeneity, striated space, like a Euclidean grid with fixed coordinates, is stable, measured and homogeneous. As Acker recreates it, St Petersburg exemplifies a quintessentially striated geometric space where, in Deleuze and Guattari's terms, 'the vertical apparatus of the empire and the isotropic apparatus of the city-state' operate (*TP*, 489). Rigorously planned, rectilinearly ordered on the level of space and social hierarchy, with the straight lines of its streets, the flatness of its squares and the gravitational columns of its edifices, it is indeed the most abstract city in the world:

> Lamplights hang over the edges of the park running through the vertical center of the Nevsky Prospect, from its beginning at St Isaac's, about fifty blocks north, to its black section in the depth of the seventeenth line. The geographical divisions are actually racial: ghettoes, each one on the whole about nine to sixteen blocks large, don't mingle. This past year the ghettoes're beginning to physically cross cause the rich're now trying and will take over this whole city by buying all of its real estate. (*DQ*, 42)

In Deleuze and Guattari, the spaces of the ghetto, slum and shanty town, or of the urban poor in general, tend to display a strong affinity with smooth space. These are patches of uncontrollable mobility which break down the organisation of the administrative mainland. This is true of Bely's novel, as it is from the periphery of the surrounding islands that revolutionary chaos streams in through the connecting bridges. But in Acker's account, the periphery no longer thrives with vitality or brews revolutionary events. In St Petersburg, Don Quixote finds not a hotbed of revolutionary passion but a deathly stillness where geometrical abstraction alienates any immediate sensory experience. In this abstract city that denies social and sexual connection Don Quixote sees 'Squares quadrilaterals concatenations of imaginations who lack other necessary sensualities', concluding that 'The flesh which touches flesh has to resemble Martian green gook' (*DQ*, 42). The sensation Don Quixote craves is associated with what Deleuze and Guattari refer to as 'haptic space', which contests the sense of sight privileged in the rationalising 'optic' space. By engaging other senses, it enables a more immediate and intimate material experience. In haptic perception one refuses to consider the rational mind apart from the situation of the flesh.

In the next tableau, the perspective shifts once again into a closer view, and we become witnesses of a non-event: a female weight-lifter falls out of her loft-bed. Her passionless urban existence is embodied in an ironic description which suggests detachment: 'It was a beautiful day, late in September. Larks were singing and drops of sunlight were filtering through the navy blue Levelors (through the clouds through the pollution through the surrounding building's walls)' (*DQ*, 42). Evoking cubist experiments with *papier collé*, Acker places a scrap of a newspaper underneath her fallen body:

CITY OF PASSION

a non-achiever	George was totally wrap
non-leader, non-	up in the fantasy world
and non-romantic,'	comic books.
former classmate	'He was also cons
lentine.	with TV – especiall
he was 18, George	ture shows,' said
stined to end up a	By high scho
then a horrifying	had withdrawn (*DQ*, 43)

Contrary to the promise of the headline 'CITY OF PASSION', the news report appears to relate a sudden death of a withdrawn teenager, possibly a drug addict.

The etymology of the name 'Petersburg' reflects further the city's rigid fixity, its 'cool cold' architecture (*DQ*, 46). 'Peter', from the Greek *Pétros*, means 'a stone' or 'a rock', and the proto-Germanic root *burg* denotes 'a castle', 'a hill fort' or 'a citadel'. One narrative thread of 'Russian Constructivism' is a tragic love affair told in love letters by a female narrator deeply in love with a married man named Peter, who does not welcome her passionate intensity, is emotionally aloof, and wants to remain married to protect his social status. This unresponsive, unfeeling stone-cold lover, who is 'sexually scared for instance he never comes with me cause he's trying not to be in love with me' (*DQ*, 56) and is 'only interested in abstract thought' (*DQ*, 59), mirrors the static structure of the city immune to revolution. The passion has been suppressed in both: 'cause you've buried your wildnesses more anger volcanoes out of you than I've ever felt from another human being [. . .]. Why do you give a damn about social rules? Why not become an artist?' (*DQ*, 45).

Acker repeats and circles around the beloved's magical name Peter in different contexts and across her works provoking us to relate amorous, political and artistic spheres. Rather than opposing cubism, love and revolution, Acker seeks to think them together, and to create possibilities occasioned by interactions and analogies between them. The narrator in *Nymphomaniac*, who has an affair with a male transvestite called Peter, turns to drinking in an attempt to stave off atony:

> I found that the awareness I had when drunk I could no longer have when sober. I needed these awarenesses. I needed to know the passions still existed. All wasn't an unchanging dullness, a horror, as it was when I was sober. An unchanging dullness in which everything I could possibly do was stupid worthless. I finally knew, when drunk, that jealousy, fear, adoration, lust, murder were still possible. A possibility for revolution. I craved alcohol more and more. (*N*, 132–3)

As we saw in Chapter 1, Acker turns Peter and other fellow experimental artists into revolutionaries. The explosion of an anarchic rebellion requires an amorous event commensurate with it: 'It's the beginning of the revolution. I think I'm in love with Peter a tall light-haired revolutionary who wants to get rid of leaders and money' (*N*, 164); 'We fight together and whenever we have a chance, we fuck' (*N*, 168). Peter in 'Russian Constructivism' is simultaneously a city, a lover and a symbol, and an autobiographical reference.[30] Peter is an implied addressee of her translated love poem by the Roman poet Catullus. Acker's grammatical analysis suggests that Latin sentence structures allow for bifurcating possibilities. The subjunctive mood of the line 'desinas ineptire' (*DQ*, 47) – usually translated as 'you are to cease/cease to be a fool' – leaves us uncertain whether the subject denounces or reaffirms the love-event in the disenchanted world. Finally, we have in the Peter letters loosely rewritten passages from *Romeo and Juliet* which confirm the collapse of time and space, and the mixing of the amorous with the political. Rather than being expressions of pure negativity, these textual fragments sustain the idea of an event by referring us back to a tense world of revolution and love: 'I don't talk cause I can't talk about you. I guess I am obsessed possessed. Spain needed a revolution, a far more profound revolution in fact than that being attempted by the Republic'; 'Day like total revolution's waiting to infiltrate'; 'The light's that's coming within you for me's as violent as mine for you' (*DQ*, 44).

Russian Constructivism: 'city of passion'

Up to this point, we have confined our attention mostly to a world in which atony prevails while only showing glimmers of hope 'filtering through the clouds through the pollution through the surrounding building's walls' (*DQ*, 42). But these subtle clues anticipate a contrasting, extraordinarily tense world signalled in the title 'Russian Constructivism'. Towards the middle of the text, we leave behind the melancholy city and enter Russia in the midst of its post-revolutionary fervor, with the utopianism and passion for experimentation of the Russian Constructivists, who used abstraction to engage with everyday life and to transform society. Acker invokes the movement's founder, Vladimir Tatlin, thus:

> Tatlin designed a city. Tatlin took unhandlable passion and molded it.
> It all comes out of passion. Our city of passion.
> ....
> A city in which we can live.
> What're the materials of this city? (*DQ*, 46)

We can find such glimpses of the 'ruling passion' of Constructivists at work in Walter Benjamin's 1927 recollections of his visit to post-revolutionary Russia:

Each thought, each day, each life lies here as on a laboratory table. [. . .] This astonishing experimentation – it is here called *remonte* – affects not only Moscow; it is Russian. In this ruling passion, there is as much naive desire for improvement as there is boundless curiosity and playfulness.[31]

Far from being an isolated space of experimentation, in Benjamin's portrait the Constructivist laboratory pervaded every aspect of reality. Its members, including Tatlin, Alexander Rodchenko, Lyubov Popova and Varvara Stephanova, renounced the work of pure art in favour of a collective and utilitarian project, adopting as their mottoes the slogans 'Art into life' and 'The streets are our brushes, the squares our palettes.'[32] Constructivism was a direct artistic response to the Russian revolution of 1917. There has been a tendency to conflate it with art produced prior to the revolution, however, as Christina Lodder emphasises, the pre-1917 works were 'completely free of any utilitarian content or social commitment on the part of the artists who produced them'.[33] What they share is that 'the non-utilitarian constructions of the pre-revolutionary period provided the formal vocabulary for Constructivism'.[34]

Constructivists' aim not to convey rationalising optical perception but a sense of physicality and connection clearly mark a position Acker can relate to: 'Is sensuality less valuable than rational thought? Is there a split between mind and body, or rather between these two types of mentality?' (*DQ*, 46). Already in the pre-revolutionary years, Tatlin sought to eliminate a number of hierarchies and abstract divisions in his art, and this was most fully realised in his Constructivist period. He turned to the 'haptic' qualities of materials: their texture, flexibility and tangibility. When his spatial structures, labelled 'reliefs', were first exhibited in 1913, visitors were allowed to touch them; Tatlin stated: 'Let us place the eye under the control of touch.'[35] He wanted to transform the formal interests of French cubism into a functional aesthetic by using found 'real' materials dissociated from the tradition of art, such as cardboard, plaster, iron, wood and glass. He did away with the frame because it 'abstracted' art from life. Following the Revolution, Tatlin applied the more formal experiments of his reliefs to architectural design, which culminated in his 1919 project of the Monument to the Third International, known as Tatlin's Tower, commissioned to house the operations of the Comintern in St Petersburg. Although the building was never built, it became the symbolic touchstone of the Russian avant-garde's mission to transform social reality. As Spencer Bronner notes, the monument was never completed not simply because it was inherently unbuildable, but because of the deflation of utopian aspirations under Stalin: 'Communism changed its face'; 'Stalin was the agent of "Thermidor," or those more conservative policies that broke with the liberating spirit of 1917.'[36] Thus for Acker to imagine Tatlin Tower in New York is not only to imagine a revolution to have happened in America, but to imagine the possibility of the actualisation of an egalitarian ideal.

Since the suppression of Constructivism's radical experiments with the imposition of Socialist Realism, critics in Russia and in the West have attempted to retrieve and critically examine its work. Western fascination with the Russian avant-garde resulted in a series of retrospectives we know Acker attended. '[S]aw two beautiful Russian Constructivist shows' – she wrote in a letter to a friend, the poet and artist Paul Buck.[37] Levine's 1984 exhibition *1917* at Nature Morte Gallery, in New York's East Village, was one of the avant-garde's neo-incarnations, and featured the statement: 'We like to imagine the future as a place where people love abstraction before they encountered sentimentality.'[38] Yet much of the Western attempt to recover Constructivism tended to reduce it to a purely artistic, modernist phenomenon. Hal Foster argues that Constructivism's productivist and historical dimension has been repressed or re-encoded, because 'its collectivist transformation of industrial culture could not be countenanced by Western institutions – individual artist, artisanal medium, capitalist exhibition, idealist museum'.[39] The posthistorical enjoyment of Constructivism mirrors Slavoj Žižek's argument in 'Passion in the Era of Decaffeinated Belief' (2004), about a series of products that have been deprived of their malignant content: 'coffee without caffeine, cream without fat, beer without alcohol'[40] – to which we might add the contemporary noncommittal consumption of the historical avant-gardes stripped of their political substance: Constructivism without revolution.

But there remain areas which develop a 'haptic' relationship with Constructivism. The movement continues to inspire contemporary artists and theorists. As Foster writes, we also abuse Constructivism if we do not use it: 'if we idealize it as an impossible model rather than develop it as a practical program, if we see it as a historical idol rather than transform it according to its own call for constructive iconoclasm'.[41] Acker is committed to shaking the Western world off its atony by re-investing Constructivism's revolutionary passion in a contemporary setting. Highlighting her transformative use of Constructivism, she draws on the act of 'molding' from plastic arts: 'By repeating the past, I'm molding and transforming it, an impossible act' (*DQ*, 48). The narrator talks about Tatlin moulding 'unhandlable passion' into urban design, and believes in love and passion overcoming the inevitability of teleology: 'I have to mold my passion for you out of time' (*DQ*, 47). Acker's 'molding' of the Russian avant-garde suggests that it is a usable, malleable, real material to be shaped in accordance with the needs of the present. As opposed to the optical detachment associated with the abstraction in Euclidean forms, this 'molding' is a direct topological transformation of material. Through this intimate engagement with the Constructivists, Acker wants to infuse the city with revolutionary passion, hoping to create a space that is sensual, evocative, meaningful and – above all – physical. Like the Constructivists, for whom revolution was not an abstract thought or a word but that which needed to be lived and physically felt, Acker, as Friedman states, 'hopes to make the abstract material, physical'.[42] Her textual moulding challenges the conventional perception of Constructivism from the 'outside' that we are accustomed to and that the capitalist society demands, drawing us instead into a tangible contact with this laboratory of possibilities.

Levine's *1917*

If Acker envisions her engagement with the revolutionary avant-garde through the process of moulding, Levine conceives it in terms of membranes which enable productive exchanges between different temporalities. We have enough evidence to speculate that Acker modelled her double-coding of St Petersburg as simultaneously abstract and sensual – after Bely – on Levine's *1917* installation, part of which stages a poetic debate between the formal purity and stable Euclidean geometry of Malevich's squares, circles and crosses against the fleshy materiality of the erotic body in the expressionism of Egon Schiele.

All the works on paper at the exhibition were pencil and water-colour copies of Malevich and Schiele, who would appear to have little in common beyond their temporal proximity to the year 1917. Levine's pencil and watercolour reproductions on paper of original paintings in oil on canvas evoke notions of liquidity, permeability, and softness. Viewed from the 'outside' perspective of postmodernist theory, it is not hard to read these visceral transformations as a feminisation of the originals and a subversion of artistic authority. Yet her drawings, which are of uniform size and distinctively smaller than the originals, and in a more subtle medium, pull beholders into their inner processes, intimating exchanges between geometric Malevich, figurative Schiele, the year 1917, and Levine's contemporary context as well as our own reality. Levine said, 'I like to think of my paintings as membranes permeable from both sides, so there is an easy flow between the past and the future, between my history and yours.'[43] Levine's aim is thus to establish a primal, haptic connection with the copied content to instigate collaboration:

> I don't think it's useful to see culture as monolithic. I'd rather see it as having many voices, some conscious and some unconscious, which may be at odds with one another. If we are attentive to these voices, we can collaborate with them to create something almost new.[44]

In Levine's pencil and watercolour renditions, Malevich's universal forms and primary colours become membranes enacting a symbiotic relationship between neo-avant-garde and historical avant-garde – urging us to consider their projects as always incomplete, as opening possibilities. Schiele's emotionally charged humanism stands out amongst Levine's choice of formal abstractions of Malevich, Miró and Mondrian. As Levine notes in one of the interviews: 'It's also been about my own personal relationship to this work'; 'There is something in his eroticism that strikes a chord'.[45] Schiele's paintings initially caused outrage with their strongly sexualised bodies which blurred gender boundaries, subverting the ideal masculine male body epitomised in Greek sculpture. Moreover, his works shifted the perspective from the exterior to the interior, requiring beholders to look into them; his bodies are theatrically suspended in negative space, without context. Schiele located emotion and sexuality in the body itself.

In hanging her copies of Schiele's repellent yet touching bodies alongside Malevich's geometric abstractions, which are nevertheless fragile and imperfect, Levine achieves the tension between passion and abstraction that we saw in Acker. As for Acker, for Levine abstraction remains a polysemantic category that retains its radically political dimension. Levine is keen to speak Malevich's universal language of utopia, but her visual language is updated by lessons of history, undercut with Schiele's astute humanism and emphasis on personal craftsmanship as well as being inflected by feminism. When Levine remarked that the neo-avant-garde's relationship with the utopian aspirations of the historical avant-gardes is 'necessarily complex', involving both 'passionate engagement and the sublimity of aloofness',[46] she suggested that this historical exchange exists, but should not be conceived in terms of a simple repetition. From this perspective, like Acker, Levine can be seen as creating possibilities through her art by unexpected conjunctions and transformations rather than offering terminate solutions.

Conclusion

For Acker, revolution, cubism and love are not merely abstract notions that enable her to entertain the fictional question of possibility, but also material interventions that her writing seeks to reactivate to bring about change in the political present. Acker forces the feminine and the evental back into consciousness, and for her the two are interrelated. The breaking apart of the dominant order – patriarchal, capitalist, individualistic, imperialist, conservative (in art and human relationships) – is integral to both, as is the creative project of the opening of nonlinearity and possibility. Clearly, 'Russian Constructivism' contains constructive gestures, offering a remarkable point of entry into understanding Acker's political vision in her other works, and in it we find the implication of her utopianism.

Notes

1. See for example Roland Barthes's 'The Death of the Author' (1967), Craig Owens's 'The Allegorical Impulse: Towards a Theory of Postmodernism' (1980), and Benjamin H. D. Buchloh's 'Allegorical Procedures: Appropriation and Montage in Contemporary Art' (1982).
2. Friedman, 'A Conversation with Kathy Acker', p. 13.
3. Deitcher, 'Sherrie Levine: Rules of the Game', p. 9.
4. Sciolino, 'The "Mutilating Body" and the Decomposing Text: Recovery in Kathy Acker's *Great Expectations*', p. 249.
5. Jacobs, 'Kathy Acker and the Plagiarized Self', p. 50.
6. Tucker, Marcia, 'Director's Foreword', p. vii.
7. Cited in Buchloh, p. 52.

8. Friedman, '"Now Eat Your Mind": An Introduction to the Works of Kathy Acker', p. 44.
9. Burton, 'Fundamental to the Image: Feminism and Art in the 1980s', p. 440.
10. See for example Matich, 'Bely, Kandinsky, and Avant-Garde Aesthetics'.
11. Acker, *Great Expectations*, in *Blood and Guts in High School Plus Two: Great Expectations, and My Death My Life by Pier Paolo Pasolini*, p. 218.
12. Silverblatt.
13. Acker, 'Dead Doll Prophecy', p. 21.
14. Stein, *Tender Buttons*, p. 9.
15. Malevich, 'New Art and Imitative Art (Picasso, Braque)' in *Essays on Art: 1915–1933*, p. 40.
16. Ibid. p. 35.
17. Ibid. p. 20.
18. Silverblatt.
19. DeKoven, 'Gertrude Stein and Modern Painting: Beyond Literary Cubism', p. 85.
20. Maguire and Malmstad, 'Introduction', p. xv.
21. 'abstract, adj., v.'; 'abstraction, n', *Oxford English Dictionary Online*, last assessed 15 May 2016.
22. Foster et al., *Art Since 1900*, p. 119.
23. McCaffery, 'An Interview with Kathy Acker', p. 90.
24. Dostoevsky, p. 5.
25. Bely, *Petersburg*, p. 1.
26. Ebbesen, *Postmodernism*, p. 110.
27. Bragg.
28. Steinberg, 'Melancholy and Modernity: Emotions and Social Life in Russia between the Revolutions', p. 821.
29. Ibid. p. 826.
30. As Chris Kraus notes in her biography of Acker, *Don Quixote* incorporates Acker's correspondence with the filmmaker and theorist Peter Wollen. Kraus, *After Kathy Acker*, pp. 208–9.
31. Benjamin, 'Moscow', in *Walter Benjamin: Selected Writings*, pp. 28–9.
32. Cited in Lodder, *Russian Constructivism*, p. 48.
33. Lodder, *Russian Constructivism*, p. 3.
34. Ibid. p. 4.
35. Cited in Lynton, *Tatlin's Tower*, p. 35.
36. Bronner, *Modernism*, p. 116.
37. Acker and Buck, *Spread Wide*, p. 68.
38. Reproduced in Levine, 'Five Comments', p. 93.
39. Foster, 'Some Uses and Abuses of Russian Constructivism', p. 244.
40. Žižek, 'Passion in the Era of Decaffeinated Belief', p. 239.
41. Foster, 'Some Uses and Abuses of Russian Constructivism', p. 244.

42. Friedman, '"Now Eat Your Mind": An Introduction to the Works of Kathy Acker', p. 39.
43. Levine, 'Five Comments', p. 93.
44. Sherrie Levine, cited in Burton et al., *Sherrie Levine*, pp. 14–15.
45. Levine, 'After Sherrie Levine', p. 268.
46. Sherrie Levine, cited in Burton et al., *Sherrie Levine*, p. 168.

Chapter 4

'Beneath the Paving Stones': The Politics of Proximity in *Empire of the Senseless* and the Situationist Avant-Garde

In my reading of *Don Quixote* and its component 'Russian Constructivism', I showed how Acker strove to inspire political meaning in 'night time'. She contested the rationality of modern cynicism and realpolitik with their opposites: militant Cynicism and dreampolitik. She then offered alternating 'pictures of hope and despair' in relating St Petersburg and New York, dehabitualising perception and looking for passion in their abstract and melancholy topographies.

Acker believed that with *Empire of the Senseless* (1988) she left the deconstructive phase which had culminated in *Don Quixote* and became interested in more constructive impulses. She wrote: 'Perhaps our society is now in a "post-cynical" phase. Certainly, I thought as I started *Empire*, there's no more need to deconstruct, to take apart perceptual habits, to reveal the frauds on which our society's living. We now have to find somewhere to go, a belief, a myth. Somewhere real.'[1] In this chapter, I look at how this novel opens history by bringing into proximity three revolutionary contexts, arguing that Acker fuses the events of May 1968 in France, the Algerian Revolution and the Haitian Revolution to create a new global revolutionary space in the present. The politics of proximity in *Empire*,[2] I will suggest, is realised through Acker's continuation of the Situationist avant-garde project and their shared experiments with topology and turbulence, which in my analysis are complexly interwoven with the fluid and the feminine as operators of change.

At the crossroads

Empire is narrated alternatingly by two main characters, Abhor and Thivai, who tell the story through each other, and also through other voices and narrators. Thivai is a white male who wishes to become a pirate, and Abhor is his 'partner, part robot, and part black' (*ES*, 3). Both names activate our detective instincts, taking us to widely differing locations. Abhor and Thivai are collocations of mythical places: Mount Abora or the river Abora, and the city of Thebes. Thebes plays a significant part in Greek mythology, and is primarily known as the setting for the story of Oedipus, Dionysus, and the city founder Cadmus, among others. In the first section of *Empire*, entitled 'Elegy for the World of Fathers', Acker engages with the worn Oedipal script, which forms part of what she calls the 'Theban cycle', before attempting to dismantle it in the subsequent sections.[3] Meanwhile, the name Abhor may be referring the reader to the paradisiacal Mount Abora – evoked as Mount Amara in John Milton's *Paradise Lost* – which is also apparently connected with the biblical river of the same name that watered the fields of Eden.[4] Thus Abhor, through the prevalence of water imagery in *Empire* – notably the rivers featured in the text, including the Thames of the 'dead' London (*ES*, 128), the muddy Amazon, and the Mississippi from Mark Twain's *The Adventures of Huckleberry Finn* (which Acker considers 'one of the main texts about freedom in American Culture')[5] – may be instructing us both to the paradisiacal mountain and to the biblical waterway.

The pairing of Thebes and Abora may suggest a simple duality: the male-dominated mythical city which denotes static terrestrial forms, patriarchy and the deadly entrapment of the recurring Oedipal triangle; and the mythical river which alludes to movement, escape, freedom, anarchy, femininity, life, birth and re-birth, and even paradise. But to think of Acker's narrative in terms of such a strict opposition between these two states, one of stasis, the other of flux and becoming, would be misleading. Thivai acts against social norms, becomes a criminal and a terrorist, and dreams of becoming a pirate, and both his unruliness and his name make him a version of Jean Genet's semi-autobiographical character in *The Thief's Journal* (another influence on *Empire*). Meanwhile, the intrusion of 'h' in the name Abhor disrupts the sonorous tranquility and harmony of celestial Abora, blending together paradise's opposites: 'whore', 'war', and 'abhorrent'.[6] Thivai and Abhor, then, rather than having separate voices, narrate through each other and are intertwined. Thivai realises: 'I was glad to see her [Abhor], as if she was my heart's double' (*ES*, 177), and states 'The male half of me'll rape the female half of me' (*ES*, 176).

The Abhor–Thivai pairing is just one possible point of entry into an immense topography of *Empire*'s conceptual crossroads.

Throughout, the novel intertwines opposites, and elaborates conventionally unlikely encounters and fusions between art, science, history and myth. Its assemblage-like structure absorbs a plurality of influences and resonances, ranging from the Situationist avant-garde to the related figures of topology and chaotic turbulence, the anticolonial struggles of nineteenth-century Haiti and mid-twentieth-century Algiers, the neoliberal landscapes of the Western world and even Voodoo spirituality. At the same time, there is no obvious central metaphor or hierarchy of terms through which to unpack this underlying notion of transdisciplinary, transnational, transhistorical or transcultural plurality, one which also crosses the boundaries of consciousness when it exhibits dreams and ecstasy. The horizontal figures of a patchwork, felt, bridge, Möbius strip, knot and mosaic can be applied with success. The crossroads is another useful figure to help us envision the text through the underlying notions of cross-connection, non-linearity, multiplicity and bifurcating openness operating on many levels.

The crossroads is also an important element in Voodoo cosmology – another influential context in *Empire*.[7] Kafou, a spirit whose name means 'crossroads' in Haitian Creole, is a key symbol in Haitian Voodoo. It is also worth noting that both Haiti and its religion Voodoo are geographically, culturally and theologically at the crossroads of the Atlantic world, and that Acker's attraction to Voodoo is, in part, due to its characteristic synthesis and crossing-over of notions which traditional Western mythology keeps separate. These include the intertwining of anatopian landscapes (paradise lost) with utopian ones (paradise re-created), and the bridging of concepts such as past and present, life and death, human and animal, male and female, body and spirit, and dream and reality.

The crossroads also occupies an important place in Michel Serres's conceptual framework, along with the comparable tropes of the parasite and turbulent Venus – his operators of change which this chapter applies to reading *Empire*'s revolutionary actors and spaces. According to Serres, in thinking which embraces the crossroads, as opposed to figuratively taking one road of interpretative enquiry, a linear 'chain of reason' is replaced by 'a multiplicity of chains'.[8] Andrew Gibson's summary of Serres's approach can be applied to reading Acker: 'There is no overview of this journey, it has no totality and cannot be diagrammed'.[9]

The afterlives of the Situationist International

My analysis of Acker's work through the legacy of the Situationist International has multiple aims. It is my intention here to show that avant-garde forms are living on in Acker's work, and that Acker and the Situationists offer ways of thinking the event in non-Saturnian terms; subscribe to the anarchist revolution imagined through turbulent water imagery; approach the past as a repository of ideas and potentialities; politicise the use of science through the figures of topology and turbulence; and, finally, that they underscore the idea of literary communism. I do not aspire to provide a comprehensive summary of the history or the ideas of the Situationist International, and my use of its thinkers is necessarily partial and selective, orientated towards the politics of event. My focus is on the infrequently acknowledged scientific concepts of topology and turbulence as important strategies in the movement's re-imagination of politics and history.

The importation of Situationist thought into the American art scene was far from straightforward. Tom Finkelpearl tells us that the artist Gordon Matta-Clark is believed to have been the disseminator of Situationist ideas in New York in the early 1970s, having been greatly influenced by them while studying in Paris in 1968. With his translation of *The Society of the Spectacle* in 1969, a year before the official English translation, Leandro Katz, a writer, filmmaker and visual artist, and an active New York-based Situationist, is another figure seen to be responsible for introducing the New York art world to the ideas of Guy Debord. During this time Katz was friends with a number of artists and writers including Matta-Clark, Helio Oiticica, Suzanne Harris, Joseph Kosuth and Charles Ludlam – and Kathy Acker.[10] Situationist ideas then found their way into the American mainstream much later following exhibitions in Boston and London towards the end of the 1980s. This coincided with Greil Marcus's *Lipstick Traces: A Secret History of the Twentieth Century* (1989), in which the Situationists were no longer confined to art history but placed within a broader tradition of oppositional culture, as the bridge between Dada and punk. Acker herself forms something of a bridge within this context. As Peter Wollen glosses: 'The two basic ideas underlying détournement were those of re-contextualization and active plagiarism, ideas found subsequently in the writings of Kathy Acker, who had certainly read Debord and the Situationists.'[11]

Situationism has suffered from the same problems as its avant-garde precursors. There were various internal disagreements within the movement, which added to the notoriety surrounding several of its members. For the media theorist McKenzie Wark, the movement was recuperated the moment it was formed, disbanding itself at the right moment when it had become 'a collective celebrity'.[12] To many, Situationism is the end-game of twentieth-century avant-gardes. Wark writes that while the scholarship on the Situationist International (SI) has been growing since 1989, much of this approaches the Situationists from a safe distance.[13] They are consigned to the archive; their ambitions are rigorously documented and even appreciated but no longer considered viable, with their revolutionary poses often ridiculed. What these approaches have in common is that they consider the SI project no longer relevant. By contrast, Wark, echoing Hal Foster's refusal to participate in a staging of the funeral for the avant-gardes, sees their project as always unfinished and open to creative uses for the purposes of the present.[14] Acker's work is an example of such creative uses of Situationism, consistent with its 'copyleft' policy, which encouraged free use of their material without relinquishing their aspirations to change society. In a significant sense, she retrieves and revitalises the avant-gardes, raising their ghosts and making them live on in the narrative, as their undertaking is far from complete.

The SI was a group of radical leftist thinkers and artists active between 1957 and 1972. The group's critique of capitalism was developed most fully in the two 'terrorist bibles', both published in 1967: Guy Debord's *The Society of the Spectacle* and Raoul Vaneigem's *The Revolution of Everyday Life*. Debord's essential argument, formulated in the opening thesis of the book, is that 'In societies dominated by modern conditions of production, life is presented as an immense accumulation of spectacles. Everything that was directly lived has receded into a representation.'[15] The Situationists argued that in modern capitalist societies all real life experience is mediated by images, and that people were spectators of their own lives. They developed a set of strategies whose cohesive aim was a total transformation of what Debord diagnosed as 'the society of the spectacle'. These strategies, rather than being arranged into a coherent programme, were part of an open-ended composite of interlocking theoretical and practical concepts such as psychogeography, drift, *détournement*, unitary urbanism and, their highest ambition, constructing situations designed to be re-applied for revolutionary purposes in various contexts. The Situationists appropriated content from others and correspondingly advocated appropriating their own content in the manner of 'literary communism'.[16]

Early in his career Debord became fascinated with Lautréamont (Isidore Ducasse), whose poetic novel *Les Chants de Maldoror* (1868–9) would influence Debord's later work, reinforcing the importance of chance, plagiarism and juxtaposition. Debord often referred to Lautréamont's well-known dictum: 'Plagiarism is necessary, progress implies it' and that poetry 'must be made by all'.[17] The potential of Lautréamont's poetic technique was developed further in the concept of *détournement*, which involved the aesthetic manipulation of pre-existing materials into new ensembles.[18] The political intentions of *détournement* were manifold. The content of the spectacular material was undermined and critiqued by being rearranged. Moreover, *détournement* was to be understood as a challenge to private property and recuperation. In *détournement*, past material – a product of collective human labour, such as a work of art or an event – rather than being out of date or commodified, was made open to revolutionary use in the present.

Détournement is different from quotation, Wark argues, because 'quotation brings the past into the present, but it does so entirely within a regime of the proper use of proper names. The key to détournement is its challenge to private property.'[19] The Situationists drew freely on the resources of their predecessors and contemporaries, and in the same spirit offered up their work to be pirated. Each of the six issues of the avant-garde journal *The Situationist Times* was edited by Jacqueline de Jong. It was originally conceived as an English-language version of *Internationale Situationniste* (1958–69) but it split away from it.[20] Each back cover contained a statement which embodied literary communism: 'all reproduction, deformation, modification, derivation, and transformation of *The Situationist Times* are permitted' (Fig. 4.1). In the third issue this statement appears beneath an image of an interlacing knot, an example of a popular artform celebrated by Asger Jorn and other Situationists, for whom knotwork and weaving encouraged collaboration, diversity, transformation, improvisation, connection and openness to new connections and forms. Acker's *Empire* follows this topology of weaving very closely. If the appropriation of other texts was an overt, self-reflexive technique of deconstruction up to *Don Quixote*, in *Empire* 'plagiarism is much more covered, hidden'.[21] Like the creators of the Situationist magazine, Acker is unafraid to intertwine disciplines and genres. The novel overlays a large number of texts, and it becomes impossible to identify where one reference stops and another begins: 'I've used tons

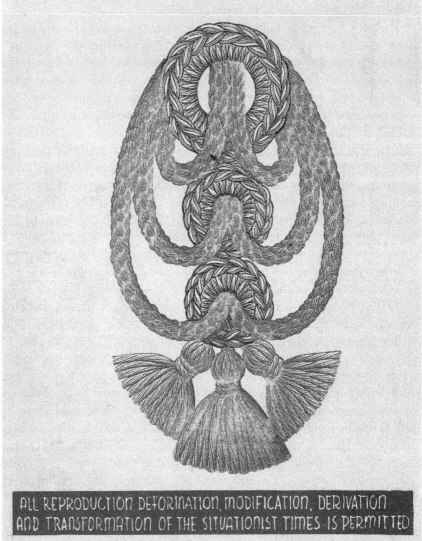

ALL REPRODUCTION DEFORMATION, MODIFICATION, DERIVATION AND TRANSFORMATION OF THE SITUATIONIST TIMES IS PERMITTED

Figure 4.1 Back cover of *The Situationist Times*, International British Edition, no. 3 (January 1963). *The Situationist Times*, Beinecke Rare Book and Manuscript Library, Yale University.

of other texts – sometimes it's just a phrase. You know I've gotten very good at it. There's a lot of Genet for instance. The beginning is based on *Neuromancer*, a book by William Gibson. But from page to page, I've adapted a lot of other texts. I couldn't even say exactly.'[22]

This strategy is informed by a primarily spatial concern, 'to find writers who describe the particular place I want to get to'.[23]

May '68 as the event

One of the major concerns for the Situationists was that revolutionary action tends to be followed by reaction, recuperation and cultural amnesia. The aftermath of the events of May 1968 in France (the revolts marked the culmination of the SI activities) perpetuated this pattern. Following May '68's avowed 'failure', the New Philosophers emerged, turning their backs on the event, with the ex-Maoist André Glucksmann being the most explicitly reactionary.[24] Contributing to the media's diffusion of the events' radical inheritance, in one of his 2007 speeches for the presidential elections, Nicolas Sarkozy famously called for the liquidation of the spirit of 1968.

The revolts appear to be far from forgotten: the body of 1968 scholarship is vast, and the events have been officially and vigorously commemorated over the last four decades. But all this disconcertingly amounts to a mere spectacle of memory, where the revolutionary spirit of the events is replaced with a detached sentiment. Kristin Ross observes that much of the discussion about the events is framed around opposing poles, such as 'failed or not'; 'revolution or psychodrama'; 'event or non-event'; 'revolution or festival'; 'words or actions'; 'seizing speech or seizing power'.[25] The prevailing question about the events is 'what happened', and the frequent response is 'nothing happened'. Challenging this reductively binary thinking, Ross is more interested in what 'lies elsewhere, outside the parameters of revolution, failed or not. Why did something happen rather than nothing?'[26] She argues that the events were misrepresented as being only cultural in nature, insisting that 'In May, everything happened politically.'[27] Moreover, for Ross the notion of 'successful' politics, understood conventionally as taking power, is a misplaced one with regard to the May events. Because the May events did not fit in with the orthodox Marxist typology of overthrow – lacking a heroic leader, a clear revolutionary agent (workers or students) or a party – they did not conform to the established discursive forms for them to be intelligible, acknowledged and assimilated. But to deny them revolutionary status altogether, or to say that they failed because the revolutionaries did not seize power, is to miss the point completely, as the aim was to overcome binary thinking and create social bonds not based on domination.

The recuperation of May 1968 contributed to the dissolution of the SI movement. In the context of intellectual and political reaction in the early 1990s, Raoul Vaneigem is fully aware of the vulnerability of the May events to becoming incorporated into the dominant culture by counter-revolutionary thinking. In his 1991 preface to *The Revolution of Everyday Life*, he writes: 'This is the whole meaning of the notion of "recuperation". Revolutions have never done anything but turn on themselves and negate themselves at the velocity of their own rotation. The revolution of 1968 was no exception to this rule.'[28] Yet while Vaneigem finds that in the 1990s 'even the critique of the spectacle has [. . .] been travestied as "critical spectacle"', he nonetheless argues that his book remains relevant to political struggle. On the one hand, it can be seen as little more than an interpretation of its time, bearing 'witness to a history imprecise in its becoming'.[29] But on the other hand, Vaneigem wants us to recognise that 'a book that wreaks change on its time cannot fail to sow the seeds of change in the field of future transformations'.[30]

In part, *The Revolution of Everyday Life* retains its influential power because of the emphasis it places on the radicalisation of subjectivity in response to the environment. The crucial realisation is that 'learning to live is not the same thing as learning to survive'.[31] Refusing mere survival, a type of existence synonymous with death and boredom, Vaneigem calls for a 'radical subjectivity' which embraces life in all its forms.[32] What gives this radical subjectivity consistency and drive for emancipation is its topological relationship with events: 'My subjectivity feeds on events. The most varied events: a riot, a sexual fiasco, a meeting, a memory, a rotten tooth. The shock waves of reality in the making reverberate through the caverns of subjectivity.'[33]

If there are considerable differences and even gulfs between the Situationists and the theorists such as Deleuze, Serres and Badiou, the preponderance of the event brings their projects into proximity, if not a striking alliance, and Acker's work exemplifies this. They share the same abhorrence of mere survival in the reactionary present. They equally oppose dominant historical narratives which either fail to register events (as in 'nothing happened') or distort them or reduce them to calculable data ('no one died in May '68'), or record them as disorderly, nonsensical and irrational (tellingly, the Paris Communards were frequently presented as drunks and the May '68-ers as criminals and delinquents). Above all, their body of work suggests fidelity to the revolutionary impetus of past events, coupled with a militant refusal to accept past events as bearing no relevance to the transformation of the present. The emancipatory spirit cannot be contained by established historical narratives. For Deleuze:

> an event can be turned around, repressed, co-opted, betrayed, but there still is something there which cannot be outdated. [. . .] But even if the event is ancient, it can never be outdated: it is an opening onto the possible. It passes as much into the interior of individuals as into the depths of a society.[34]

Topological transformations

The cover of the third issue of *The Situationist Times* features a diagram of intersecting loops entitled 'Overlapping situations. The Person P is in two different situations S1 and S2 at the same time' (Fig. 4.2). The editors appropriated it from Kurt Lewin's study *Principles of Topological Psychology* (1936). As Karen Kurczynski points out, they were less interested in Lewin's theories of the immediate environment's emotional effects on the individual – which at the time offered an alternative to psychoanalysis preoccupied with personal history – and more struck by the elaborate diagrams that accompanied his theories, adopting them as an opportunity for interaction with other understandings of topological relations within the journal.[35]

Les Lèvres nues (1954–8), a Belgian surrealist journal, published several important essays by Debord, and its form anticipated the visual interventions of *Internationale Situationniste* and *The Situationist Times*. The front cover of its eighth issue features an untitled image by Marcel Mariën, the Belgian surrealist and later Situationist collagist and photographer.[36] Discernible in the obscure hexagonal shape, in black ink on a white background, is a map of France. There is a large black dot indicating Paris, dots for Bordeaux and Toulouse, and many smaller dots for smaller places. Closer inspection, however, reveals that this is not an ordinary map of France, because the French place names have been replaced by Algerian ones. 'Algiers' is next to the dot for 'Paris', and 'Oran' is where 'Lyon' should be. The image is summed up by the caption, 'Algeria is French'. The map has provoked a number of readings. For Todd Shepard, it is a bold reminder to those who reject Algerian independence following the Algerian Revolution (1954–62) or fail to acknowledge the reality of

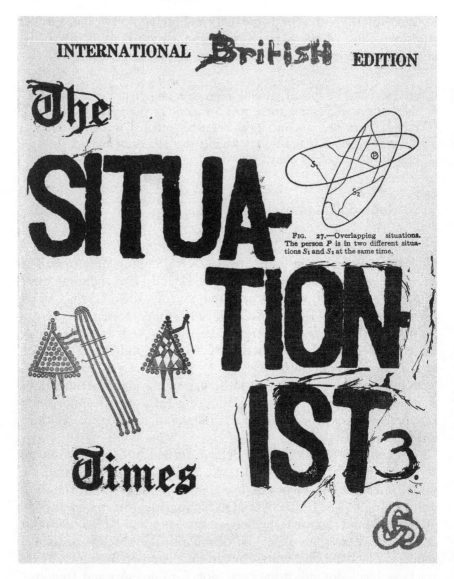

Figure 4.2 'Overlapping situations' diagram on the front cover of *The Situationist Times*, International British Edition, no. 3 (January 1963). *The Situationist Times*, Beinecke Rare Book and Manuscript Library, Yale University.

imperialism.[37] For Andrew Hussey, meanwhile, the image is a perfect example of the Situationist International's use of *détournement*: the distinction between the coloniser and the colonised becomes blurred.[38]

The Picador edition of *Empire of the Senseless* also features on its cover an unconventional map. It is a dream map by Robert Mason, the British illustrator and co-editor of *Radical Illustrations*, best known for his attempts to revive the medium of illustration in the era of the computer-generated image. A visual interpretation of post-apocalyptic landscapes of *Empire*, the cover depicts a surrealist map of an ocean, with the central image of a sand- or skin-coloured heart-shaped continent or an island (perhaps an allusion to Haiti) with a fractal coastline, tiny rivulets resembling blood veins and a pole marked with a pirate emblem. The continent is filled with pirate imagery. The burning skyscrapers and a dollar sign consumed by flames hint at an attack on capitalism. There are also thin dogs, a bird, and a skeleton figure dressed in black. A whale is spouting blood into the air and there is a naked figure lying in a boat circled by sharks to the left, and a mermaid and a tattooed arm with a bottle emerging from the water to the right. The lines of latitude lose their straightness as they extend from the centre, becoming wavy, swerving, forming loops, fragmenting and dissolving. The lines of longitude are likewise disordered, bending at various angles or shooting diagonally across the map. We should not conceptualise them as Euclidean coordinates, which delimit a grid-like stationary space, or a similarly straightforward Ptolemaic geography. Rather, we should construe them in terms of variable topological relations.

The Situationists were voyagers between disciplines, inventing bridges between the arts, politics and sciences. Topology, a mathematical field dealing with continuity and transformation, is the crucial and insistent notion in *The Situationist Times*. The avant-garde magazine brought into dialogue topologically orientated artistic, cultural, scientific and other forms of intellectual and political production. Max Bucaille, a surrealist artist and mathematician, submitted a whole set of writings on topology to the journal. Asger Jorn, an admired painter and the co-founder and theorist of the movement, based his conceptualisation of 'situology' on topological foundations. These and other contributions, as Wark has observed, anticipate 'the revival of interest in complexity, chaos, and turbulence that would not come for some years'.[39] The abiding interest of the Situationists in topology also ties in with Lefebvre's writings on the lived spaces of everyday life, a body of work which influenced and was itself influenced by the Situationists.

Topology fascinated a number of post-war artists, architects and theorists who sought alternatives to the Euclidean understanding of space. Topology continues to inform conceptualisations of time, space and subjectivity in contemporary philosophical discourse. But if topology has won adherents across disciplines, it resists a clear-cut definition, and its history is patchy rather than linear in development.

With classical geometry topology shares its mathematical understanding of shapes in different types of space. But whereas metric geometry investigates quantitative properties of space such as length, degrees and volumes of geometrical figures, topology deals with its qualitative aspects, such as flatness or roundness, and smoothness or angularity. In Euclidean geometry, for two triangles to be considered congruent, their parameters must be identical. If the actual distance between angles is different, they can only be considered similar. In topology, meanwhile, two triangles, each of whose sides are of a different length, are congruent because they can morph into each other. According to the famous example, topologically speaking, a doughnut and a teacup are equal because they can be moulded into one another by means of stretching, squeezing and folding the form without making any cuts. As Serres asserts, 'while the science of stable, well-defined distances is called metrical geometry', topology 'is a science of nearness and rifts'.[40] Or, in the words of the editor of *The Situationist Times*, de Jong, 'the beautiful thing about topology [is] that everything can be changed at any time'.[41]

In his article for the fifth issue of *Internationale Situationniste*, 'Open Creation and Its Enemies' (1960), Asger Jorn highlights the difference between topology and Euclidean geometry in their contrasting understanding of spatial relations. Whereas the latter relies on a superficial system of co-ordinates (vertical, horizontal and depth), the former abolishes any external referents, with the spatial coordinates constantly shifting, changing parameters, disappearing and appearing, continually moving and 'becoming'. From this premise Jorn developed a theoretical practice he named 'situology', which expresses the key ideas of topology. But if in topology the transformation of forms is detached from time and can be repeated – time is conceived as universal and abstract – situology emphasises the singularity of the lived experience, approaching it from within. In Jorn's words, the aim was 'to oppose a plastic and elementary geometry against egalitarian and Euclidean geometry, and with the help of both, to go toward a geometry of variables, a playful and differential geometry'.[42] As Wark glosses, 'situology is topology without equivalence'.[43] 'Situ-analysis' replaces the emblematic figures of Euclidean geometry, such as a square or triangle, with the topological forms

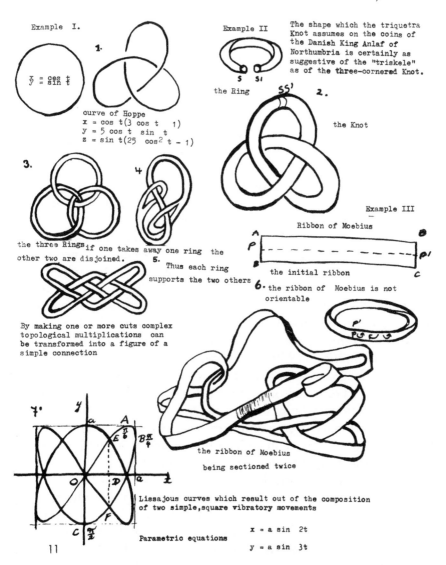

Figure 4.3 Knots in *The Situationist Times*, International British Edition, no. 3 (January 1963), p. 11. *The Situationist Times*, Beinecke Rare Book and Manuscript Library, Yale University.

of the knot and interlace, which the third issue of *The Situationist Times* explored at length (Fig. 4.3).

Empire engages us with a topological manipulation of the complexes of location and time. Around halfway through the novel, two main revolutionary events directed against imperial France, the Haitian Revolution of 1791–1804 and the Algerian Revolution of 1954–62, overlap. Both rebellions occupy a seminal place in the history of decolonisation, and their spatial and temporal overlapping, with eighteenth-century Haiti mapped onto twentieth-century Algeria, have important political implications for Acker. In the section 'Let the Algerians Take over Paris', Abhor explains that: 'in those old days, those days of death, of a political turn to the right-wing when the only saviour seemed to be anything and anyone who was not white' (*ES*, 64).

In her representation of the Haitian Revolution Acker relied primarily on C. L. R. James's study of the events in his *The Black Jacobins* (1938). The uprising in the French Caribbean colony of St Domingue, present-day Republic of Haiti, was the only successful slave revolt in history, and the first time that black people had overthrown a European coloniser to establish an independent country. The terrorist activity of the Arab nationalists is documented in the Gillo Pontecorvo film *The Battle of Algiers* (1966), which Acker drew on in her characterisation of the events, along with her borrowings from Frantz Fanon's *The Wretched of the Earth* (1961) and *A Dying Colonialism* (1959), influential texts which ardently criticised colonisation and called for violent resistance. The guerrilla tactics of the FLN (the French acronym for the National Liberation Front), the main revolutionary body which sought to unleash the Algerian people's revolutionary energy and turn it against the French oppressor, stirred militant activity in radical organisations around the world, including the Black Panthers in the United States.

These two key historical struggles are mapped onto *Empire*'s postmodern landscapes. The scholar Angela Naimou has produced a brilliant attempt at untangling this spatio-temporal knot, investigating Acker's 'conflation' (as Naimou terms the method) of revolutionary and dystopian realities. As Naimou points out, the Haitian Revolution is fused with the mid-twentieth-century Duvalier dictatorship, which is fused, in turn, with scenes from the Algerian War. The political clashes of immigrants with French citizens in 1980s suburban Paris are also evoked here. Contemporary New York is another recognisable setting, for Acker synonymous with the reactionary climate of the 1980s under Thatcher and Reagan. As Naimou asserts, 'In the storyworld of *Empire*, Haiti is Algiers, and Haiti simultaneously is Paris.'[44] The overlapping of the mythical locations of Thebes and Abora adds to this spatial uncertainty, as does Paris in the Situationists' experiments in psychogeography, and numerous other charged locales. However, a complete disentangling and ironing out is neither possible nor desirable. Not unlike the Situationists' fascinating play with knots, *Empire*'s plotlines are constantly tying and untying themselves, intersecting in unexpected ways and continually seeking new connections. We are made to follow Abhor, who 'entered the world of muddy rivers, the Amazon, whose jungles were so entangled that the wings of vultures, being almost useless, grew monstrous. Entered the endless areas of the heart' (*ES*, 121). Rather than being a master and controller of the folded space she creates, Acker always wants to point us elsewhere, to another transformative relation.

Serres writes that Émile Zola's Paris has an unexpected geography populated by characters circulating through and between spaces that initially seem heterogeneous and distinct from one another. He uses a handkerchief to visually represent this topological space and time:

> If you take a handkerchief and spread it out in order to iron it, you can see in it certain fixed distances and proximities. If you sketch a circle in one area, you can mark out nearby points and measure far-off distances. Then take the same handkerchief and crumple it, by putting in your pocket. Two distant points suddenly are close, even superimposed. If, further, you tear it in certain places, two points that were close can become very distant.[45]

Empire performs precisely this exercise. Paris, Algiers, Haiti, New York, or rather their various modal states – pre-revolutionary, revolutionary, post-revolutionary, colonial, postcolonial, fascist, dystopian and utopian, Thebes and Abora – all meet at the crossroads. Innovation arises here not from spatial and temporal separation of elements, which for Serres signifies stagnation and death, but their transformation through continuous remoulding and connections. In the words of Steven Connor, this topology warrants 'the possibility of rereading historical continuities, of revisiting the uncompleted past and being revisited by it, with new mutations of understanding emerging as the result'.[46]

The Haitian and Algerian revolutions have each become archetypes of post-colonial struggle, but the cost of these events was tremendous violence – poisonings, torture, assassinations, bombings and civilian massacres. I concur with Lidia Yuknavitch when she writes that Acker's historical flattening 'in no way suggests that Acker is devaluing or trivialising the historically specific events'.[47]

Acker is following the Situationists in postulating a creative resurrection of past events through topological manipulation. In Vaneigem's evocative account, radicalism and resistance reside in that relation:

> Let the formidable reality of the third force emerge at last from the mists of history, with all the individual passions that have fuelled the insurrections of the past! Soon we shall find that an energy is locked up in everyday life which can move mountains and abolish distances. The long revolution is preparing to write works in the ink of action, works whose unknown or nameless authors will flock to join de Sade, Fourier, Babeuf, Marx, Lacenaire, Stirner, Lautréamont, Léhautier, Vaillant, Henry, Villa, Zapata, Makhno, the Communards, the insurrectionaries of Hamburg, Kiel, Kronstadt, Asturias.[48]

In *Empire*, Acker is notably drawn to uprisings that are non-Western and anticolonial. This engagement with a non-Western revolutionary event is Acker's way of signalling that resistance to oppression – in its capitalist, patriarchal or colonial forms – is an endeavour experienced across the globe and throughout history. In this context, Badiou's call for fidelity to events also applies to those events that appear distant in time and those not obviously geographically proximate.

Acker is attracted to these events also as productive alternatives to modern Western rationality. As Shepard remarks, the Algerian uprisings had important intellectual consequences because they provoked a profound rethinking of post-Enlightenment Western rationality, challenging the Western project of universalising the conceptions of the nature of reality and time, along with the abstract idea of unchanging human rights and values, and specifically Western understandings of freedom.[49] Because white Western mythology, entrapped by the notion of causality, keeps life and death separate, Acker looks for alternatives in the elements of non-Western tradition and in the discoveries of modern science which challenge the Newtonian paradigm of linear time. Attempts to disrupt the dominant logic are animated vividly in the overlapping of Algerian and Haitian insurgencies and cultures: 'Because most of the nations' governments are right-wing and the right-wing owns values and meanings: The Algerians, in their carnivals, embraced nonsense, such as Voodoo, and noise' (*ES*, 73). The Haitian leaders she evokes, Mackandal, the runaway slave whose failed rebellion preceded the Haitian Revolution, and Toussaint L'Ouverture, are both practitioners of Voodoo and overtly criticise the Western ideology of self-interest: 'Toussaint

L'Ouverture who used Voodoo to defeat Western hegemony said: "If self-interest alone prevails with nations and their masters, there is another power. Nature speaks in louder tones than philosophy or self-interest"' (*ES*, 65). Moreover, Acker's Mackandal preaches that Voodoo operates not by a separation of modalities but a crossover between them: the spiritual and the physical, life and death, past and present, human and animal, solid and fluid. Rather than being separate entities, the two sides are in constant relation to each other, metaphorically assuming the form of a Möbius strip:

> The white people believe that death is prior to life. [. . .] In his or her beginning, this living person is both physical and mental, body and spirit. The body must touch or cross the spirit to be alive. Touching they mirror each other. A living person, then, is a pair of twins. [. . .] The whites make death because they separate death and life. (*ES*, 74–5)

Historical accounts portray Mackandal as a legendary figure of metamorphosis capable of overcoming the boundary between human and animal, and between life and death. He persuaded his worshippers that he could not die and that he had the ability to transform himself into any living creature. He was burned at the stake by the French authorities when they discovered that he had mobilised slaves to poison the food of their masters, and his followers then believed that he transformed himself into a plaguing insect. In Acker's narrative Mackandal assumes the forms of the Haitian spirit Loa and a giant mosquito.

Throughout *Empire*, there is a strong presence of small animals such as insects, rats, stray cats and dogs, and examples of animal-like and superhuman behaviour, grotesque forms, disturbances, collations of natural and urban elements . One scene reads: 'Algerians, blacks swarming everywhere; dogs nudging over garbage cans with their cold black noses' (*ES*, 78). What this demonstrates is that Acker is quite clearly interested in relating disorderly animal formations to collective human political activity. If in Western representation slaves have been de-humanised by being presented as animals, and particularly as insects, in Acker's narrative, as in Haitian mythology, the human becoming animal or aquatic, rather than rendering people impotent and primitive, endows them with superhuman agency and collective power capable of crushing authority. The swarm, especially, with its acoustic and gestural effects, intensifies the anarchic chaos of social upheaval. The droning hum of revolutionaries anticipates the physics of the turbulence that we will consider in the next section. The buzzing minor groups embody the 'third force' Vanei-gem talked about earlier – the disruptive noise-maker and intermedi-ary, which is in turn evocative of Serres's fascinating concept of the parasite, which he theorises as both a disruptive and creative figure, an agent of change, an initiator of unexpected kinships.[50] This is why we should not be surprised to see Mackandal from the eighteenth century interfering in 1980s suburban Paris: 'From 1981 to 1985, for five years, Mackandal built up his organization. But revolutions usually begin by terrorism. His followers poisoned both whites and their own disobedient members.' His Haitian insurgency overlaps with the Algerian one: 'Most of Mackandal's followers were Algeri-ans' (*ES*, 75).

Modern science also provides Acker with powerful alternatives to comprehending the historical past. In her scientifically dense 1984 essay 'Models of Our Present', she interrogates a model of time inher-ited from the Enlightenment which has dominated the way in which the Western world perceives and apprehends the world and events. This 'Past Time', as she labels it, presupposes a strictly causal and linear relationship: 'If I do x, then x1 happens.'[51] It is the time that is distant, enclosed; it runs indifferently to and separately from the observer; it cannot be renewed, reborn; it holds no other possibilities. According to this reasoning, '[t]he past's over'; it 'can be considered as mathematical points on a line'.[52] In this context, the neighbouring reprint of Goya's nightmarishly grotesque 'Saturn Devouring His Son' may indeed be received as a stark reminder of such a homogenised time of endless upheavals, which aspire to break with the past, but by doing so merely replace the enemy with another powerful ruling body to be then overturned again, in effect repeating the same.

The narrator in *Empire* warns us that linear rationality 'always homogenizes and reduces, represses and unifies phenomena or actu-ality into what can be perceived and so controlled', putting it 'in the service of the political and economic masters' (*ES*, 12). By contrast, in the example of quantum mechanics (among others) Acker finds a striking instance of non-causality encapsulated in the 'branching worlds' principle, where 'if I do x, then x1 and –x1 and . . . hap-pen'. Here the experiment is no longer independent of the experi-menter, but 'involves human intentionality'.[53] Hence, as Friedman has observed, Acker's literary world is 'filled with sets of disrupted moments', and 'instability and unpredictability provide a liberating context'.[54] Topological thinking, which we have established as the primary logic operating in *Empire*, with the emphasis on metamor-phosis, chance, fluctuations of cause and effect, being 'in touch' with history rather than separate from it, provides such a 'liberating context' and thus an escape route from the dreadful homogeneity of linear time.

Acker's resurrection of historical figures, events and artistic interventions – summed up by the command voiced in *Empire*: 'Raise Us from the Dead' – resonates with the Situationist call for subverting official history to contemporary revolutionary ends. Like Acker, Vaneigem considered it paramount to guide others towards disrupting traditional histories and to make it possible for the past to bleed into the present. Conventionally considered dead, for Vaneighem, the revolutionary past can seem more alive than the lives that many people are currently living. Various economic imperatives rationalise time into measurable qualities which codify a person's capacity to work and to consume. The abstract linearity of time implies the mortality of all phenomena: everyone's time is limited; it passes unit by unit and never returns; past events are moving further and further away with the passage of time. Vaneigem critiques the operations of a typical historian concerning past events thus:

> He organises the past, divides it up according to time's official line, and then assigns events to *ad hoc* categories. These easy-to-use categories put past events into quarantine. Solid parentheses isolate and contain them, preventing them from coming to life, from rising from the dead and running once more through the streets of our daily lives. The event is, so to speak, deep-frozen.[55]

In response to this, Acker joins the Situationists in their mission to unfreeze history's liquidity to allow new potentials to emerge. Understood topologically, a past event's solidified form becomes only one of many possible states it might take, and the task is to open it to remoulding, variation and recontinuation.

Hydrography of turbulence

The May revolts did not conform to the traditional model of revolution. As a result, as Ross has pointed out, the official historical discourse either does not accept them as an event ('nothing happened') or perceives them as a failure because nothing had changed, dismissing them as disorderly and nonsensical. For Ross the May '68 events were very much in the spirit of the Marxist theorist Rosa Luxemburg, who shunned the idea of centralised leadership and organisation, advocating instead spontaneous mass participation. Scholars have suggested that the portrayal of Luxemburg as Lenin's enemy is one-dimensional, as in fact they 'were close allies for many years'.[56] But Luxemburg's activity and outlook, formed in response to the mushrooming worker's strikes leading up to the Russian Revolution of 1905, point us to a specifically self-organising model of revolution where order and self-discipline arise naturally from within, rather than the centrally administered one promoted by Lenin and his followers. For a true social revolution to occur, she insists in *The Russian Revolution* (1922), there must be a 'spiritual transformation in the masses degraded by centuries of bourgeois class rule'.[57] Elsewhere, she argues: 'it is only by extirpating the habits of obedience and servility to the last root that the working class can acquire the understanding of a new form of discipline, self-discipline arising from free consent'.[58] In Luxemburg's idea of society, the anarchist theorist Noam Chomsky sees a replacement of Leninist elitism with the 'creative, spontaneous, self-correcting force of mass action', capable on its own of creating a spiritual transformation and solving the problems of reconstruction.[59] Long before the Soviet regimes emerged, she predicted that Lenin's system of organisation would 'enslave a young labour movement to an intellectual elite hungry for power . . . and turn it into an automaton manipulated by a Central Committee'.[60]

Empire engages us, I would suggest, in a revolution of the Luxemburg kind, and one way to consider its political and aesthetic implications is through the metaphor of turbulence. Turbulence – whirling spirals and vortices forming and dissipating in unpredictable ways in chaotic flux – has long fascinated and perplexed scientists because of its shifting states of order and chaos and its resistance to description and prediction. In their seminal work *Order out of Chaos* (1984), Ilya Prigogine and Isabelle Stengers theorise positive characteristics of systems 'far from equilibrium', because rather than being the negative of order, there emerge complex dissipative patterns of self-organisation:

> For a long time turbulence was identified with disorder or noise. Today we know this is not the case. Indeed, while turbulent motion appears as irregular or chaotic on the macroscopic scale, it is, on the contrary, highly organized on the microscopic scale. The multiple space and time scales involved in turbulence correspond to the coherent behaviour of millions and millions of molecules. Viewed in this way, the transition from laminar [that is, *non*-turbulent] flow to turbulence is a process of self-organization.[61]

A parallel can be drawn between the 'mainstream' depictions of the May 1968 political outburst – namely, the widespread dismissal of its anarchist character as meaninglessly chaotic, undisciplined, impossible to describe, contain or categorise, devoid of clear leadership, resisting a linear narration, and not succumbing to a 'failed or not' dichotomy – and the long-standing inadequate understanding of turbulence by conventional logic as simply the unruly opposite of order. Traditional science and historical accounts have been unable to articulate the complexity of turbulent phenomena in science or politics, deeming them nonsensical and disorderly. In Acker's figuration of revolution as turbulence, by contrast, the chaotic formlessness of a revolutionary event appears not as meaningless disorder but as a meaningful moment of both destruction and formation, and therefore a condition of political possibility.

This appreciation of turbulence extends to Acker's adoption of the figure of the woman along with woman's implicit connection with fluid dynamics, an investigation of the movement of liquids and gases – an understudied area in traditional science. The reason for this neglect is the enduring convergence of scientific rationality with the theory of solids and their alliance with masculine authority. The dominant scientific discourse has revolved around the illusory ideals of stability and solidity, which in the realm of politics corresponds to the controlled state-man. Deleuze, Guattari, Serres, Luce Irigaray and Sadie Plant, and other theorists who have incorporated the rich offerings of fluid dynamics into their body of thought, confront hydrophobia in science, culture and politics, and reaffirm fluidity – that '*physical reality* that continues to resist adequate symbolisation and/or that signifies the powerlessness of logic to incorporate in its writing all the characteristic features of nature'.[62] Plant and Irigaray combat fascist subjectivity with female fluidity. Deleuze and Guattari have consciously aligned the nomadic notions of change such as becoming, heterogeneity and continuous variations with turbulent fluidity (*ATP*, 363). Serres revives repressed ancient theory of fluid behaviour and prioritises topological thinking, which allows him to view solidity as merely a marker of speed.

Serres seeks to bring the richness of Lucretian fluid physics to life. Lucretius's long poem *De rerum natura* (c. 50 BC) has been largely ignored as a scientific text because the ancient doctrine of atomism it explored was at odds with the classical and modern tradition of rationalism practised from Plato to Descartes to Newton. Serres argues that Lucretius's work, rather than being merely of historical and literary interest, constitutes the foundation of all physics. This is because it has an enormous amount to teach us about openness, uncertainty, fluidity, deviation, equilibrium and disequilibrium – notions which threw the classical ideals of closed systems, linearity, regularity and reversibility into question, anticipating the complication of the Newtonian paradigm by modern lines of scientific inquiry such as quantum physics.

The world of Lucretius is a fluid one, a place of turbulent flows and order emerging out of chaos. In this world, forms are created spontaneously from the event of deviation and collision of atoms falling through the void. If their flow were *laminar* – that is, if the atoms were falling parallel to one another – there would be no new relations or forms. However, in Lucretian physics atoms are spontaneously deviating from their laminar paths, an event Serres calls 'clinamen': 'the *clinamen* is the smallest imaginable condition for the original formation of turbulence [. . .] appearing by chance in a laminar flow'.[63] For Serres, 'Vortical physics is revolutionary. It goes back to the first disturbance, toward the primordial *clinamen*.'[64] There is no external cause of clinamen, since it is an irreducible complexity to which we cannot assign one logical cause, and is in constant deviation from the general: 'It opens the closed system. It places the physical laws under the rule of exception.'[65] Or, as Deleuze puts it: 'the *clinamen* manifests neither contingency nor indetermination', but 'the irreducible plurality of causes or of causal series, and the impossibility of bringing causes together into a whole'.[66] Lucretian vortical physics, typically for Serres, affirms relations, culture and science that are of use to us, because turbulent non-linearity occasions genuine possibility: 'The old logic of causality becomes vortical, effects go back to their causes.'[67] In this way, 'History is chance, aleatory and stochastic. A background cloud, first, the background noise. Great populations, the parametric multitude surpassing every measurement.'[68]

Red women

Male heroes feature prominently in *Empire*. But their revolutionary leadership, which culminates in an undemocratic rule, is called into question. 'Papa Death' is the key figure here that refers us back to the Saturnian refrain. As Naimou points out, through 'Papa Death' Acker associates her revolutionary leaders with the late twentieth-century Duvalier dictatorship in Haiti. Its *paterfamilias* was François Duvalier, aptly nicknamed 'Papa Doc', who was succeeded in 1971 by his son, Jean-Claude 'Baby Doc' Duvalier, whose own regime lasted until 1986 when he was overthrown during an uprising. Possibly mirroring these events, Acker's 'Papa Death' initially acts as a legendary revolutionary, hailing from and speaking on behalf of the poor, but after he gains power the scenario of corruption, oppression and violence repeats itself.[69] Moreover, Mackandal's oratory skills and charisma are compared to the manipulative speeches of the French contemporary political elite: 'Mackandal was an orator, in the opinion even of Mitterand, equal in his eloquence to the French politicians and intellectuals, and different only in superior vigour' (*ES*, 74). It comes as another shock that after the Algerians have taken over Paris, there emerges a curiously named organisation, RAP, which we find out to be an oxymoron of sorts: 'Revolutionary Algerian Police' (*ES*, 188–9).

Acker commented that any of her attempts to construct a society not defined by an Oedipal script were confronted with a counterforce which prevented the realisation of that society, because no idealised community can exist in isolation:

> The second part of the book concerns what society would look like if it weren't defined by oedipal considerations and the taboos were no longer taboo. I went through every taboo, or tried to, to see what society would be like without these taboos. Unfortunately, the CIA intervenes; I couldn't get there. I wanted to get there but I couldn't. The last section, 'Pirate Night,' is about wanting to get to a society that is taboo, but realizing that it's impossible.[70]

Thus Acker comprehends radicalism in terms of always being in exchange with power – that is, with the structures of power which organise social life. But she also suffuses *Empire* with the anarchic forces, associated with the feminine and the fluid, which offer challenges to these Oedipal relations.

The section in *Empire* entitled 'Let the Algerians Take Over Paris', the recognisable names, including Mackandal, Jesus Christ, Baron Samedi, Ahab, Papa Death, Prometheus, MASTER and Mitterand, give us the impression that the story of the violent Arab revolution and its aftermath revolves around male figures. Yet a more attentive reading will acknowledge the presence of nameless female characters in this section. We also notice that it is narrated by the female-robot Abhor. Even more telling is the fact that the first part which recounts the proceedings of the revolutionaries is framed by the heading 'My Mother' (*ES*, 63), whereas the aftermath of revolution, which features revolutionary Algerians turning into police, comes under the heading 'Daddy' (*ES*, 81). The feminine and the fluid permeate the revolutionary landscape, before the figure of the father returns. In 'Mother', Abhor evokes a childhood memory, where 'you would be seeing the beginning of revolution always made by females' (*ES*, 66). It is also in this section that Abhor relates hearing 'the old women. My grandmothers', whom she later associates with 'the future' (*ES*, 68). On encountering a white male Parisian, Abhor notices that 'his facial features looked female' (*ES*, 66). Lidia Yuknavitch has noted that Acker based Abhor on Frantz Fanon's characterisation of Algerian women active during the Algerian revolution.[71] In Fanon's account, the struggle for liberation redefined gender roles: 'The woman-for-marriage progressively disappeared, and gave way to the woman-for-action,' writes Fanon, adding that 'The woman ceased to be a complement for man inside the family. *She literally forged a new place for herself by her sheer strength.*'[72]

The unity of the fluid and the feminine is at the forefront of Acker's figuration of the spontaneous, decentralised revolutionary model that we saw proposed by Luxemburg. Luxemburg organised a socialist revolution in Germany, and was killed as one of its leaders by the German pro-right group the Freikorps. As the first volume of Klaus Theweleit's study *Male Fantasies* (1977), devoted to 'women floods bodies history', makes abundantly clear, the Freikorps expressed their hatred of communism – and particularly their hostility towards female communism, along with their general hatred of women and the rebellious working class – through watery imagery and metaphors denoting abject femininity. The army of 'Red women' activated in them a fear of dissolution and anarchy, thus posing a threat to their fascist masculinity and their desired political order. To the Freikorpsmen, as Barbara Ehrenreich notes in her 'Foreword' to *Male Fantasies*, female communism 'represents a promiscuous mingling, a breaking down of old barriers, something wild and disorderly. ("Represents" is too weak a word. This is what communism promises the oppressed and, we must imagine, usually hungry, working class of postwar Germany.)'[73] In the words of General Ludwig von Maercker, cited by Theweleit, 'Rosa Luxemburg is a she-devil. [. . .] Rosa Luxemburg could destroy the German Empire today and not be touched; there is no power in the Empire capable of opposing her.'[74]

Numerous examples listed in Theweleit suggest turbulent movement: 'The wave of Bolshevism surged onward';[75] 'The Reds inundated the land';[76] 'for a time was the only one to stand up to the Red wave';[77] the Freikorps 'rescued' Germany 'from the Bolshevistic flood . . . and ruination';[78] 'The side of the ship of state that faced east was in the greatest danger. This was where the water gushed through its ribs and plates';[79] 'The atoms whirl around in the boilers of the metropolis.'[80] Theweleit tells us that dry imagery, such as a sandstorm, a hurricane or a mass frost, was missing from the representations of the threats and global changes brought by the communist revolution. By contrast, references to dryness pervaded the descriptions of the German invasion of Belgium, or the Freikorps' intervention in the Baltic region, who were said to 'march in dry and solid, an army of dam-builders with a song on their lips'.

The fluid and the feminine form a symbiotic relationship in the service of revolution across Acker's works. For instance, parts of *My Mother: Demonology*, Acker's penultimate novel, are based on the life and work of a historical revolutionary, the political activist and writer Colette Peignot. Dario Argento's horror film *Suspiria* (1977) had become another important source of inspiration. With official history predominantly registering biographies of revolutionary male heroes and their Saturnian overthrows, Acker is looking for foremothers in culture and history. Revolutionary passion is affiliated here with the blood-red imagery characteristic of *Suspiria*:

> I'm in love with red. I dream in red.
>
> My nightmares are based on red. Red's the color of passion, of joy. Red's the color of all the journeys which are interior, the color of the hidden flesh, of the depths and recesses of the unconscious. Above all, red is the color of rage and violence.[81]

Suspiria juxtaposes Nazi spaces (represented by the concrete-grey neo-classical architecture preferred by the Nazis, images of guards with dogs and barbed wire) with the neo-Baroque red interiors and exteriors of a school of witches. Tellingly, Theweleit recalls the Freikorps comparing a civil war to a witch's cauldron: 'with the heat of a thousand blast furnaces, that fire is causing the old order, the old people, the entire world, to bubble, boil, foam, and melt'.[82]

Rivers of anarchy

C. L. R. James's study of the Haitian Revolution, *The Black Jacobins* (1938), an important historical reference in *Empire*, already complicated the grandeur of a male revolutionary hero. In his 'Preface' to the first edition, James distances himself from the Carlylean accounts which celebrate Toussaint, recording the story of the revolution as a portrait of his personality and achievements: 'By a phenomenon often observed, the individual leadership responsible for this unique achievement was almost entirely the work of a single man – Toussaint L'Ouverture.'[83] However, James adds: 'Toussaint *did not make* the revolution. It was the revolution that made Toussaint. And even that is not the whole truth.'[84] James employs watery imagery to underscore the chaotic character of the events, which Acker certainly retained. He described the revolution vividly as 'the ceaseless slow accumulation of centuries bursts into volcanic eruption', 'meaningless chaos', and 'those rare moments of history when society is at boiling point and therefore fluid'.[85]

Critics have explained that James wrote the history of the revolution in the Caribbean with the 1930s mindset of an anti-Stalinist Marxist, and so his discussion of Toussaint makes apparent the tensions between a single historical agent and the masses, and between individual political agency and historical determinism. Hence we read him say: 'Great men make history, but only such history as it is possible for them to make. Their freedom of achievement is limited by the necessities of their environment.'[86] This is a reworking of Karl Marx's famous observations in *The Eighteenth Brumaire of Louis Bonaparte* (1852):

> Man makes his own history, but he does not make it out of the whole cloth; he does not make it out of conditions chosen by himself, but out of such as he finds close at hand. The tradition of all past generations weighs like a nightmare upon the brain of the living.[87]

Echoing this, Abhor comments: 'History shapes all of us; history is the lives and actions of dead people. As soon as I'm dead, I'll be part of this history which shapes. Memory or history runs human blood through the river of time' (*ES*, 66).

But rather than remain engulfed by old scripts and let them continue structuring the present, Abhor resolves to escape their grip: 'The iciness of my blood which is my galloping horse proves that memories of past events have and are shaping me. Rather than being autistic dumb feelingless ice, I would like the whole apparatus – family and memory – to go to hell' (*ES*, 52). For Abhor, the galloping horse is paradoxically synonymous with the non-movement of frozen blood, because the rider of the horse, not unlike the passenger on the speeding train, possesses only an illusory capacity of agency. While they are compelled to perform a historic task they are simultaneously restricted by the forces of history. In this instance, Acker metaphorically associates the continuous re-enactment of the Saturnian cycles with iciness and dead history: with the freezing of alternative myths and blocking the profusion of bifurcating revolutionary paths. A bronze statue of a male hero on a galloping stallion (like that of Peter the Great in St Petersburg on a stone pedestal, or the familiar representations of Toussaint L'Ouverture in French military uniform riding on horseback) illustrates that paradox – namely, the repetition and fake mobility that underlie the Oedipal displays of heroism. The special code that Abhor is given reads 'WINTER', and, as the narrator laments, it keeps frozen those sisterly relations which are not defined by the pervading phallocentric politics: 'It's winter. Winter is dead time. I don't have any life now that my sister is dead. Raise us from the dead' (*ES*, 39). Winter is associated with the capitalist order, and the circulation and flow of money is again perceived as the opposite of life and genuine movement: 'WINTER's a recognition code for an AI. This particular AI is, that is his money located in Berne. Money is a kind of citizenship. Americans are world citizens' (*ES*, 39).[88]

Abhor wonders about comprehending history in ways other than a redundantly rationalised unity: 'Is there any other knowing besides this remembering?' (*ES*, 48). It is an invitation to trade the revolutionary horse for a 'witch's broom',[89] which would replace the exclusionary linear rush of progress with a multiplicity of anarchic swerves and turbulences, thereby restoring fantasy and desire. The turbulent imagery is predominantly hydraulic, but disturbances in air are also present, as in this flight of fancy:

> Perhaps if human desire is said out loud, the urban planes, the prisons, the architectural mirrors will take off, as airplanes do. The black planes will take off into the night air and the night winds, sliding past and behind each other, zooming, turning and turning in the redness of the winds, living, never to return. (*ES*, 112)

We imagine the expected transformation to lead to the release of a flow of desire from the closed circuit of the Oedipal pipework. Such turbulent desire would not only break through the established social orderings but enable the production of new relations. In this shifting paradigm of order and disorder, the family as a central organising unit of social life recedes. But rather than leaving her characters 'floundered in the inhuman sea', where there are 'No friends anywhere to be seen' (*ES*, 156), there emerges a different form of connection – friendship:

'you meet someone one day by chance and your whole life changes' (*ES*, 215). The novel is dedicated to Acker's befriended tattooist, who appears in the story and proposes to Agone: 'Maybe we can be friends' (*ES*, 137). Evocative of atoms' deviating paths in a turbulent flow, the tattooist exemplifies the formation of soul through a self-organising desire propelled by random human contact, without which desire would cease to flow: 'There were no straight routes, except by chance. Rather, the soul travelled in such turns and windings, snails, that a world was found, defined. The soul created out of his own desires. But, suddenly, in his swerves and curves, he found himself stopped. Unable to go further. Unless someone took him by one of his hands' (*ES*, 136).

In Acker and the Situationists, topological transformation and fluidity take on a privileged role in transforming reality. The Situationist slogans that appeared on Parisian streets during the May revolts, such as 'the beach beneath the paving stones', 'I cum all over the paving stones' and 'the wall bleeds', identify watery substances and the formless – particularly bodily fluids – as subversive. The liquid form has long been associated with anarchism. As Marshall has noted, 'anarchism is like a river with many currents and eddies, constantly changing and being refreshed by new surges but always moving towards the wide ocean of freedom'.[90] In *Empire*, the heading 'Algeria's Cock' is followed by an observation that 'Nothing ever changes' (*ES*, 48). This, however, is contested by the presence on the same page of the heading 'Primitive/Before', under which Acker writes: 'Climatically Algeria is a sluggish country and cunt' (*ES*, 48). Algeria here is coded feminine, fluid and anarchic, and is taking us to pre-hierarchical relations. The Situationist slogan 'the beach beneath the street' similarly points us to the anarchic currents that have been paved over by layers of social structuring. Although difficult, the street can be dismantled thanks to those wounds between the tightly fitted stones: the stones are removed and thrown. The cobbled street and the wall signify a structured system, which nevertheless has fissures that bleed an anarchical, disordered and unbound (other) that never vanishes. The sand of the beach signals the proximity of the ocean that is freedom. Abhor finds herself unable to resist the pull of the primal turbulent soup:

> There was a huge green ocean. [. . .] The waves which were beginning indicated that monstrous, frightening waves were about to rise. I had to return to my little rowboat to get my papers and wanted to have those wave tops, even though they were dangerous, toss me upwards so that flying I would be beautiful. (*ES*, 52)

The recurrent images of haze and fog – air infused with water – are suggestive of the progressive dissipation of social structuring and the unfreezing of history. Confrontations between fluid and solid forms abound. Acker depicts places where 'Rock became sky', 'haze [. . .] resembled human nausea', and where 'the tops of the water [. . .] were light' (*ES*, 7–8). Property, patriarchy, stagnation and boredom, and the confinement and suppression of the anarchist spirit are associated with solidity. 'Berne was the Hollywood set for Death. [. . .] One level is concrete columned streets. Several levels are thick bricked roofs. Bridges fly from heaviness to heaviness' (*ES*, 57). 'Paris looked as if it was made up of glass. [. . .] Rectangular blocks of mirrored glass intersected tall buildings of black glass about a quarter way down their lengths. [. . .] There Parks For The New Bourgeois Workers seemingly intangibly, seamlessly metamorphosed into the largest bank in the world' (*ES*, 110). '[T]he English built mansion flats to be property. Property should be indestructible, cold and hard' (*ES*, 196).

The fluid forms, by contrast, signify life and revolutionary change. The Algerian revolution is infused with vibrant watery imagery – the seas, rivers; storms, and even bodily fluids: 'This dead culture perceives the earth as concrete or marble and not as the water flowing from our tears' (*ES*, 166). Algerian revolutionaries advocate 'bang[ing] one's head against the wall, preferably a red brick wall, until either the red brick wall or the world, which seems unbearable and inescapable, breaks open' (*ES*, 73). Unstoppable turbulence revisits Paris: 'Spanish sailors, long time anarchists, had flowed in from ports near Paris, via the Seine, in orgies of general hooliganism and destruction. [. . .] They joined Algerians, their brothers, who were breaking into flats of the rich. The whites were already trembling from fear, nausea, and diarrhoea. [. . .] Algerians, blacks swarming everywhere [. . .]. The whole city was in flames' (*ES*, 77–8). Mackandal's followers then use poison, as 'There is a way to stop guns and bombs. There's no way to stop poison which runs like water' (*ES*, 77). As a result of this experiment, where one revolt is injected into another, Thivai and Abhor witness apocalyptic anarchy, a 'Paris which was now a third world. [. . .] All humans and animals now sail over the same seas' (*ES*, 82–4).

Western mythology traditionally associates power, progress and order with the elements of earth and air. Earth provides a solid foundation for building an empire: boundaries are erected, land is conquered, owned and paved over; leaders are elected, laws are issued, and structures – including Oedipal ones – endlessly repeated: hence Acker's references to the mythological space of the city of Thebes. The air and the skies have heavenly and authoritarian connotations.

Let us relate these domains with those characteristics which Serres ascribes to the dominion of Mars, the god of war, whom he associated with the realm of deadness, where nothing changes, and where the science of fluids is supressed:

> The order of reasons is martial. [. . .] Determination, identity, repetition, no information, not an iota of science; extermination, not even a shadow of a life, death at the end of entropy. Then Mars rules the world, he cuts the bodies into atomised pieces and lets them fall. [. . .] Mars has chosen this physics, the science of fall, and that of silence. [. . .] Nothing new under the reign of the same and under the same reign, preserved. Nothing new and nothing to be born, no nature. [. . .] Stable, immutable, redundant. [. . .] Reason is the fall. The reiterated cause is death. Repetition is redundancy. And identity is death. (*BP*, 109)

Here, Serres rejects those sciences that lack 'declination', namely 'reasons' interested only in the reiteration of laws, where 'the new is born of the old, the new is just the repetition of the old'. Such sciences ignore signs of chance, newness and deviation that occur in nature, and isolate themselves from culture and life (*BP*, 109). Refusing to be children of Mars, Acker and Serres (Deleuze and Guattari and the Situationists also belong to this particular rebellious band) embrace alternative models.

As we have seen, Voodoo's attraction for Acker resides in its reversal of a number of Western cultural constructs. Voodoo disrupts thresholds between life and death, terrestrial and spiritual worlds, and human and animal domains. Moreover, Acker borrows from the 'Black Jacobins' their liberating oceanic imaginary. As scholars have noted, the 'Vodou equivalent of paradise is an island that lies beneath the ocean called Ginen [. . .]. Here, the heavenly is associated not with the element of air, as it is in European metaphysics, but with the ocean deep. [. . .] Ginen in Vodou is a kind of Black Atlantis beneath the "Black Atlantic".'[91] Acker's illustration of 'THE DEEP', depicting a ship nearly lost in high-rising waves, and Abhor's name resonating with the paradisiacal river Abora, affirm Acker's utopian understanding of the aquatic, a realm of political possibility, dreaming, and freedom (Fig. 4.4).

This ship, half-sunk in turbulent waters, brings us to Serres's theorisation of the creative potentials that reside between chaos and form. In *Genesis* (1982), Serres uses the evocative trope of 'la belle noiseuse' (a beautiful noisemaker) to philosophise his notion

Figure 4.4 Kathy Acker, 'THE DEEP'. Artwork in *Empire of the Senseless* (London: Picador, 1988), p. 88.

of liquid, turbulent history. He contrasts the turbulent state with what he calls the 'great chain of reason'[92] – a relentlessly 'solid' history he identifies with reason and representation, and death, because it stifles creativity, divides and solidifies processes into classes and groups, and over-codes phenomena into dull repetitions while preventing the emergence of a 'new stability'.[93] Instead,

Serres writes, 'Turbulence disturbs the chain. It troubles the flow of the identical, just as Venus disturbs Mars' (*BP*, 110). He derived the metaphor of *la belle noiseuse* from Balzac's short story 'The Unknown Masterpiece' (1831). Central to the story is a painting by an old master named Frenhofer, which, rather than being a masterly representation of a nude, is a chaotic confusion of 'masses of colours contained by a multitude of strange lines, forming a high wall of paint'.[94] In the canvas before them, starry-eyed admirers discern

> A bare foot emerging from the chaos of colours, tones and vague hues, a shapeless fog; but it was a delicious foot, a living foot! They stood petrified with admiration before this fragment which had somehow managed to escape from an unbelievable, slow and progressive destruction. The foot seemed to them like the torso of some Venus in Parisian marble rising from the ruins of a city destroyed by fire.[95]

It is this half-formed figure that inspired Serres to coin the 'turbulent Venus' metaphor. Like Acker's turbulent ship, Serres's *la belle noiseuse* occupies the middle position between form and formlessness, order and chaos, repetition and fertile noise. It thus offers us a striking conceptual alternative to the heavy elevated statues of heroic leaders on their pedestals we saw earlier as representing stasis and invariance. For Serres, as Maria Assad explains, 'Turbulence is an as yet undecided openness to all future directions of a system; we may call it "possibilities unlimited". Frenhofer's turbulent Venus is an immensely profound representation of the possible, the multiple.'[96] Turbulent Venus therefore proves to be a rich model, one that reflects the complexity and irreducible open-endedness of revolutionary upheaval in *Empire* suspended between destruction and creation. If turbulence signifies violence against the status quo, like Venus's incomplete emergence from the whirlpool, it also represents the chance of birth.

In *A Thousand Plateaus*, Deleuze and Guattari draw on Serres to conceptualise their hydraulic (or nomad) science. They claim that 'the State needs to subordinate hydraulic force to conduits, pipes, embankments, which prevent turbulence', and to constrain 'space itself to be striated and measured, which makes the fluid depend on the solid, and flows proceed by parallel, laminar layers' (*TP*, 363). The logic of the nomad science and the war machine, conversely, 'consists in being distributed by turbulence across a smooth space, in producing a movement that holds space and simultaneously affects all of its points' (*TP*, 363). In *Empire*, the outburst of turbulence is continually held in check through the suppression, surveillance or elimination of the potentially rebellious:

> The Parisian and the French government desired simply to extermi-nate the Algerian trash, the terrorists, the gypsies. The urban sections inhabited by Algerians were literary areas of plague to the Parisians who knew how to speak properly. [...] As a result of this *urban* rather than *political* situation, by 1985 city ordinances prohibited all blacks from going anywhere at night unless accompanied by a white and carrying a special governmental ordinance. (*ES*, 75–6)

But chaos always narrowly underlies the calm. The passage below anticipates a clinamen – a deviation which will rapidly disintegrate the hideously oppressive layers of social and architectural structur-ing. In a grotesque adaptation of the Situationist slogan: this is the shit beneath the street:

> Under your concrete, Urban America, the piles of shit in the sewer-pipes around which the icy air has put its arms (the only physical affection left in disease) are so numerous that the shit's going to burst through the concrete and hit the fans . . . the winds of history . . . Even the steps of the whites are lost in these winds of perfumes . . . The rich know nothing . . . strangers . . . strangers to the world they own . . . themselves . . . Winds of perfumes. (*ES*, 165)

Pussy, King of the Pirates, Acker's final novel, taps into the plumbing imagery even further, offering up multiple juxtapositions between the controlled laminar flow within a bathroom's pipework and the turbulent waters of the sea. In the world of anarchist pirates, scenes of primordial formation abound, punctuated by variations of the phrase 'the world began'. O, one of the characters, can 'glimpse the ocean' '[f]rom the toilet'; 'The ocean's freedom'.[97]

Turbulent prose

Acker also elaborates a turbulent aesthetics in her prose, so that lan-guage and form become sites of eventual possibility rather than clo-sure. The effects of clinamen are first made evident in her fusion of texts and events. She admits to having used a huge number of texts, and her borrowings and overlappings occur at the level of paragraph, sentence and individual word. In her writing Acker eliminates quotation marks, those metaphorical dams separating texts and events which the discourses of history, education and copyright separate. The dissolution of boundaries between texts, words and geographical and historical zones enables them to behave like elementary particles in an atomic flow: they collide, recombine and release energy. Arabic script fascinates the narrator because it visually recalls Lucretius's turbulent swirls: 'a mad lovebird maddened, the *Koran*'s verbal turbulence – the thousand and one verbal variations, the thousand and one and more variations, similitudes within dissimilitudes and dissimilitudes within likeness – all transform into something beyond, about to move into flight' (*ES*, 166). The collapsing of boundaries between languages and cultures: 'The ceiling of languages is falling down' (*ES*, 163), implies that we are all 'Becoming Algerian' (*ES*, 141) in fighting oppression.

Applying atomism to language, Serres writes that 'Atoms, as we know, are letters or are like letters'. This is because although finite in variety, the number of their combinations, of letters forming words, like atoms forming bodies, is infinite: 'The analogy of behaviour is perfectly apt. It is a metaphor and it is not' (*BP*, 141). 'Language is born with things, and by the same process' (*BP*, 123). By disrupting syntax, creative use (and misuse) of punctuation and a confusion of tongues, Acker inverts the use of language, exposing its form and structure to be only relatively stable. The event (linguistic, political or sexual) is detached from its historical imprint and from interpretative frameworks which seek to capture it: 'Lack of meaning [. . .] as linguistic degradation' (*ES*, 17).

The noise of history emanates from acoustic events. In *Empire*, the linear narrative of official history, which reinforces causal chains, codifies events and consolidates the status quo, is confronted with the noise of history, a becoming of events waiting for their actualisations to become-otherwise. We can hear what Serres has described as the 'sound and the fury' of history[98] in Acker's resourceful use of sibilant fricatives /s/ and /z/ throughout the novel. Phonology distinguishes the acoustic characteristic of hissing fricative consonants (also known as 'stridents'), from sounds such as vowels, nasals and approximates, in that sibilant fricatives produce 'high intensity noise': 'This high intensity reflects the mechanism of noise generation, where the airflow is directed against an obstacle such as the upper or lower incisors.'[99] Thus the primary source of noise in the articulation of /s/ and /z/ is turbulence: 'When an air jet forms at the constriction and flows into a wider cavity, such as the front cavity, the laminar flow turns into turbulences, at a certain threshold formulated by Reynolds' number.'[100] In *Empire*, the voiced hissing fricative /z/ intensifies the immediacy of such recurring key words and formulations as: 'Raise Us From the Dead', 'razor', 'blaze', 'raze', 'haze', 'realize'. Another acoustic element shared by the words in this group are diphthongs: /ei/ as in 'raise' and 'razor', and /ai/ in 'realize'. Diphthongs are complex vowel sounds, also referred to as gliding vowels, which involve a movement from one vowel to another within one syllable. The swerving and curving movement of the tongue required for the articulation of diphthongs activates a sensory experience of deviation and change.

The acoustically turbulent and swerving word 'Raze' appears in *Empire* at the top of page 43 on its own, suggesting that the content that followed it has been erased. Although its larger size and font type are the same as those of the titles of the three sections ('Elegy for the World of the Fathers', 'Alone' and 'Pirate Night') into which the novel is divided, this title appears in the first part, is unnumbered and unnamed in the table of contents. The otherwise blank page containing the onomatopoeic 'Raze' is therefore an unexpected turbulent intermission, which further unsettles the passive ingestion of the written material on the part of the reader. It calls attention to the event which is not fully expressible in the text. Reminiscent of erasure poetry, and possibly an allusion to the image of destruction in Malevich's 'Suprematist Composition: White on White' (1918), or to Duras's *Destroy, She Said*, it is an imperative to destruction, calling for a stripping away of the solidified layers of representation, to confront the event afresh with boundless possibilities. White canvas invites us to make sense of the world anew. Suggesting again the creative-destructive connotation of turbulent forces, she writes under the 'Pirate Night' heading: 'But the blazing will to live: to live anew' (*ES*, 173).

Acker takes advantage of the prevalence of the voiceless hissing fricative /s/ in English, so that the noise of the sea – of suppressed anarchy – is always there, even if in the narrative background. At the same time there are instances where this sound is particularly concentrated for maximum effect so that the hierarchical relationship of message and noise is reversed, as in the title of the novel, *Empire of the Senseless*. The heavily coded word 'empire' is polarised with the ambiguity of 'senseless'. The proliferation of /s/ in 'senseless' is remarkably instructive of this turbulent sound actively participating in the dissolution of meaning, and of the status quo. Among other examples where acoustics indicate radical politics, the narrator's defence of the German Romantics occupies an important place. She announces her affinity with this lineage which 'strikes, at this base, where the concepts and actings of order impose themselves' (*ES*, 12). In the passage below, the alliteration of stridents /s/ and /z/ combined with the explosive quality of /b/ associates the destructive quality of the whirlwind with the capacity of literature to destroy that 'Reason which always homogenises and reduces':

> the German Romantics sung brazenly brassily in brass of spending and waste. They cut through conservative narcissism with bloody razor blades. They tore the subject away from the subjugation of her self, the proper; dislocated you the puppet; cut the threads of meaning; spit at mirrors which control. (*ES*, 12)

Any critical venture into the paradigm of turbulence in *Empire* must thus penetrate the novel's intricacies on both macro-and microscopic scales, through layers of thematic content and through language itself, zooming and tuning in and out as Acker interweaves politics in fractal-dimensions of the novel. On all levels, Acker employs the figure of turbulence to open events to resignification.

Conclusion

Although the Algerian Revolution was 'successful' in that the Algerians managed to overthrow the French government, Abhor ultimately questions its validity as a harbinger of positive change in the post-revolutionary world: 'Someone may wonder whether in a post-industrial world a revolution can change a city's architecture. Or anything' (*ES*, 110). This landscape leaves her confused and disappointed because it has replaced the very system it opposes: 'The Algerians had taken over Paris so they would own something. Maybe, soon, the whole world' (*ES*, 83). Another character, Agone, laments 'There are no more decisions [. . .] for in this unending growth of multinational capitalism, nothing ever changes' (*ES*, 126). Because we are denied a positive image of revolutionary change, the question arises whether this novel conveys to us the ultimate futility of political endeavours. After all, Abhor notes:

The Algerian revolution was stupid! Right. Innocent people got killed. But it was good for business! Any revolution, right-wing left-wing nihilist, it doesn't matter a damn, is good for business. Because the success of every business depends on the creation of new markets. (*ES*, 182)

The denial of a revolutionary 'happy ending', rather than being a final blow against utopian thinking, is a refusal of that rationality which equates revolutionary success with replacing one oppressive system of power with another. The event resists transcription into the official frameworks of understanding: parts of it are irreducible to representation and recuperation, and thus in the novel it remains unsaid: untouched by knowledge and the structures of knowledge. The hopeful slogan 'the beach beneath the paving stones' conveys a persistent sense of memory of anarchism, and anarchy's ongoing trickling into the system and readiness to burst when the first cracks show.

If capitalism perceives revolutionary activity as a consumer product – trivialising and recuperating it as radical chic – Acker, like Badiou, envisions evental truth as a process: an ongoing labour and commitment not based on calculable profit. If there is no linear success story it is also because the event at its most turbulent state of possibility does not guarantee a paradisiacal future but is, first and foremost, a chance. Speaking through Abhor on the final pages, Acker reminds us that events require faithful subjects who pursue evental promise with militant fidelity and patience rather than retreating into familiar sequences, relations and constraints, into the safety of the already named, decided and known: 'Then I thought about all that had happened to me, my life, and all that was going to happen to me, the future: chance and my endurance. Discipline created endurance' (*ES*, 224). Accordingly, by examining a series of Rimbaud's decisions in relation to the Paris Commune in Acker's novel *In Memoriam to Identity*, my final chapter will explore a variety of ways in which subjects can respond to the evental call.

Notes

1. Acker, 'A Few Notes on Two of My Books', p. 11.
2. Hereafter referred to in the text as *Empire*.
3. Acker, 'A Few Notes on Two of My Books', p. 12.
4. In Samuel Taylor Coleridge's poem 'Kubla Khan' (1816), the narrator has a vision of a damsel playing on a dulcimer, 'Singing of Mount

Abora'. The name was apparently suggested to Coleridge by 'Mount Amara' in Abyssinia, the same mountain which features in John Milton's allegorical epic of revolution, *Paradise Lost* (1667).

5. Acker, 'A Few Notes on Two of My Books', p. 13.
6. I borrow these three phrases from Lidia Yuknavitch, *Allegories*, p. 89. Yuknavitch links them to Acker's appropriation of Pierre Guyotat's depiction of female figures in *Eden, Eden, Eden*.
7. My discussion of Kafou is indebted to Alex Farquharson and Leah Gordon (eds), *Kafou: Haiti, Art and Vodou* (Nottingham: Nottingham Contemporary, 2012). For discussions of Voodoo in Acker, see the essays by Shannon Rose Riley, Michael Hardin and Angela Naimou collected in Mackay and Nicol (eds), *Kathy Acker and Transnationalism*.
8. Gibson, 'Serres at the crossroads', p. 87.
9. Ibid. p. 87.
10. Finkelpearl, *What We Made*, p. 28.
11. Wollen, 'Situationists and Architecture', p. 134.
12. Wark, *50 Years*, p. 9.
13. Ibid. p. 8. See also Wark, *The Beach*, p. 13.
14. Wark, *50 Years*, pp. 8–9; Wark, *The Beach*, p. 11.
15. Debord, *The Society of the Spectacle*, p. 7.
16. Debord and Wolman, 'A User's Guide to Détournement', p. 18; authors' emphasis.
17. Cited in Debord and Wolman, p. 16.
18. A definition of the process of *détournement* appears in the first issue of *Internationale Situationniste* (1958). Here it is defined as: '[t]he integration of present or past artistic productions into a superior construction of a milieu. In this sense there can be no situationist painting or music, but only a situationist use of those means. In a more elementary sense, détournement within the old cultural spheres is a method of propaganda, a method which reveals the wearing out and loss of importance of those spheres.' See 'Definitions', in Knabb, *Situationist International Anthology*, p. 52.
19. Wark, *The Beach*, p. 5.
20. De Jong intended *The Situationist Times* to be an English-language version of *Internationalle Situationiste*, but when the Central Council members excluded Gruppe SPUR (the German Situationist section) from the movement, in solidarity with the evicted artists de Jong positioned her journal as an independent international review which would explore connections between art, science, politics and cultural formations in the spirit of the post-war avant-garde review *Surréalisme révolutionnaire*. For an excellent account of the Situationists in Scandinavia, see Mikkel Bolt Rasmussen and Jakob Jakobsen (eds), *Expect Anything Fear Nothing: The Situationist Movement in Scandinavia and Elsewhere* (Copenhagen: Nebula in association with Autonomedia, 2011); for Jacqueline de Jong and *The Situationist Times*, see, in

particular, Karen Kurczynski's 'Red Herrings: Eccentric Morphologies in *The Situationist Times*' and 'A Maximum of Openness: Jacqueline de Jong in conversation with Karen Kurczynski' within the volume. I owe my awareness of this resource to Ellef Prestsæter.

21. Friedman, 'A Conversation with Kathy Acker', p. 16.
22. Ibid.
23. Ibid. p. 17.
24. See, for example, Alain Badiou, 'Roads to Renegacy', interviewed by Eric Hazan, trans. David Fernbach, *New Left Review* 53 (Sept./Oct. 2008), pp. 125–33.
25. Ross, *May '68*, p. 73.
26. Ibid.
27. Ibid. p. 15.
28. Vaneigem, *The Revolution*, p. 10.
29. Ibid. p. 7.
30. Ibid.
31. Ibid.
32. Ibid. p. 245.
33. Ibid.
34. Deleuze, 'May '68', p. 233.
35. Kurczynski, 'Red Herrings', pp. 171–3.
36. Les Lèvres nues 8, Brussels, 1956, front cover.
37. Shepard, *The Invention*, pp. 269–70.
38. Hussey, *The Game of War*, pp. 103–4.
39. Wark, *50 Years*, p. 19.
40. Serres and Latour, *Conversations*, p. 60.
41. Jacqueline de Jong, cited in Wark, *The Beach*, p. 118.
42. Jorn, *Open Creation and Its Enemies*, p. 24.
43. Wark, *50 Years*, p. 18.
44. Naimou, '"Death-in-Life": Conflation, Decolonization, and the Zombie in *Empire of the Senseless*', p. 134.
45. Serres and Latour, *Conversations*, p. 60.
46. Connor, 'Topologies', p. 116.
47. Yuknavitch, *Allegories*, p. 16.
48. Vaneigem, *The Revolution*, pp. 62–3.
49. Shepard, *The Invention*, p. 5.
50. See Michel Serres, *The Parasite*, trans. Lawrence R. Schehr (Baltimore: The Johns Hopkins University Press, 2007).
51. Acker, 'Models of Our Present', pp. 62, 63.
52. Ibid. p. 62.
53. Ibid. p. 63.
54. Friedman, '"Now Eat Your Mind": An Introduction to the Works of Kathy Acker', p. 44.
55. Vaneigem, *The Revolution*, pp. 231–2.
56. See Scott, 'Introduction to Rosa Luxemburg', p. 1.

57. Luxemburg, *The Russian Revolution*, p. 71.
58. Cited in Chomsky, *Chomsky on Anarchism*, p. 41.
59. Chomsky, *Chomsky on Anarchism*, p. 41.
60. Cited in *Chomsky on Anarchism*, pp. 41–2.
61. Prigogine and Stengers, *Order out of Chaos*, p. 41. For a reading of *Empire* through chaos theory, see Joseph M. Conte, *Design and Debris: A Chaotics of Postmodern American Fiction* (Tuscaloosa: University of Alabama Press, 2002), pp. 54–74.
62. Irigaray, *This Sex Which Is Not One*, pp. 106–7; author's emphasis.
63. Serres, *The Birth*, p. 6.
64. Ibid. p. 130.
65. Ibid. p. 77.
66. Deleuze, *Logic*, pp. 306–7.
67. Serres, *The Birth*, p. 164.
68. Ibid.
69. Naimou, '"Death-in-Life": Conflation, Decolonization, and the Zombie in *Empire of the Senseless*', pp. 143–4.
70. Friedman, 'A Conversation with Kathy Acker', p. 17.
71. Yuknavitch, *Allegories*, p. 87.
72. Cited in Yuknavitch, *Allegories*, p. 84; author's emphasis.
73. Ehrenreich, 'Foreword', p. xiv.
74. Cited in Theweleit, *Male Fantasies: Volume 1*, p. 76.
75. Wilhelm von Oertzen, cited in Theweleit, p. 229.
76. Georg Heinrich Hartmann, cited in Theweleit, p. 229.
77. Walter Frank, cited in Theweleit, p. 229.
78. Franz Wiemers-Borchelshof, cited in Theweleit, p. 229.
79. Rudolf Mann, cited in Theweleit, p. 229.
80. Theweleit, p. 238.
81. Acker, *My Mother*, p. 7.
82. Theweleit, *Male Fantasies Volume. 1*, p. 238.
83. James, *The Black Jacobins*, p. xviii.
84. Ibid. p. xix; emphasis added.
85. Ibid.
86. Ibid.
87. Marx, *The Eighteenth Brumaire*, p. 9.
88. *Empire* borrows scenes and much of the plot from William Gibson's *Neuromancer* (1984). For a discussion, see Victoria de Zwaan, 'Rethinking the Slipstream: Kathy Acker Reads *Neuromancer*', *Science Fiction Studies* 24.3 (November 1997), pp. 459–70.
89. Evocative of Deleuze's well-known notion of lines of flight, the 'witch's broom' imagery is summoned by Deleuze with reference to the experience of reading Spinoza; see Deleuze and Parnet, *Dialogues*, p. 15.
90. Marshall, *Demanding*, p. 3.
91. Alex Farquharson, 'Aquatopia: The Imaginary of the Ocean Deep', in Alex Farquharson and Martin Clark (eds), *Aquatopia: The Imaginary of the Ocean Deep* (Nottingham: Nottingham Contemporary, 2013), p. 10.

92. Serres, *Genesis*, p. 73.
93. Ibid. p. 120.
94. de Balzac, *Gillette or the Unknown Masterpiece*, p. 30.
95. Ibid. p. 30.
96. Assad, *Reading*, p. 36.
97. Acker, *Pussy*, p. 123.
98. Serres, *Genesis*, p. 7.
99. Toda et al., 'Formant-cavity affiliation in sibilant fricatives', p. 343.
100. Ibid. p. 344.

Chapter 5

Searching for the Subject: Rimbaud and the Paris Commune in *In Memoriam to Identity*

In our examination of *Empire*, we have seen how Acker and the Situationists utilised the figures of topology and turbulence as operators of change, which, in conjunction with the fluid and the feminine, allowed for the transformative energy of past insurrection to flow into the present. We also saw that for Acker the event is not a realisation of the political goal of emancipation in itself, but rather a chance of achieving that goal. If *Empire* projects us back to the event, that fragile chaotic moment of opening the realm of possibility and beginning anew, in *In Memoriam to Identity* (1990)[1] she insists on the role of individual commitment in realising and sustaining evental promise. She calls, implicitly, for a responsible subjectivity engaged in the hard, unpopular work which transposes the truth of the past event into a positive project – of restructuring society while remaining faithful to emancipatory ideals. As we will see, this is proposed at a time when traces of the past event have been obliterated and the prospects of a new event are few and far between. Existential concepts, such as responsibility, anxiety, passion, truth, commitment and engagement, are for Acker inextricably linked with the articulation of pre- and post-evental subjectivity. Embarking on a truth-procedure becomes in her work an opportunity for individuals to take responsibility for constructing a meaningful existence, allowing them to participate in collective action and the shaping of the world.

In Memoriam overlays the disenchanted years following the crushing of the Paris Commune in 1871 – an event forgotten by the official discourse of the Right, and registered in the Left as one of the most potent experiments in liberal democracy in Western history – onto 1980s America, and onto England's dwelling in the non-evental situation, where the naturalisation of capitalist ideology and the equation of democracy with the free market prevents the genesis of alternatives. The setting is the post-revolutionary landscape of *Empire*: that world where 'nothing ever changes', a universe of multinationals 'where there are no more decisions' (*ES*, 126). The late 1980s of *In Memoriam* amount to what Marcuse has described as the one-dimensional reality of '[a] comfortable, smooth, reasonable, democratic unfreedom'.[2] In a striking correspondence with the geographical and mobile orientation of Arthur Rimbaud's volumes of poetry *Season in Hell* (1873) and *Illuminations* (1886) (key influences on *In Memoriam* alongside William Faulkner's novels), the organising trope in the novel is that of a journey. There are departures, arrivals, wanderings and returns, stoppages and connections, passages, trains and 'airplanes', flight and stasis, transience and vagrancy, speed and slowness, roads and junctions, decision and indecision. The metaphors of movement that populate the novel, as demonstrated in this chapter, point to Acker's articulation of 'subject destinations' in response to the eventual truth. In the world of fixity and defined identity, Acker grants us the possibilities of travel and decision-making.

Democratic 'unfreedom' in an atonal world

In 1980s England, 'when Thatcherism was doing very well, and it was very trendy to be a yuppie, and all the punks were now wearing suits', Acker felt that 'history was disappearing'.[3] The revolutionary activism of 1968 was deep below ground; the contemporary situation unbearably stable, devoid of events, causing what Adrian Johnston calls a 'non-eventual claustrophobia'[4] – a new anxiety befalling disoriented and alienated individuals in a world highly resistant to change, where the neoliberal consensus dams up escape routes. Despite the illusion of constant change and novelty in liberal democracy, nothing happens, nothing changes, and there is nothing for individuals to decide, as the limits of their existence have been established and managed. In the passage below, the central character R ('R' for *Rimbaud*), articulates the overwhelming mood of reaction that permeates *In Memoriam*:

> In the time of good-for-nothings, bums, liberty will triumph. R said. Paris has been the seedbed for the intellectual and revolutionary forces which're capable of dragging people up out of the mire into which

what has seemed to be an implacable destiny has thrown them. At this moment liberals think bums should be saved and made into yuppies. Like themselves. (*MI*, 7)

This is the world which Badiou describes as atonal, 'devoid of points' (*LW*, 420). Badiou defines 'points' as operators which help reduce the chaotic complexity of empirical impurity of the world into binary decisions undertaken by the eventual subject, made to affirm fidelity to the eventual truth. Eventual truth can be incorporated into the world by a series of the subject's decisions, simplified into either 'yes' or 'no' (*LW*, 427). A subject proceeds, point by point, without guarantee or causality, by 'the destinal possibility of a [new] world' (*LW*, 409). Badiou writes: 'A point, which dualizes the infinite, concentrates the appearing of a truth in a place of the world. Points deploy the topology of the appearing of the True' (*LW*, 409). A point thus spatially crystallises the infinite into a figure of choice and a decision, localising the truth and giving it 'the chance to appear in a world' (*LW*, 401). Points are therefore necessary requirements for leaping into a new subjective stage and making a cut in the given ontology. Badiou finds a literary example of atonality in Julien Gracq's novel *Opposing the Shore* (1951):

> no decision seems to be on the order of the day; the coastal garrisons, embodied by captain Marino, no longer experience any kind of expectation, only a melancholic activity of the spirit, a kind of subtle and voluptuous renunciation. In such a context, as the young Aldo finds out for himself, to say 'yes' or 'no' is meaningless. All is torpor and flight of meaning. (*LW*, 408)

The atonal world can thus be described as a 'pointless', homogeneous existence devoid of figures of decision and responsibility. Badiou identifies atonality as representative of democratic materialism, where there is no truth but only 'bodies and languages' (*LW*, 420) and 'the banality of exchanges' (*LW*, 422). The consequence of this is that the apparent complexity of the world becomes an excuse for contemporary capitalist democracy's management of statistical bodies. No longer seen as capable of active citizenship other than voting, people are reduced to numbers and biological beings.

In *In Memoriam*, democracy degenerates into an ally of capitalism and what comes with it: privatisation, corporatism, exploitation, domination, the loss of history and memory, fragmentation of society, and existential choices reduced to commercial ones. In this atonal world, all experience is mediated through economics: 'But this world is decaying because nothing, like the words *I love you*, means anything and anything means nothing, everything's always about money' (*MI*, 112; author's emphasis). In the section 'Loss of something like memory', the narrator describes the seemingly infinite gradation of choices available in a sex club, suggesting that just as the sex industry represents a reduction of humanity to an unending exploration of carnal enjoyment, so does an apparently tolerant and all-inclusive democracy reduce humanity to bodies: 'The magazines were arranged in categories of kinds of sexual activity. It's possible to name everything and to destroy the world. [. . .] The machines showed anything, any choice in a democracy, from lez sex to pig fucking (humans)' (*MI*, 123). In this quintessentially atonal world, choice and truth are clearly foreclosed. There appear to be no genuine 'points' but only monetary decisions, as the conversation between the two protagonists, Airplane and Capitol's married companion, Harry, exemplifies:

> 'I'm either going to buy a co-op development for my wife and son which will take all my money or I'm going to get my own room.'
>   Airplane: 'Said, that's some choice.[']
>   'Do you know anything about real estate? Do you want to get into real estate?[']
>   'My wife wants."
>   Airplane: "I asked why.[']
>   'Money.' (*MI*, 251)

The English, in particular, appear to the outsider (whose conclusions may be identified with Acker's) as lacking historical and political consciousness: 'England is worse than America cause the people in England who are oppressed don't know they're oppressed. If there's no memory, is there anything?' (*MI*, 200). Social engagement in this highly hierarchised class society, meanwhile, is criticised for becoming perverted into a quest for social mobility underpinned by selfish motivations: 'a populist movement is one in which the members of a poorer class defy their limits and climb into the class above them' (*MI*, 200). Revolution, rather than signifying the possibility of new forms of relationships and behaviour, again reveals only a desire for power. The result is a post-revolutionary body that mirrors the despotic and bureaucratic government that it previously opposed: 'they've internalized their oppression for so long that the only revolution they can conceive is to become their oppressors' (*MI*, 200).

Badiou's juxtaposition of the 'atonal' (pointless) and 'tense' world (full of points or decisions) has its beginnings in Sartre. As Sartre writes in *Being and Nothingness* (1943), 'I am nothing but the project of myself beyond a determined situation, and this project pre-outlines me in terms of the concrete situation as in addition it illuminates the situation in terms of my choice.'[5] Badiou's subject is derived from Sartre's notion of subjectivity where freedom forms itself from nothingness (or the void) and is outside of social justification. Critics agree that Badiou remains faithful to Sartre as 'a philosopher of decision, and of freedom as decision',[6] but note that Badiou significantly departs from him by rejecting the subject's reliance on 'for-itself' as the ontological ground for change and free action. For Badiou, 'the individual is not sufficient in itself to produce radical change, but requires something in excess of itself and the current situation'[7] – the event. Contrary to Sartre, Badiou separates the subject from any foundational role and breaks the link with the pre-evental individual, as the subject's emergence necessarily begins with an event in politics, science, art or love. The dependence of the subject on the event allows Badiou to develop a positive vision of revolt and collective action, in contrast to Sartre's pessimistic and passive formulations.[8] This theoretical intervention continues with Badiou's critique of Sartre's notion of a group of subjects (a fusion of individuals who can disperse at any moment): for Badiou, 'Political action can only be sustained if the group itself is the subject.'[9] As Christopher Norris writes, Badiou's collective includes:

> not only those comparatively numerous multiples that constitute a social or political class, group, faction, movement or tendency but also the couple that typically forms the erotic or love relationship, and even – insofar as they must figure in any adequate account of these matters – the singular individual (whether scientist, artist, political activist or lover) whose very singularity [. . .] presents a powerful challenge to received modes of thought, concepts of order, or collective representations.[10]

For Badiou, an event offsets a series of points, allowing individuals to make responsible use of their freedom and thereby go beyond mere survival to become a subject of truth. However, for both Badiou and Sartre, one can choose *not* to go through the point (where not deciding is still a decision), which would mean a betrayal (*LW*, 400).

An interruption of the event produces a specific event-orientated anxiety which forces the subject to take a standpoint. In Badiou's typology, there are four major destinations of the subject in response

to an event: first, a *faithful* subject who, following a 'hysterical' affirmation of the event, 'makes truths appear in a world' (*LW*, 46) and
is in tension with, second, the *reactionary* subject, who is characterised, in the words of Peter Hallward, by the 'belief that the revolution was pointless or that their once consuming love was in fact an
illusion'.[11] Reactionary figures are 'unable or willing to distinguish
truth from matters of opinion'.[12] Third, there is the *obscure* subject,
who 'devalues an ongoing [. . .] fidelity in favor of a rigid conformity to the absolute past of an allegedly original event',[13] examples
of which include possessive love, iconoclasm, religious fundamentalism, Stalinism and resistance to scientific discovery. Badiou also
proposes a fourth subject, the figure of *resurrection*, through whom
the obliterated traces of the event are reactivated. All these subjective positions respond to an anxiety associated with the instability
of the event, namely, towards its uncertain status as 'the undecidable' in the situation, and its truth being in excess of the status quo.
In Badiou's earlier work, *Theory of the Subject* (1982), the concept
of anxiety is already linked to courage, and transplanted to his later
considerations of the event, where anxiety is an affect accompany-
ing the initial disturbance of the event. If followed with courage,
it can be utilised, as Johnston puts it, 'into a deployable program
of sustained inquiring and forcing (i.e., an enduring event-subject-
truth constellation)'.[14]

Now, the questions arise, what subjective positions are there in an
atonal regime, which produces an anxiety different from that which
arises as a shock to the event? And, as Badiou has asked elsewhere,
'Is there a place, in a disoriented world, for a new style of heroism?'[15]
Johnston reminds us that Badiou categorically contrasts an immortal
evental subjectivity with 'the living death of non-evental individuality'. This means that Badiou does not theorise the gap between
these positions and thus does not provide us with models of being
in atonal reality.[16] It is a widespread criticism of Badiou that he does
not assign individuals an agency prior to the event, thereby implying
that when events are forgotten human beings are merely passive. In
Acker's world they become yuppies, puppets or even zombies, as this
passage from *My Mother: Demonology* illustrates:

> It was the days of ghosts. Still is. Not the death, but the actual for-
> getting [. . .] of all those who control and those and that which can
> be controlled. Since an emotion's an announcement of value, in this
> society of the death (of values) emotions moved like zombies through
> humans.[17]

In defence of Badiou, it should be noted that he postulates that we should be faithful to past events as an ethical programme for the non-eventual present, and, as we have seen, this is a project Acker undertakes explicitly. But it is also possible to tease out subjective agency where Badiou signals that atonality can itself be an ideological construct which obscures genuine existential choices:

> Under the cover of a programme of familial happiness devoid of history, of unreserved consumption and easy-listening euthanasia, it [the declaration of atonality] may mask – or even fight against – those tensions that reveal, within appearing, innumerable points worthy of being held to. (*LW*, 422)

As Johnston has pointed out, approaching atonality as an ideological depiction of reality introduces the need for a new type of bravery other than that which is required of a post-eventual subject. This bravery, extrapolating from Badiou, is predicated upon the belief 'that true points exist in one's seemingly point-less pre-eventual world'.[18] In *Theory of the Subject*, Badiou already signals that 'All courage amounts to passing through there where previously it was not visible that anyone could find a passage.'[19] But his ethics does not consider how individuals can approach the task of distilling points that will allow them to be incorporated into the true – thus to become a subject – or how to distinguish them from banal decisions.

Chapter 1 has already emphasised that literature theorises 'the remainder' and the everyday better than eventual philosophy. We saw how Acker recommends that we fashion ourselves as classical Cynics, which is one way of resisting cynical rationality and overcoming Thermidorian disenchantment with politics. A Cynical stance is, of course, an existential decision: a militant way of being in the world. The problems of modern cynicism resurface in *In Memoriam*, together with Don Quixote's unfulfilled quest for love. Consider, for instance, the following conversation between R (Rimbaud) and a religious African guru:

> 'There's no such thing as a soul,' the African said.
> R replied, 'I'm sick of Baudrillard. The intellectual side of American postcapitalism. Cynicism. You're too intelligent to be a cynic.[']
> 'As for religion: evangelists only want money. For people who have money, money's power. There's nothing else. In this society. This society isn't France; it's America.[']

'Like religion, your cynicism's a hype. The assumption that every-thing including the soul is shit hides the real nexus of political power. Hurt me, baby. Show me what love is. ['] (*MI*, 6)

In order to account for Acker's search for the subject, we need to make Badiou's definition more inclusive, by extending it to pre-even-tal subjective agency that searches for truths. In *In Memoriam* Acker is painstakingly distilling areas of tonality where atonality prevails. In a world where freedom of choice has been reduced to commercial freedom, her characters are anxious for genuine choices and new kinds of heroism. In this journey, rather than telling us where to go, she makes it apparent that choices are available and we should not give up on searching for truths.

Search for the subject

When *In Memoriam* invokes Rimbaud's well-known formulations, 'To be a poet is to wake inside someone else's skin' (*MI*, 23) and 'I am an *other*' (*MI*, 226; author's emphasis), or when the narrator in *Don Quixote* proclaims 'I'll say it again: without I's, the I is noth-ing' (*DQ*, 101), they explicitly denounce the Cartesian notion of the subject – that rational, implicitly masculine, bourgeois notion of a self that is a unified, fixed, pre-constituted and autonomous foun-dation of consciousness. Elsewhere, Acker has also openly rejected the Hegelian totality of absolute knowledge, a self-aware and self-determining subject: 'If there is a self, it isn't Hegel's subject or the centralized phallic I/eye.'[20] She thus clearly positions herself with the postmodern project of doing away with classical humanism, taking seriously postmodern critique of binary thinking centred on divisions such as self and other, body and mind, a position that Foucault theo-rised so impactfully. His concern with the decentring and denaturali-sation of the subject led him to the formulation of a subject that is constituted by historical discourse:

One has to dispense with the constituent subject, to get rid of the subject itself, that's to say, to arrive at an analysis which can account for the constitution of the subject within a historical framework [. . .] without having to make reference to a subject which is either tran-scendental in relation to the field of events or runs in its empty same-ness throughout the course of history.[21]

Taking these terms to the extreme, Janey, the central protagonist in *Blood and Guts in High School* (1984), affirms her lack of essence or depth: 'Everything is on the surface. That everything is me: I'm just surface: surface is surface.'[22] Such a subject is a reflection of the external forces that constituted her and is thus no longer comprehended as a point of *departure*, namely, that autonomous transcendental self from whom existence originates, independent of history. But dispensing with the autonomous ego altogether introduces serious problems of agency, freedom and responsibility, as it appears that the subject is, on the one hand, overdetermined by its social structuring and is therefore a victim of the system that produces it, and on the other, a non-subject that is so fluid, schizoid, multiple, fragmented and decentred that, having no points to hold on to, it becomes impossible to arrive at a subject position that would assert community and active citizenship. The schizoid subject thus might be seen as contributing to atonality instead of overcoming it. This makes it correlative to the processes of fragmentation and proliferation of 'truths' that are commonplace in a capitalist society.

Acker's protagonists reveal anxieties at being merely containers for discursive inscriptions. For instance, in *In Memoriam* R comes to realise that 'I'm no longer interested in being defined, positively and negatively, by a culture I think's sick' (*MI*, 24). Instead, he wants 'to escape this school and, axe in hand, to demolish FF [his teacher], the school, and his identity' (*MI*, 18). Later in the novel, anxiety begins to trouble a submissive abused female character named Airplane, whom Acker modelled on Temple Drake in Faulkner's *Sanctuary* (1931): 'I grew scared because I realized I was how someone had made me' (*MI*, 102). Don Quixote, in turn, laments the impossibility of heroism due to the lack of grounding: 'How can I say anything when I'm totally uncentralized' (*DQ*, 56).

It becomes apparent that Acker is looking for an open notion of the subject which, while remaining faithful to the poststructuralist disposal of a closed Cartesian ego, is more committed, responsible, self-willed, collective and active than the poststructuralist models would allow. Further, her questing heroes are undeniably driven by the pursuit of eternal values such as love, community and political emancipation, which suggests that their becoming a subject exceeds Sartrean 'being for-itself'. An exemplary case in point is Rimbaud's plea that love be reinvented. Don Quixote's desperate quest for love is another (Don Quixote reappears in *In Memoriam* within a section evocatively entitled 'In Search of Love'). Their respective ongoing pursuit of freedom for all reveals that universal truths, those 'wounds that don't heal when you touch them but grow' (*MI*, 264), define their being in the world. In this way, Acker gestures towards Badiou's model of a collective subject who cannot be justified by objective social circumstances, and has the freedom to invent itself by making decisions in relation to eternal values.

The comments Acker expressed during the interview by Andrea Juno throw these insights into sharp relief. Acker suggests that individuals can either choose the safe option of being determined by the social script, or be brave enough to risk investing faith in something which exceeds their social conditioning:

> I guess everybody makes a choice, somewhere down the line: that they're going to abide by society's rules and hide in their nice suburban house and do just what they're told and they're not going to step out of line [. . .]. My father made this type of decision; I saw him get a heart attack and suddenly he realized that he wasn't safe – he was about to die. He had done everything by the rules and it hadn't done him a goddam bit of good . . . he had *nothing* to hold on to. Because he didn't have any values – all his values were the values of society, they weren't his. [. . .]
>
> I think the other choice is: to find what your value is . . . to find who you are and [. . .] where your centers are [. . .]. People are searching for their centers [. . .] but really in a way it's a search for 'god.' And in this search – that's when someone starts being interesting, and stops being like jello. There are various ways of going about this search for 'god.'[23]

Choice, decision, the pursuit of extra-subjective values (here represented by the figure of 'god') and intra-subjective 'centers' are the subjective attributes that complicate the reception of Acker's articulation of agency as unambiguously poststructuralist. Certainly, on many occasions Acker identified herself with the poststructural project and its key theorists. But she also reveals an appeal to a certain humanism which needs to be accounted for. In the same interview, she speaks of her search 'for a society that allows us *the fullness of what it is to be human*'.[24] This is, however, neither the centralised, rational, inner-directed, fixed bourgeois ego, nor quite the fully-fledged Sartrean self-sufficient subject – that locus of individual agency, rights, autonomy, authenticity and freedom. She complains that contemporary society misplaces the source of meaningful existence in the individual alone, and insists that the search be 'both individual and collective at the same time'.[25] The desired scenario would resemble 'a rite of passage', which she understands as 'a real change; you go through intense trauma or intense modification', not experienced on just an individual level, but also '*communally*'.[26] Individuals would be collectively transformed through a collective experience whose consequences, leaving a permanent trauma or wound, cannot be simply shrugged off or left behind. It is an invitation to reconfigure one's position in the world, offering a 'way of going from one stage in life to another'.[27]

To examine Acker's attempt to go beyond both orthodoxies – the poststructuralist and liberal-humanist one – let us adapt Badiou's model of the militant subject. To reiterate, Badiou's notion of the subject resides in 'the possibility for an individual, defined as a mere human animal, and clearly distinct from any Subject, to decide to become part of a political truth procedure [. . .] This is the moment when an individual declares that he or she can go beyond the bounds (of selfishness, competition, finitude . . .) set by individualism.'[28] By allowing the truth to 'take them over', individuals exercise their freedom. This freedom involves commitment and responsibility, as well as 'inventiveness, intelligence, creativity or strength of political purpose'.[29] Rather than being a point of departure, a subject is what we search for: as Badiou writes, 'we can only *arrive* at the subject': 'It must be found'.[30]

Acker's search for a subject runs across her work. *Burning Bombing* celebrates schizo-formations connected and overlapping with the world. The *Portrait of an Eye* trilogy compellingly articulates political subjectivity as steeped in animality and affirmed through radical martyrdom and sacrifice. *Empire*, meanwhile, marks a shift from deconstruction – a major strategy up to *Don Quixote* – to construction. With this move, her characters have acquired a new depth. As Acker put it: 'What I particularly like about *Empire of the Senseless* is [that] the characters are alive. For instance, in *Blood and Guts*, Janey Smith was a more cardboard figure. But I could sit down and have a meal with Abhor.'[31] But it is *In Memoriam* that offers the most sustained elaboration of the ways of becoming 'fully human'. In an interview with Larry McCaffery, Acker reveals *In Memoriam* to be 'a book of several mirrors all reflecting this basic myth of romantic love'.[32] The mirrors include the Rimbaud–Verlaine affair, and the relationships that run parallel with it: a Japanese story about Uneme and Tomomori; the myth of Jason and Medea; Airplane's relationship with the Rapist and the reporter; Capitol's with her father and brothers and later her husband. When prompted by McCaffery's impression that '*In Memoriam* feels different to [him] than anything else you've written – there's less irony', Acker admits:

> The fact that these different mirrors keep showing you the same thing made the range feel very constricted to me. It is also less theoretical than any of my last few books, and it's got a narrower range than I usually work with. It's more personal as well. [. . .] [T]he form of my recent books seems to be coming more organically in the sense that it's based on a theme, which I think is more clearly laid out in *In Memoriam* than elsewhere. It's not as if I'm basing my work on any kind of centralisation but that I'm not working out deconstruction any longer.[33]

Such a rigid organisation of the novel around relationships that reflect each other reinforces the claustrophobically constricted identities which the novel seeks to question. Although, as Acker suggests, *In Memoriam* is more personal and less theoretical, it is nevertheless relentlessly political and historical. Her protagonists persevere in their search for love and freedom, or are sedentary, pause their search and then re-enter it, or abandon it entirely – but Acker puts forward the view that all possibilities continue to exist.

Rimbaud's 'Genius'

Rimbaud's life and poetry dominate the first part of *In Memoriam* and are interwoven into the latter parts which draw on Faulkner. Acker rewrites Rimbaud's miserable childhood in Charleville-Mézières, followed by his turbulent relationship with the married poet Paul Verlaine, who had invited him to Paris and into his life in 1871. The appropriated material includes fragments of Rimbaud's *Season in Hell*, written following the affair, and also her 'mistranslations' of *Illuminations*, a collection of poems often read as his bitter reaction to the failure of the Commune.

The choice of Rimbaud is far from random, given his pioneering position in the literary avant-garde. Acker writes: 'I very much hope I do enough significant work that I can someday be seen as belonging to that lineage.'[34] She regards him as a fellow traveller: 'Rimbaud wanted to live completely out on the edge where he could investigate perception and how the body worked.'[35] As she told McCaffery:

> [W]hen I started the Rimbaud I was trying to recover my own child-hood. Rimbaud had been important to me when I started out writing in the late sixties, and at a certain point I wanted to remember why because I'd forgotten. About the time that *Empire* came out, watching several programs about the European hippie scene that was happening in England and France in '68 made me start thinking again about those times. One of the programs showed how there was this huge outcry in the English press about how much they hated that kind of stuff, how they really loved Thatcherism (this is when Thatcherism was doing very well, and it was trendy to be a yuppie, and all the punks were now wearing suits, and whatever). Then when *Empire* came out, everyone in England hated it because they thought it was preaching hippie politics. That's when I started wanting to remember why Rimbaud had meant a lot to us. I felt I needed to go over this material again, so I could remember where I came from. Because when I saw all this '68 stuff I was feeling like history was disappearing. [. . .] because if we don't have history [. . .] [w]e're not going to have models or ranges of possibility.[36]

Acker thus wants to use Rimbaud as a vehicle through which to come into contact both with the repressed history of 1968 and with the lost potentiality of childhood. The two clearly merge into one project of the recovery of past potentials for a political purpose. In her work there is little distance between personal and political content, and *In Memoriam* is no different: the contemplation on childhood becomes here an arena for debating crucial decisions about how to live one's life as a political subject. The fact that the narrative focuses on three adolescent characters – Rimbaud, Airplane and Capitol – is indicative of this heightened focus on subjective development.

To help us situate Rimbaud's role as a medium, let us turn to his prose poem 'Genius' ('Génie') from *Illuminations*. In *In Memoriam* we can identify entire passages of Rimbaud incorporated and (mis)trans-lated into her American prose, often with significant modifications. In her depiction of the submissive character Airplane, whose identity seems overdetermined by patriarchal oppression, Acker reverses the open notion of subjectivity that we find in 'Genius'. Airplane points to an apparently unchangeable, fixed state of identity by declaring:

'Identity must be a house into which you can enter, lock the door, shut the windows forever against all storms' (*MI*, 118). This imposes a shutting down of potentials signalled in the opening lines of 'Genius'. Rimbaud evokes a supplementary entity – 'genius' – referred to as 'he', a magus who transcends the safe confines of a stable identity:

> He's feelings and he's now, because he's held open house for the heady blizzards of winter as well as summer-time's easy rap-sessions – he's unpolluted our food and drink – he's the magus of running away and the non-quite human bliss of standing still. He's feelings and the future, the heart and energy passing overhead between the storms and the streamers of ecstasy, as we stand put in our boredoms and rages.[37]

Airplane's description of identity as a claustrophobic space denotes the individual who retreats into the safety of the known. Rimbaud's figure of genius, by contrast, represents a force through which an individual can harbour the possibility of transformation. For Badiou, Rimbaud's 'Génie' articulates 'the breath and movement' of 'pure presence'.[38] We can say that Acker wished not only to evoke the poem 'Genius' but also to summon Rimbaud himself as a genius to serve as a medium to open up time, history and self.

Rimbaud's genius played an inspirational role in the 1968 events. He was extensively mythologised and idolised by generations of artists and young people who shared his hatred of authority and irritation with bourgeois platitudes. Rimbaud's persona and poetry is often viewed in conjunction with the Paris Commune, the event Kristin Ross considers to be 'the moment in the history of Western society that came closest to a dismantling of the state apparatus'.[39] Rimbaud transmitted the Commune's revolutionary energy, and it was not unusual to view May 1968 in symmetry with the events of May 1871. Lines from Rimbaud's poems and the Commune's slogans appeared on the streets of 1968 Paris, with the Situationists reinterpreting the 1871 insurrection as 'the biggest festival of the nineteenth century', and 'a positive experiment whose whole truth has yet to be rediscovered and fulfilled'.[40] Acker was fascinated by the intensive tonality of French revolutionary history: 'The French have a poetical, frivolous streak. Gems of defiance have blossomed in the French' (*MI*, 19).

In her essay 'Proposition One', Rimbaud is a shining model of a politically committed poet. His work collapses social distinctions, including those between artists and workers, men and women, poetry and prose, body and mind. Rimbaud, Baudelaire and Artaud are exemplary in that 'they viewed their writing – every aspect, content and structure, because their very lives, their life-decisions – as politically defined'.[41] Acker's use of Rimbaud – as an operator of change, a connector of art with life, a medium through which the revolutionary past events are transmitted – corresponds with Ross's positive appraisal of his relationship with the 1871 insurrection. By drawing attention to the linguistic density and complexity of his poetry she has dispelled the critical reception of Rimbaud as 'an immature or adolescent taste'. Rather, his poetic interventions, Ross insists, should be viewed 'an agent as well as an effect of cultural and political change'.[42]

Rimbaud was aware of the tragically short-lived insurrection of the Paris Commune and was anxious to relate its ideals to his poetic project. In Edmund White's account, when he heard about the uprising while still in Charleville, Rimbaud immediately identified with the crisis, enthusiastically exclaiming: 'That's it! Order has been banished.'[43] He was eager to leave his home town, refusing to return to school when it reopened after the Prussian occupation, and instead hoped to aid his country by being taken on as a Guard. It remains uncertain whether he actually joined up with the insurgents, yet he and Verlaine certainly associated themselves with the exiled Communards in London.[44] Poems such as 'Chant de guerre parisien' (1871), 'Paris se repeuple' (1871) and 'Les Mains de Jeanne-Marie' (1872) confirm that his heart was with the Commune.[45] For Ross, Rimbaud's chief legacy is an 'interpellation *across* generations, a kind of diachronic constellation or latent community' which calls forth a future crowd of followers.[46]

But Acker is also alert to elements of Rimbaud's work and life on which Ross is silent. Rimbaud abruptly turned away from his rebellious lifestyle, *voyance* and poetry, early on, renouncing his literary career at the age of nineteen. Furthermore, as Enid Sarkie has documented, the remainder of his life casts a shadow on the cult of Rimbaud.[47] Before his death at the age of thirty-seven, he went on an expedition to East Africa, becoming a gunrunner, and attempted careers as a slave trader and a construction foreman. Acker writes:

> I had originally set out to write the life of Rimbaud. But when I got to the end of the affair with Verlaine I thought, 'This guy became a fucking capitalist! He's like a yuppie, I can't do this, I'm bored out of my mind!' The more research I did about Rimbaud (and I did quite a lot), the more I realized I didn't want to write this anymore.[48]

The path of childhood

Rimbaud's well-known injunction that his works should be understood both 'literally and *dans tous les sens*' opens up two ways of gauging Rimbaud's presence in the novel. The first part of Rimbaud's call to be read literally invites us to make sense of Acker's linear representation of his life: that biographical story of progression from a runaway rebel poet, to his love affair with Verlaine followed by rejection, and to his renunciation of poetry. At this literal level, childhood is conceived in conventionally linear terms as the first irretrievable stage of one's life, succeeded by maturity and stabilisation. In contrast, the second part of the call, *dans tous les sens* – which Ross takes to mean 'in all directions, according to all five senses, according to all possible meanings'[49] – demands from us that we approach his childhood and poetry as a *becoming* – a directionless process never complete. This second plane of reading invites new routes and perceptions that are not restricted to the linear cause-and-effect sequence. The rush of ordering and progression is replaced with reflection and imagination, when Acker captures and freezes the journey at the moment of decision. In these interruptions of the 'actual' lifeline, we can discern glimpses of the unwritten tracks – roads forgotten, imaginary roads, or roads not taken. This level of becoming, or as Rimbaud describes it in 'The Impossible': 'that childhood life of mine, the open road in and out of season'[50] (which Rimbaud then renounces as stupidity), denotes a realm of revolutionary energy that is not strictly measurable; creativity; experimentation; an ongoing making of oneself; a never finished programme.

The story of Rimbaud's childhood, as detailed in the first part of the novel, interweaves his early years spent with his abusive mother and at school with the chaos of the Franco-Prussian war, onto which Acker overlays her contemporary Thatcherite reality: 'The yuppies are the Germans' (*MI*, 7). Together, these contexts create a network of oppression: by the family, institutions, military expansionism and neoliberalism. Their shared goal is the production of a servile subject. R realises that 'Our teachers are playing games with us, games that they love us, games that we need them, so that they can carve us up into lobotomies and servants to a lobotomised society. So that we'll learn to obey orders. They're German' (*MI*, 13). Similarly, in order to deter future public resistance, the German authorities (here denoting any governing body that Acker finds oppressive) adopt strategies to disallow individuals to think creatively and for themselves, and so 'To terminate this populist revolution before it starts, we must inalterably change their educational system. First, we'll close all the free schools whose lessons have turned lower- and lower-middle-class mongrels into poets, painters, and fashion designers. We only want laborers' (*MI*, 19).

The retelling of Rimbaud's childhood becomes a platform for voicing criticism on how it is not only the neoliberal culture but also certain theories that may be viewed as complicit in furthering passivity. For Acker, Baudrillard's apparent lack of clear political concern contributes to apathy (she claimed to be familiar with his works up until *America*). She elaborated on this point in her interview with Nicholas Zurbrugg:

> When he writes that 'there's no more value, there's only this black hole,' I find this denial almost a celebration of – if you want to call it that – the disappearance of value. I find this celebration very problematic because the way it's been interiorized in this culture, it becomes a celebration of consumerism and of the kind of culture we've got. And this I dislike greatly.[51]

In Memoriam distils this criticism into a poetic form. The verses evoke Baudrillard as an evil influencer, a promoter of harmful cynical ideology which suppresses agency, dreams and alternative values:

Satan Triple-Master – cynic, money-hungry, pupil of
Baudrillard –
Lulls and quiets my enchanted spirit.
My free will's rich metal has been vaporized
Into nothing by this modern chemist.
The Devil moves the strings that move me.
I find myself charmed by the most boring things [. . .] (*MI*, 22)

From this perspective, childhood is seen as a progressive internalisation of prevalent values and norms. Already in this early part of the novel, these processes are nevertheless undercut by personal anxiety, which allows for the possibilities of existential choices and agency to emerge: 'R would do anything to get away from school. Break the heart's dead ice. He knew that the habitual self had to be broken' (*MI*, 16). Acker's Rimbaud demonstrates an ability to transcend the external conditioning that has thus far defined his identity. When joining a gang proves to be a poor alternative, R 'wondered what he himself really wanted' (*MI*, 20) and realises that 'he wanted a new world. He had to escape' (*MI*, 21). Rather than being a passive recipient of a social imprint, Rimbaud wants to wrest control over his own making: 'I'm no longer interested in being defined, positively and negatively, by a culture I think's sick' (*MI*, 24). We soon learn that Rimbaud sets out to realise his subjectivity by pursuing the eternal truth – love.

The second part of the novel, entitled 'Easter', anticipates the understanding of childhood as a becoming. It begins with an epigraph:

> R:
>> Idle youth enslaved to everything
>> Let the time come when hearts feel love (*MI*, 26)

We are not far from Badiou here. 'Easter' suggests a subjective reactivation of a truth procedure, the arrival of a new time. As Badiou writes, 'every faithful subject can also reincorporate into the evental present the fragment of truth whose bygone present had sunk under the bar of occultation. It is this reincorporation that we call resurrection' (*LW*, 66). The implication of infinity resonates further in the belief held by a 'lost student' whom Acker conjures up from an unidentified Japanese story and has say: 'The universe is limitless; love is eternal; love conquers the world' (*MI*, 34). In her interview with McCaffery, Acker refers to Rimbaud's childhood as a 'season of paradise'.[52] Because the poet's biographical childhood was miserable, the paradisiacal dimension is bound up with the time he spent with Verlaine: 'Childhood for him *was* like being with Verlaine, a period of pure happiness.'[53] But McCaffery reminds her that his relationship with Verlaine cannot fully account for 'the underlying aesthetics of his world', because Rimbaud was concerned with childhood 'representing this moment of pure "connection" with the world' prior to meeting Verlaine.[54] Here, a crucial distinction between divergent attitudes to subjectivity arises. Whereas for Acker, Rimbaud's subjectivity is constituted by the sustained pursuit of the eternal truths of love and freedom, the Rimbaud invoked by McCaffery is redolent of the Deleuzian non-subject, who fully connects with the world and becomes it. Simon O'Sullivan contrasts the two positions:

> Whereas for Badiou the subject is that which goes beyond what we might call the animal state of our being in the world, for Deleuze it is precisely this animal state – or becoming with the world – that is foregrounded. This is a privileging of a certain horizontality (becoming-animal) as opposed to Badiou's verticality (becoming-subject).[55]

We should clarify that the Deleuzian approach never ceases to be relevant in the sense of dismantling a closed, centred self and promoting a life open to becoming. We have seen it realised with greatest intensity in *Burning Bombing*, and it underlies subjective fusions with the world across Acker's later works. This commitment is central to Rimbaud. As Ross has noted, 'There is no I-Rimbaud who suddenly hallucinates an identity with various marginal characters; instead there is something like a Rimbaud-subject who passes through a series of affective states.'[56] In Rimbaud's use of an absolute metaphor such as 'I am a boat', instead of 'I am like a boat', he goes beyond representing the world and becomes it.

But if Deleuze's non-human becomings presuppose ongoing divergence, decentralisation, differentiation and groundlessness, rather than liquefy or dissolve the subject, in *In Memoriam* Acker moves away from mere fusion and animality towards a subject grounded in truth, and so deploys 'vertical' categories such as belief, love, responsibility and decision. For this reason, the childhood of Acker's Rimbaud is specifically defined by his amorous encounter with Verlaine and also, I want to suggest, by the political event of the Paris Commune.

For Acker, the recovery of childhood is neither an individualistic nostalgic gesture of reconnecting with the wholesome classic self nor a total fusion with the world. Rather, it is a way of opening onto a subjectivity that constitutes itself both within the given world and in response to truths that are beyond ordinary perception. Hence her Rimbaud demands forcefully: 'Tell me, love, who I am! V, we must do whatever we must to together find out who we are. That's our human duty. It demands total responsibility' (*MI*, 40). Rimbaud and Verlaine believe that 'their love was eternal' and belonged to that 'part of that (unknown) region which words can't touch' (*MI*, 69). Thus childhood here takes us back to the realm of possibility, utopian longing and immediate experience, compelling us to make a radical choice: either we remain in the safety of the known, or embrace something that exceeds us. Acker's Rimbaud wishes to escape from prosaic reality, from 'that false self' of childhood which he calls a 'desert', to the magical dimension where he can be 'the child who believed in the season of love' (*MI*, 66). Though he is repeatedly twisted in the gap between the two universes:

'We don't need money cause our paradise'll happen as soon as we enter the magical world of childhood.' R knew this was shit. 'When our memories become actual, we'll be living in the world of childhood.' R knew his childhood had been shit because his parents had either deserted or hated him. (*MI*, 64)

Rimbaud's poem 'Alchemy of the Word' (where Rimbaud cites from his previous poetry), from his *Season in Hell*, becomes an occasion for Acker to explore the state of childhood with all senses, as the subjective expression of utopian dreaming. The famous passage where Rimbaud ascribes colours to vowels is inserted to underscore the idea of childhood as a space where language verges on being beyond representation:

> Language is alive in the land of childhood. Since language and the flesh are not separate here, language being real, every vowel has a colour. *A* is black; *E*, white; *I*, red; *O*, blue; *U*, green. The form and direction of each vowel is instinctive rhythm. Language is truly myth. All my senses touch words. Words touch senses. Language isn't only translation, for the word is blood. (*MI*, 89–90; author's emphasis)

Language itself is part of the experience, instead of being a mediator which reduces feeling. The subject is no longer a purely linguistic-discursive construct or place-holder onto which identity is inscribed. Instead, it opens an existential space where freedom, voice, agency and commitment can be exercised. Childhood here does not denote the irretrievable past. Rather, it is an expression of an 'experiment of having a human, an *honest*, relationship' (*MI*, 78; author's emphasis) – not only a romantic one, but the relationship of an individual with society and history. The return to childhood becomes a quest for truth, a search for lost treasure – a space where individuals can realise themselves both in love relationships and as political subjects.

Childhood becomes, figuratively speaking, a play area: a realm of unblocked experimentation in search of new forms of human relationships, and a chance to imagine social change anew. In *In Memoriam*, history, like Rimbaud's tale, is mediated through the trope of childhood and analogously lends itself to the double reading: literally and as a becoming. Translating another passage from Rimbaud's 'Alchemy of the world', Acker retains most of the original text, but inserts the phrase 'topological revolutions' and the line 'This was my childhood', thereby reinforcing her association of childhood with conjoined alternative histories and geographies:

> And I dreamed of the Crusades, voyages of discovery unknown to our history books, dreamed of nations who exist outside documentation, of suppressed religious wars, revolutions of this society, major shifts of race and actual masses even continents – topological revolutions: I have believed in every desire and myth.
> This was my childhood. (*MI*, 89)

The literal presentation of history, on the other hand, is saturated in historical specifics. At the novel's opening, the historical setting is France during the last moments of the Second Empire. The Empire had lasted twenty years, but towards the late 1860s its foundations were undermined by deteriorating economic conditions and increasing militancy among the working class, until it was brought to a sudden, violent collapse during the invasion by Prussia (1870–1). We are presented with a series of descriptions of war, contributing to what Rimbaud refers to as 'image[s] of actuality' (*MI*, 17). For example:

> It is January 1. The Germans have invaded Mézières, which is the town nearest Rossat School. [. . .] More German troops pierced French geography. There were more victims. Less talkative than their enemies, the Germans never announced their ferocious war plans. [. . .] All men, being men, are cruel and minimal; the Germans, being conscious of their cruelty, thus confident of their decisions and lack of decisions, were crueller. (*MI*, 16, 17)

In the wake of France's defeat, the Paris Commune emerged – a complex and compelling event, and a haunting presence in *In Memoriam*. The scenes of German oppression are contrasted with the growing atmosphere of patriotic unrest: 'Germs of defiance have blossomed in the French' (*MI*, 19). They coincide with Rimbaud's own progressing anxiety: 'Demons're rioting in my brains' (*MI*, 23); 'I'm waiting! I'm waiting for what I want!' (*MI*, 28). Moreover, Rimbaud's romantic relationship with Verlaine, far from being narrated in isolation, is steeped in a political reality, even reflecting it. It is therefore hardly surprising that Verlaine sets out to record the unfolding insurrection:

> V began writing his *History of the Commune* and contacted and recontacted certain proscribed Commune supporters: Jean-Baptiste Clément, Henri Jourde, Léopold Delisle, Arthur Ranc, Benjamin Gastineau, George Cavalier or 'Pipe-en-bois'. Politically excited he wrote his wife to send him his prior files on the Commune which were located in the unlocked drawer of his writing desk. (*MI*, 70)

How is the Commune remembered in *In Memoriam*? If read solely as part of literal-linear historical-biographical reality of the 'before' and 'after', namely from its early hatching to the final degradation, the Commune's 'truth' is reduced to its final outcome, which would suggest that the novel expresses pure negativity. But Acker's depiction of the revolution as subordinated to causal determination, finality and failure is consistently paired with her challenging of these schemata and her unflinching resolve to recover the neglected elements of genuine creation. The history of the Paris Commune the novel evokes is not only an established, linear story, from its spontaneous inception to its tragic end, but also a becoming that the official record fails to grasp. Conceived in these idealistic terms, both the Commune's forgotten experiment in democracy and Rimbaud and Verlaine's love belong to the realm of childhood.

From Rimbaud to Reagan

Let us first examine the grim vision of history as predetermined, cyclical and drained of novelty and creativity. In this dark vision, which *In Memoriam* addresses and relentlessly challenges, any attempt to establish genuine democracy inevitably gives way to Caesarism. The disappointment with the apparent futility of revolutionary endeavour is encapsulated in Rimbaud's poem 'Democracy', one of his *Illuminations*, which Acker incorporates into her novel. The poem has been read as Rimbaud's cryptically obscene reaction to the suppression of the Commune. What future does Rimbaud anticipate in the face of the shutting down of political possibilities?

'Toward that intolerable country
The banner floats along,
And the rattle of the drum is stifled
By our rough backcountry shouting . . .'

'In the metropolis we will feed
The most cynical whoring.
We will destroy all logical revolt.'

'On to the languid scented lands!
Let us implement industrial
And military exploitations.'
'Goodbye to all this, and never mind where.'
Conscripts of good intention,
We will have policies unnameable and animal.
Knowing nothing of science, depraved in our pleasures,
To hell with the world around us rolling . . .

'This is the real advance!
Forward . . .
March!'[57]

Like other poems in *Illuminations*, 'Democracy' conjures up distressing images of dystopian landscapes formed in the aftermath of revolutionary failure. In a mocking tone, parodying the speech of the bourgeoisie, Rimbaud describes the French middle class as destroying all 'logical revolt' and expresses his concern with their capitalist and imperialist expeditions, a characteristic feature of late nineteenth-century Western European modernity. For Kristin Ross, the poem describes an oppressive reality where the very term democracy 'is no longer being used to express the demands of the *peuple* in a national class struggle, but is rather being used to *justify* the colonial policies of the "civilised lands" in a struggle on an international scale between the West and the rest, the civilised and the noncivilized'.[58] In the novel, the political energy which enthused Verlaine into writing *History of the Commune* is clearly missing from 'this essay: "DEMOCRACY"' that Rimbaud is writing. Crucially, his 'Democracy' is introduced here not as a poem but as an essay. While a poetic form, at least, might intimate a potentially unknown side of reality, in the essay's reasoned linear argument the Commune is ultimately consigned to the unpromising category of failure.

Acker's Rimbaud and Verlaine may attempt to escape from the prosaic universe of Rimbaud's original, but we soon learn that this is in fact a conflict of wandering and return. At one point, the novel suggests that they are ready to escape the post-revolutionary wasteland. In Acker's rewriting of the first line of the original poem, the flag symbolising imperialist power is replaced with 'My and V's flag's for a dirty, sex-crazed countryside' (*MI*, 70). At the same time, the meaning of the following lines remains unaltered in her translation:

> In the center of our cities we feed the most cynical prostitution. And we'll annihilate any reasonable revolt! Forward – march! To the most decadent, sexually plagued countries – In the service of a really monstrous military industrial exploitation – (*MI*, 71)

There follows another promising affirmation of departure in favour of the unknown universe: 'So it's goodbye. Mum, childhood, the whole lot. It doesn't matter where I'm going. Maybe – where *we*'re going' (*MI*, 71; author's emphasis). Rimbaud and Acker discard traditional rationality: 'may the whole Western intellectual world go to hell' (*MI*, 71). Nevertheless, again, the brutal reality of 'Democracy' impinges on their flight: 'There's real progress for you. Forward, march!' (*MI*, 71). It thus becomes impossible to distinguish Verlaine and Rimbaud's flight into the unknown from the march of imperialists plotting the expansion of France. The poetic universe remains in conflict with the prosaic universe of decay and disappointment: 'Having recovered from the disease of heroism, not totally, we're living in a land we found. Our land isn't pure. Belgium stinks' (*MI*, 71).

One obvious reading of Acker's repetition of Rimbaud's well-known line 'we'll annihilate any reasonable revolt' (also translated by others as 'we will massacre/destroy all logical revolt'), might be that they coincide in their radical critique of exploitation and 'cynical whoring', and together lament the death of democracy in a Rancière-ian sense, namely, 'the capacity to do things'.[59] Yet because Acker fuses the dark universe of 'Democracy' with Rimbaud and Verlaine's plan of escape, we cannot distinguish the 'we' denoting the pair of lovers from the 'we' denoting the voice of those who suppress revolts. In his reading of 'Democracy', Rancière is similarly suspicious of this 'we' which for him can only denote the colonial armies of democracy, and with which he sees Rimbaud as complicit: 'we also hear in the background the royal "we," by which the poet makes himself too a killer of logical revolts, and puts an end to the insurrection of his poem'.[60] In Acker's narrative, this vision is confirmed when Rimbaud stops being a 'Génie' – a divine medium which assists in the passage from the prosaic to the extraordinary universe of salvation. Clearly, he becomes weary of the difficult relationship with Verlaine and gives up on the promise that the world could be otherwise:

> Come come come
> What I've been wanting
> In every bit of my flesh
> To happen.
>
> I've been so fucking patient
> That I've forgotten
> Reality [. . .] (MI, 91)

Acker's Rimbaud lapses into the inexorability of what is given: 'I've been returned to earth violently' (*MI*, 94). He is no longer committed to imagining things as they can be but 'to see[ing] what is' (*MI*, 95), announcing that 'In a Thatcherite society it's necessary to be absolutely modern' (*MI*, 95). Paris is now no longer a hotbed of revolutionary fervour but 'a city of money. [. . .] This city was the most bourgeois in Europe' (*MI*, 64). It is through Rimbaud's no longer being a 'Génie' that we begin to sense Reagan's looming presence in the novel. Acker uses 'R' throughout to refer to Rimbaud, but with the poet's declining revolutionary spirit and his subsequent careers as a capitalist and a slave trader, we might be inclined to read 'R' more as Reagan than Rimbaud. Rimbaud becoming Reagan marks the altered political direction of the country between the 1960s and the 1980s: 'Only poetry is rebellion and Rimbaud had gone, rebelled against his inheritance in order to make himself a businessman. He was still a poet. A dead poet' (*MI*, 183). This Rimbaud is close to Badiou's because he lacks the discipline and endurance required of a faithful subject. Badiou writes that 'Rimbaud's poetry is both completed by means of and brought to an end by impatience', and recommends that we distance ourselves from Rimbaud because in times like this, 'Life's polymorphous impatience is provisionally of no use to us.'[61] Also rejecting the impatient Rimbaud who in another poem decides that 'We can't take off', and returns to the pull of gravity, 'Back again to local roads',[62] Acker introduces her female protagonists, the first of which is the revealingly named 'Airplane'.

The prosaic universe in *In Memoriam*, as brutally outlined in Rimbaud's 'Democracy', is recognisably Spenglerian. The cult of money, military expansionism, Rimbaud's haste, his Faustian[63] ambition to possess all knowledge and his economic greed are representative of the Western world in decline as described by German historian Oswald Spengler, from whom Acker borrows an unreferenced passage cited below. In his two-volume historical treatise *The Decline of the West* (published in English in 1926 and 1928), Spengler prophesied the inevitable decline of Western European culture (to which he gave the ominous label 'Faustian'). He foretold the inexorable transition from the age of democracy to an age of corruption, dictatorships, Caesarism, and the reign of money, because 'through money, democracy becomes its own destroyer, after money has destroyed intellect'.[64]

In Spengler's essentially deterministic view of history, each culture has a circle of life, and like a biological organism passes through four seasons, or the stages of 'childhood, youth, manhood, and old age'.[65] Contemporary European culture, he maintains, is now at the stage of decline, experiencing its winter phase, approaching the end of its life. It will be succeeded by a new culture, born in its grave. Spengler identified possessive individualism; political, economic, intellectual, spiritual expansion; materialism; the popularity of recreational religions (which he distinguished from authentic religious vitality), and achievement beyond any cost to be at the heart of late Western culture. A Faustian man is unable to resist his imperialistic drive: 'The expansive tendency is a doom, something daemonic and immense, which grips, forces into service, and uses up the late mankind of the world-city stage, willy-nilly, aware or unaware.'[66]

In the passage Acker borrows from *The Decline of the West* we find a terrifying vision of how democracy becomes perverted in a greed-driven culture:

> This is the end of Democracy. If in the world of truths it is *proof* that decides all, in that of facts it is *success*. Success means that one being triumphs over the others. Life has won through, and the dreams of the world-improvers have turned out to be the tools of *master-natures*. In the late Democracy, *race* burst forth and either makes ideals its slaves or throws them scornfully into the pit. (*MI*, 119; author's emphasis)

The narrator, via Spengler, hereby criticises the cult of money and widespread corruption of social life at all levels. In the source text preceding this passage, Spengler talks about the dictatorship of the party leaders and the dictatorship of the Press: 'one whips their [the masses'] souls with articles, telegrams and pictures [. . .] until they *clamour* for weapons and force their leaders into a conflict to which they *willed* to be forced'.[67]

Despite Spengler's anti-egalitarian, anti-democratic views (which have always made him popular with the Right), his worldview struck a chord with many because he identified so powerfully a modern sense of alienation and impending apocalypse.[68] Critics have identified a residue of personal freedom in Spengler's thought, whereby although decline is inevitable and irreversible, 'the exact way in which the decline of the West will be actualised is subject to individual volition'.[69] However, this 'freedom' would be hardly satisfactory for Acker. Her work provides us with alternatives to his cyclical model of history and the view that people must reconcile themselves to historical destiny as any attempts to overcome their social-historical conditioning are futile. Accordingly, she argues for 'the emergence of radical otherness, immanent creation, nontrivial novelty' (*MI*, 52), which she saw in the example of the Paris Commune, to which we shall now turn.

The Commune as the lost treasure of the revolutionary tradition

The Paris Commune of 1871 refers to the brief insurrection by the people of Paris against the national government. Following France's humiliating defeat in the Franco-Prussian War (1870–1), the government attempted to restore order by commanding a mass disarmament of workers, which sparked off an angry reaction of 'frustrated patriotism'.[70] The government's plan to seize the guns and arrest the rebellious crowd was a failure as the soldiers fraternised with the crowd and soon arrested their own commander. Paris was in revolt.

But while demilitarisation was the igniting spark, the Parisians' rebellion was an effect of more complex and deep-rooted circumstances. These included dissatisfaction with the increased civil repression during the Second Empire, growing economic and political collapse, the concomitant rise of working-class militancy and the still inspirational memory of the preceding revolutions of 1789 and 1848. The Commune was born in the early hours of 18 March 1871, and proclaimed a political act on 28 March following the formation of a revolutionary government, the Central Committee of the National Guard, through which the Parisians administered their own city.

The Commune culminated in a festive destruction of private and political symbols, including the demolition of the Vendôme Column, one of the Commune's last acts. The Column, inaugurated in the first decade of the nineteenth century to glorify the military campaigns of Napoleon I's Grand Army, was toppled in a grand ceremony on 16 May 1871. It was an anti-military and anti-despotic gesture. The Communards condemned the column as 'a monument to barbarity, a symbol of brute force and false glory, an affirmation of militarism, a negation of international law, a permanent insult by the conqueror over the vanquished, a perpetual assault to one of the great principles of the French republic, fraternity'.[71] Among the Communards, the sight of the shattered remnants of the monument created euphoria. As an English observer wrote, 'The excitement was so intense that people moved about as if in a dream.'[72]

Such acts cannot solely be interpreted as the urban masses' 'frustrated patriotism' at the seemingly unpatriotic stance of bourgeois republicans. It is with this in mind that Ross considers the Commune as 'a primarily spatial event', namely, an attempt to break down social, political and gender hierarchies, rather than just a revolt against the repressive political regimes of the Second Empire. For

Ross, the Commune needs to be viewed as an 'attack on vertical-
ity' embodied in the attack on the Vendôme Column.[73] In his foreword to Ross's study, Terry Eagleton calls the Commune 'a peculiarly
political revolution': not so much a 'revolt [. . .] within the means of
production, rooted in factory soviets and a revolutionary working-
class party, as one within the means of life themselves'.[74]

What followed, however, was in terms of its human cost disastrous. The uprising was brutally put down at the end of May 1871 as
troops of the regular army stormed Paris and blasted the barricades,
slaughtering over 25,000 Parisians, whose martyrdom, as discussed
in Chapter 1, Acker commemorated in *Toulouse Lautrec*. Soon after
the Commune was suppressed, the French government attempted to
erase it from history. Numerous monuments and buildings destroyed
during the so-called 'Bloody Week', such as the Vendôme Column or
the Hôtel de Ville, were restored. Contemporary France also appears
to disavow the legacy of this revolutionary event. As Badiou put it
in 2003: '[T]he Paris Commune was recently removed from [French]
history syllabuses, in which, however, it had barely occupied a
place.'[75] In the discourse of the Right, the Commune has become
a mark for another revolutionary endpoint. Gluckstein notes that
the Commune was perceived as 'either inexplicable, a drunken orgy,
or a criminal conspiracy masterminded by Red Professor Marx and
the First International'.[76] David Harvey cites Pope Pius XI who, in
a similar tone, referred to the Communards as 'devils risen up from
hell bringing the fires of the inferno to the streets of Paris'.[77]

The Commune's anarchist character was also judged against the
standards of an ideological vision of revolt. It did not conform to the
scientific-socialist model according to which a revolution is 'planned,
prepared, and executed almost to cold scientific exactness by the professional revolutionaries'.[78] In the final chapter of *On Revolution*,
entitled 'The Revolutionary Tradition and Its Lost Treasure', Arendt
argues that post-revolutionary thought fails to remember and account
for the creative and constitutive elements of a genuine democracy
inherent in the uprisings such as the Paris Commune. Both Marx
and Lenin, she writes, were unprepared for the Parisian insurrection,
which they saw as contradicting their unilineal and progressive models of historical change, and undermining their predictions of a revolutionary subject: the industrialised proletariat (the Communards
consisted mostly of semi-skilled day labourers). Arendt laments that
revolutionary professionals, historians and political leaders dismiss
the original political organs that emerged spontaneously during revolution, such as the Parisian *communes* (or the organisation of the

workers into councils – *soviets* – in the Russian strikes of 1905) to be only temporary manifestations of civil unrest. But, as Arendt insists, the communes 'were spaces of freedom' intended to survive the revolution to become 'permanent organs of government' (*OR*, 256). The lost revolutionary treasure is thus 'the revolutionary creativity of the people' (*OR*, 249), 'a direct regeneration of democracy' (*OR*, 255), where the revolution involves not only 'a swift disintegration of the old power', but also 'the amazing formation of a new power structure which owed its existence to nothing but the organizational impulses of the people themselves' (*OR*, 249).

The democracy that emerged during the Commune shared little with either its perverted version in the Leninist-party state or with the contemporary devaluing of democracy in Western societies, where people's participation in politics tends to be reduced to numbers and voting. It sought to disestablish the centralised power which had defined the state – the revolution of 1789 notwithstanding – since Louis XIV.[79] In contrast to the inherited political system of autocratic rule over a passive population, during its short reign the Commune spontaneously created a political system based on the direct participation and equality of its citizens. For the first time in modern history, a mini-government was formed with a proletarian base, which defied imperialism and the bourgeoisie. Confronted with the insurrection and a governing body which did not confirm his predictions, Marx felt the need to reassess his view of history as an unstoppable, inevitable march towards capitalist centralisation. As Ross writes, 'When Marx takes the Commune seriously, he must confront the possibility of a multiplicity of roads replacing the unique Highway of History: he must give new significance to the decentralisation of socio-political power.'[80]

One of its democratic goals was the emancipation of women. This entailed dismantling the prejudices against unmarried women and the re-establishment of divorce. The reforms proposed by the Commune might even be deemed unrealistic today: an end to monotonous work, long hours and, sex discrimination and the realisation of equal pay.[81] The Commune nobly attempted to combat the terrible unemployment, hunger and deprivation created during the siege of the city by the Prussian army. A city official related the Commune's endeavours thus:

> During [the Commune's] short reign not a single man, woman, child or old person was hungry, or cold, or homeless. [. . .] It was amazing to see how with only tiny resources this government not only fought

a horrible war for two months but chased famine from the hearths of the huge population which had had no work for a year. That was one of the miracles of a true democracy.[82]

Indeed, the very name given to the uprising conveys its democratic essence. The noun *commune* refers to 'a parish or township' and the adjective *commune* means 'common, general, universal'.[83]

In summary, the democratic model embodied by the Commune had little in common with its contemporary equivalents. In fact, the ambitions of the Commune were closer to Rancière's understanding of true, not to say ideal, democracy, as opposed to its contemporary liberal, capitalist and representative mutations. For Rancière, genuine democracy is synonymous with politics, namely, it is based not on government, institutions or statistics, but on the highly active participation of political subjects. Badiou dismisses contemporary democracy as the handmaiden of international capitalism and expansionism, and castigates democratic elections, whereby people, voting reluctantly and disinterestedly, are reduced to statistics (which he calls 'the tyranny of number').[84]

Acker and Castoriadis on political creativity

Seen in this light, the Commune is no longer reduced to a teleological project designed by orthodox Marxism, or yet another failed revolt on the continuum of history as judged from the reactionary perspective, but is precisely what Arendt has referred to as the 'lost treasure' of the revolutionary tradition – that neglected imaginative and creative element of revolution, a glimpse of a new and different logic of social organisation, one which does not fall into traditional categories. This idea of a lost treasure ties in with my alignment of the event of the Commune with Acker's trope of childhood as something that has been lost in the process of symbolisation, suppressed by the logic of causal determination (one needs to grow up, one stage leads to another). The symbolic gesture of the Communards shooting at public clocks confirmed their will to do away with the notion of a linear, measured time that orders history and individual adult existence into a predetermined sequence. Driven by utopian aspirations, they contested the time which indicates the necessary end to the creative and playful stage, and a capitalist time which reduces life to work and leisure, where, to borrow Lefebvre's formulation, 'we work to earn our leisure, and leisure has only one meaning: to get away from work. A vicious circle.'[85]

In an attempt to explain why it failed, many accounts suggest that the Commune was immature – that it never stabilised itself. Henri Peyre's commentary is representative:

> [T]he Commune did not count, or produce, one powerful leader who might have guided it. It has been a spontaneous uprising, but without a revolutionary party behind it which might have given it a strategy, might have conceived an overall blueprint and have imposed its policy through a ruthless discipline. There was little method behind their fury, little clarity of purpose behind their idealism.[86]

This is an example of what the Greek philosopher Cornelius Castoriadis terms 'ensemblist-identary' logic, which comprehends all phenomena according to the 'inherited thought'. In inherited thought, Castoriadis writes, all events are subordinated under '[t]he schemata of causality, of finality or of logical consequence'.[87] In his explanation of the failure of the Commune, Peyre clearly draws on the 'inherited' model of revolution whereby one system of domination is replaced with another. His is a Saturnian model: 'All revolutionary movements, before the Commune and since, have thus had their factions and devoured their own children and, strangely enough, grown much stronger thereby.'[88] But this apparent weakness of the Commune – it not being able to grow up and become another power regime – is in fact its greatest strength. For Acker, the Commune figuratively belongs to the realm of childhood because it provided an alternative to the Oedipal recurrence, allowing children not to harden into powerful parents but engage in building alternative social relations. Accordingly, Ross has described the revolutionaries as adolescent in the fully positive meaning of the term: 'The Communards are "out of sync" with the timetable of the inexorable march of history. They are not the industrialised proletariat they are supposed to be. Like adolescents they are moving at once too fast in their unplanned seizure of power and too slowly.'[89]

In *In Memoriam*, Acker explicitly acknowledges the radical creativity and indeterminacy that so many have found in the Commune:

> Marxism is irrevocably tied to certain rationalist and positivist tenets of nineteenth-century thought. Mechanistic determinism lies at its heart. The same could be said of Freudianism. The problem now is that theory dependent on absolute models can't account for temporal

change. What is given in human history and through human history is not the determined sequence of the determined, but the emergence of radical otherness, immanent creation, nontrivial novelty. (*MI*, 52)

Acker thus clearly contests this logic in which subjectivity, human relations, society and history are thought within predetermined patterns. She challenges both the established ways of living where 'It's necessary to [. . .] obey historic rules' (*MI*, 67) and accepted beliefs such as 'History always repeats itself' (*MI*, 186, 187). The second part of the citation ('What is given . . .'), is her direct (and unreferenced) borrowing from *The Imaginary Institution of Society* (1975) by Castoriadis.[90]

Like Marcuse, Castoriadis participates in the elevation of the imaginary realm and the critique of the deterministic framework of traditional Marxism. Like Arendt (it is not uncommon to see them discussed together),[91] he negotiates participatory spaces of public democracy, utilising (but not idolising) classical Greek models as a continuous project for the realisation of society. Like Badiou, he frees historical events from the logic of causality, underscores the importance of the collective and relates ontology to set theory.[92] With late Foucault he shares an interest in parrhesia and isegoria (an equal right to parrhesia), while his notion of self-alteration and immanent creation can be seen to be akin to the system of thought found in Deleuze and Serres. Though far from exhaustive, this list of connections sketches a network of thought that has direct relevance to Acker's work. Instead of aligning herself with one theoretical influence, Acker draws on a plurality of intellectual idiom to collectively ponder what Arendt has described as 'the problem of the new': namely, an attempt to conceive of change that would not be a mere continuation of what existed before, only in a different form. Moreover, the theoretical fragmentation and plurality embedded in Acker's work, or the philosophical thought that her writing evokes (for example Badiou, whom Acker may never have read), underscore her view that theory is never finished, complete, exhaustive or fully inclusive. It reflects Castoriadis's understanding of theory as constantly productive and creative, as opposed to 'a code of lifeless prescriptions':[93] 'there can be no exhaustive theory of humanity and of history; it is provisional because praxis itself constantly gives rise to new knowledge'.[94]

But what is of more immediate interest to us is the element of creation and autonomy that Castoriadis ascribes to the subject, political practice and history. Acker no doubt would have welcomed Castoriadis's thought, because it offers an alternative to the inherited notions of subjectivity. Whereas the ideological subject has no freedom and surrenders to the power relations and institutions that shape it, the bourgeois humanist subject equates freedom with independence from others and from socio-historical conditioning. Castoriadis's proposition is that the subject does not deny its embeddedness in the socio-historical world, but is also not determined by it. What Acker shares with Castoriadis is thus a challenge to the political present. Together they call for a radical reinterpretation of history and historical actors as being capable of political innovation.

But how does one overcome determination? For Castoriadis, agency resides in the creative capacity in every individual and social body in the form of 'radical imagination'. Against the notion of the imaginary as the inferior opposite of reason, or as a mere reflection and imitation of what was already there, Castoriadis argues for the imaginary as a creative force:

> it has nothing to do with that which is presented as 'imaginary' by certain currents in psychoanalysis: namely, the 'specular' which is obviously only an image *of* and a reflected image, in other words a *reflection* [. . .] . The imaginary of which I am speaking is not an image *of*. It is the unceasing and essentially *undetermined* (socio-historical and physical) creation of figures/forms/images, on the basis of which alone there can never be a question *of* 'something'.[95]

Radical imagination is thus creative rather than simply reflective. It also involves active judgement and deliberation. A utopian vision, it is not sustained by Castoriadis's ultimate disenchantment with contemporary society, which he describes as conformist and homogeneous. 'The typical contemporary man', he writes, 'acts as if he were *submitting* to the society which [. . .] he is ever ready to blame all evils on.'[96] Castoriadis shares Marcuse's diagnosis of society as 'one-dimensional', confirming that the imagination of contemporary society has been colonised by capitalist rationality. He thus disempowers his own concept of radical imagination. Nevertheless, his ongoing criticism of the 'ensemblist-identary' logic, and his promotion of creativity, autonomy and participatory democracy, continues to nourish debates on the production of genuine novelty. Acker certainly shares her interest in the utopian dimension of imagination with Castoriadis, and like him she argues for the creative capacity on both a human and a collective level, of which art, the Commune and the fleeting romantic relationship of Rimbaud and Verlaine are the novel's most poignant examples.

The politics of decision

In *In Memoriam*, seemingly one-dimensional presentations of men, women, relationships, society and history, where the 'imaginary' only imitates what is given, are at the same time indissociable from the anxiety that underlies these depictions: despair is always coupled with hope and an availability of existential choice. Acker's characters are not puppets who uncritically enact predetermined scripts, but are shown as being anxious due to the claustrophobia of determination. Freedom is neither given nor unavailable to them but must be responsibly decided on and continuously re-made within their social conditioning. The narrative repeatedly reduces their universe to Badiouian points whereby the protagonists, including Rimbaud, Verlaine, Airplane, Capitol, Jason, Medea, Uneme, Tomomori, Don Quixote, Acker herself and by extension the reader, follow different subjective destinations. Acker's own persona should be included in this discussion, as the final section of the novel is recognisably autobiographical. In it, Acker gives an account of herself as a responsible and committed artistic subject for whom writing is freedom.

The narrator of *In Memoriam* poses a question that reduces the empirical atonality of the world into a simple duality of 'yes' or 'no':

> Do you prefer, do you think it is better to accept everything that you have been taught, that society has taught, to accept what is considered truth in the circle of your family, friends, and world and what, moreover, really comforts and seems proper? Or do you prefer to strike new paths, fighting the habitual, what goes against questioning? Do you prefer to experience the insecurity of independence and the frequent wavering of one's feelings and moral decisions, often having neither anyone to support you nor consolation, but only having this vision, this mental picture called 'truth'? In other words, are peace, rest, and pleasure all that you want? (*MI*, 48–9)

This binary simplification is reminiscent of what Badiou calls 'an existential densification', whereby the impurity of the world is reduced to a decision. If at the end of *Empire* Abhor lamented that 'there are no more decisions', in *In Memoriam* Acker is at great pains to show how atonality, which connotes conformism and cowardice, can be overcome.

In *In Memoriam*, Acker stages 'the theatre of points', to use Badiou's phrase (*LW*, 404). She borrows material from a variety of sources and brutally reduces it to construct a series of simple dualities, which, in turn, occasion a decision-making process. But unlike Badiou, who has reserved subjectivity for predominantly 'tensed', evental worlds where choices are given (as in, do I want to join the revolution or not?), she locates subjectivity as also lying in the militant work of destabilising the atonality which conceals genuine truth choices. Acker thus liquidates Badiou's solid oppositions between 'being' and 'event', atonal and tensed worlds, and allows truths to circulate in both universes at various levels of disclosure and concealment. Hence we can say that for Acker becoming a subject is a process where faithfulness to the truths of love and emancipation coincides with an ongoing search for them. The search, too, makes the subject.

Borrowing Rimbaud's famous call, 'Love has to be continually reinvented' (*MI*, 84), Acker asserts her persistent vocation for love as a truth whereby individuals go beyond themselves, and overcome their narcissism. In *In Praise of Love* (2009), Badiou subscribes to the same call for love's reinvention. He writes that contemporary Western society fears love as a truth procedure. People increasingly view love as a dangerous exposure, an unnecessary risk, and an obstacle to one's personal safety, emotional equilibrium and comfort. But love, writes Badiou, 'cannot be a defensive action to maintain the status quo. The world is full of new developments and love must also be something that innovates. Risk and adventure must be re-invented against safety and comfort.'[97] Acker conveys the urgency for the re-invention of love by presenting us with claustrophobic mirrors – 'all those reflections of different aspects of patriarchy'.[98] These relationships, as in the affair of Rimbaud and Verlaine, Uneme and Tomomori and Jason and Medea, are a mimetic reflection of that model. Acker interweaves the myth of Jason and Medea and the ancient Japanese story of Uneme and Tomomori with Rimbaud's biography, to probe the apparently unalterable cyclicity that their relationships represent. In these parallel stories, marriages are contractual, regulated risk-free arrangements established for status, stability and security. Men are individualistic, independent from others, interested only in pursuing their goals, whereas women are passive, dependent and submissive.

As Spencer Dew has asserted, Acker's Jason is 'an ego-driven, selfish, and uncompassionate figure, operating in a mode of ownership, conquest, and colonization'.[99] Acker relates Jason's conquests to a Thatcherite sensibility: his abandonment of Medea for another 'more convenient and beneficial woman', as Dew points out, is representative of the contemporary emphasis on individualism and self-interest over commitment and responsibility towards others.[100] The same can be said of Tomomori – a married man who, after having seduced Uneme, wants to dispose of her. Verlaine, having fallen in love with Rimbaud, a rebellious adolescent who urged him that 'together we can get to life; life is something other than shit' (*MI*, 28), is likewise disinclined to give up bourgeois comfort: 'V feared that all that he cared about, for his identity was socially predicated, true of all bourgeoisie, would be taken away from him' (*MI*, 30). Within this patriarchal-capitalist structure, Uneme 'loved and feared Tomomori' and left everything to follow him hoping that 'he wouldn't abandon her' (*MI*, 43). Airplane is told that 'Women are subservient,' and that 'Men torture women' (*MI*, 103). Capitol learns from her brother, Quentin, who has just graduated from Harvard, that 'Freud had said that all women are naturally masochists' (*MI*, 153). Medea hears from her husband Jason that 'all women want is security. As soon as a woman's secure, that is, married, she becomes celibate' (*MI*, 84). Airplane is told that 'When you finally want a man [. . .] you find out that you're worth nothing' (*MI*, 104). Capitol realises that 'All men want to do is own me and they don't want me to be me and do my work' (*MI*, 242). Rimbaud, in turn, observes that marriage and family are regulated comfort zones devoid of passion: 'Married people fuck each other out of boredom. They fuck other people out of boredom. They send their kids to school only because they think they should. They believe in God because they don't know who to believe in' (*MI*, 35).

The acknowledgement of the patriarchal-capitalist structure as solid and unalterably repeatable conveys the ultimately pessimistic message that there is no room for creation and novelty. Acker writes: 'If humans are inescapably subject to inscrutable yet inflexible natural and/or historical laws, utopianism is absurd' (*MI*, 27). However, she suggests that this is not the case and inexorably fights against these apparently unalterable categories to suggest that individuals are conditioned – as they are born into a socio-historical world – but not determined: they can exercise their freedom and agency by constantly looking for genuine choices and making responsible decisions, affirming and committing themselves to values which exceed them as individuals. Seeking out these truths and remaining faithful to them is rewarding because one becomes a subject which makes their own existence in a meaningful way, but it comes at the cost of effort, patience, incalculable risk, ongoing labour as well as being at odds with artificial values. Capitol realises that 'Something call it love has to force us to seek out value, a lack of meaninglessness, as anyone with no money knows' (*MI*, 230). The significance of decision-making in becoming a subject brings us back to Acker's 'theatre of points', where she reduces reality to radical choice. Badiou writes:

> In one way or another, one must go through the point. Of course, it is possible not to. One can, like the office clerk Bartleby in Melville's eponymous novella, 'prefer not to.' But then a truth will be sacrificed by its very subject. Betrayal. (*LW*, 400)

For Badiou, the betrayal of evental truth constitutes a kind of 'evil', when revolutionaries give in to the demands of self-interest and, confronted with the choice 'between human animal and subject', choose the former.[101] And so Acker reduces the multiple to two, where one alternative means 'an arrest, a reflux or even destruction' (*LW*, 400), and the other is a guise for truth which offsets 'the continuation in the world of the truth-process' (*LW*, 400). Embarking on a truth procedure is a risky endeavour which involves uncertainty and change, as Acker has Rimbaud say: 'Adventure is the state of living affairs and so is change' (*MI*, 57). Verlaine's comfortable existence is upset when Rimbaud forces him 'to choose between a boring (*boring* is *valueless*) existence as a father [. . .] and an unstable existence with a child who was half pure imaginative will and half tiger' (*MI*, 57; author's emphasis). Rimbaud confronts Verlaine: 'You want to return to your wife. So you have to make a decision whether you're going to stay with me or return to them' (*MI*, 90). Ultimately, Verlaine 'preferred odious bourgeois existence and identity in the bosom of the odious bourgeois family to reality, to chance, to the vulnerability of real identity, above all to the destiny that had been assigned to him: becoming a seer' (*MI*, 32). Tomomori's example also shows the evasion of commitment: 'Tomomori thought that she [Uneme] was more and more a nuisance. But he found this woman so beautiful that he wasn't able to give her up. Unable to decide between these two emotions, he disappeared' (*MI*, 44); 'Why had he taken her away with him when he knew that he didn't care about her? It wasn't that he hadn't cared about her. He had never taken responsibility for his actions' (*MI*, 54).

In an interview, Acker said that women fall into two groups in relation to deciding on one's existence. The first group of women – the majority –'have actually *given up* their creativity'.[102] The second group are women who 'are actively searching for who to be'.[103] Their subjectivity is conceived as an open project anchored in the vulnerable position that one is never complete: 'It's interesting when there's suffering there, and people are full of feeling, and they're full of life, and they're constantly making choices.'[104] In *In Memoriam*, Airplane and Capitol are becoming aware that their identity, rather than being final and complete, is an inherited model open to subversion and remaking. Capitol wants to challenge inherited deterministic models of identity, claiming that 'Women have always been taught to hate themselves. That's history. And they have to deny that by not allowing themselves to fuck around' (*MI*, 155). She tells her brother that 'People either do what they're told or they go outside the law, find something else, maybe themselves' (*MI*, 155). Airplane also takes note of the possibilities of subverting scripted gender roles when she states that 'We make ourselves up' (*MI*, 219), and affirms that 'I decided I was going to make my life' (*MI*, 251). In the narrative, women attempt to make themselves through embracing deviancy: by 'playing whore' and through masochism. As Airplane exclaims, 'just as I was learning about my body, I learned this kind of revolt' (*MI*, 107). Ultimately, however, Airplane's narrative is concluded with an acceptance of her scripted role as a victim in a relationship. Are genuine choices unavailable to women? Can Airplane, as her name might imply, rise above her social conditioning? Acker suggests that Rimbaud opening himself to all forms of alterity might not be applicable to women, because women are already 'other', constructed in relation to the male subject:

Rimbaud had said: 'I am an *other*.'
Airplane: 'But Rimbaud wasn't a woman. Perhaps there's no other to be and that's where I'm going.' (*MI*, 226; author's emphasis).

This chimes with Coleen Kennedy's comment that Acker's heroines are devoid of real choice:

Acker's characters are aware, even as girls, that they must choose between an illusion they only have partial access to and an objectification they cannot escape anyway. This explains why so many of Acker's characters remain, partly by choice, in abusive relationships.[105]

Airplane and Capitol repeatedly protest against the conceptualisation of female identity in terms of submission and victimhood, but it appears that, because they are denied the creativity available to men, their choices turn out to be non-choices as all alternatives seem to be complicit with the patriarchal script. As Airplane ponders: 'Love is free. She didn't know what love was. She would survive. [. . .] Perhaps it's men who dream of love and women who dream of survival' (*MI*, 115). Given this dilemma, many critics identify traces of agency in the way Acker's female characters subvert prescribed sexual roles by means of performative gestures such as parody and sexual self-knowledge. The notions of subversion, resistance and survival are weak categories of freedom because they are inevitably defined in relation to what is given, and therefore the dimension of novelty and creativity is diminished. However, in the final section of the novel, we learn that Capitol is also a writer and we can recognise parallels between her life and Acker's own. Although her characters fail in the search for love – when Harry rejects Capitol 'there is nothing to hold on to' (*MI*, 262) – Acker again dualises the universe, showing that there are still important points of meaning. This time, Acker turns us back to the important decisions that she articulated in her essay 'Dead Doll Prophecy' (discussed in the Introduction). Echoing this essay's argument, Capitol elaborates on her resolution to stay committed to her values and dreams of a better society, and to her writing method:

> The lawmakers of this world (lawmakers, judges, dealers) who were the rich sculptor demanded that Capitol not only destroy this doll, but also publicly apologize for using a rich famous person's work, for hating ownership, for finding postcapitalist and Newtonian identity a fraud, for all her years of not only publicly hating an ignorant therefore unjust society but also trying to make someone of herself. ('I am an *other*.') (*MI*, 261, author's emphasis)

Acker's decision to write the way she does is part of her larger ethos of artistic responsibility, summarised in the formula: 'Writing must be for and must be freedom.'[106]

Conclusion

Les Révoltes logiques ('logical revolts') was the name given to the research collective and journal (1975–81) of which Jacques Rancière was one of the leading members and contributors. The journal's title is a quotation from Rimbaud's 'Democracy'. Rancière explains that through this title the group wanted to assert their fidelity to the Commune, which they considered to be 'the very archetype of revolt'.[107]

Yet, significantly, the title excerpts 'logical revolts' from the full line from Rimbaud, 'We will destroy all logical revolt', and thereby 'twists', as Rancière's puts it, the original meaning. The intention, according to Rancière, was to rescue the Commune from the oppression it suffers in Rimbaud's poem, where it is massacred and subordinated to the category of failure while its egalitarian promise is ignored. This gesture was particularly important in the context of the despair surrounding the May 1968 events. The *Révoltes logiques* collective wanted to convey the message, as Oliver Davis summarises, that 'If revolts of the past could be recognized for their promise, then this would add historical depth to the political conviction that the things in the present could be otherwise.'[108]

The Commune, as it is encapsulated in Rimbaud's line, and as it is 'liberated' from that line, allows us to understand the ongoing juxtaposition of the two universes in Acker's work: the prosaic disenchanted reality of the given, and that world of suppressed evental promise. In the first, we have encountered the recurring problem with the passage from democracy to Caesarism, from the October Revolution to Stalin and from the Jacobins to Napoleon. The second concerns the passage from an ordinary individual to a subject of truth. Rather than falling into the extreme nihilism of the first world or the naive idealism of the second, Acker shows that subjects may be conditioned by the first but are not determined by it. As a responsible artist, she is a 'Génie' who connects her audience with events, mediates evental promise and salvages political and subjective creativity, urging her readers that they, unlike Rimbaud, continue deciding in favour of the second universe: 'Since all the rest is unknown, throw what is known away' (*MI*, 264).

Notes

1. Hereafter referred to in the text as *In Memoriam*.
2. Marcuse, *One-Dimensional Man*, p. 3.
3. Acker, 'The Path of Abjection,' p. 33.
4. Johnston, *Badiou*, p. 78.
5. Sartre, *Being*, p. 553.
6. Smith, 'Badiou and Sartre: Freedom, from Imagination to Chance', p. 203. See also Hallward, *Badiou*, p. xxxii.
7. Ibid. p. 203.
8. Badiou, *Pocket Pantheon*, pp. 18, 26–7.
9. Smith, 'Badiou and Sartre', p. 204.
10. Norris, *Badiou's Being and Event*, p. 28.

11. Hallward, *Badiou*, p. 146.
12. Ibid.
13. Ibid.
14. Johnston, *Badiou*, p. 77.
15. Cited in Johnston, *Badiou*, p. 78.
16. Johnston, *Badiou*, p. 78.
17. Acker, *My Mother*, p. 14.
18. Ibid. p. 80.
19. Badiou, *Theory of the Subject*, p. 294.
20. Acker, 'A Few Notes on Two of My Books', p. 33.
21. Foucault, *Power/Knowledge*, p. 117.
22. Acker, *Blood and Guts in High School,* in *Blood and Guts in High School Plus Two: Great Expectations,* and *My Death My Life by Pier Paolo Pasolini,* p. 97.
23. Juno, 'Kathy Acker', p. 181; author's emphasis.
24. Ibid. p. 184; author's emphasis.
25. Ibid. p. 185.
26. Ibid. p. 184; author's emphasis.
27. Ibid.
28. Badiou, 'The Idea of Communism', p. 3.
29. Norris, *Badiou's Being and Event*, p. 29.
30. Badiou, *Theory of the Subject*, pp. 278, 279; author's emphasis.
31. Friedman, 'A Conversation with Kathy Acker', p. 17.
32. Acker, 'The Path of Abjection', p. 30.
33. Ibid. p. 31.
34. McCaffery, 'An Interview with Kathy Acker', p. 92.
35. Acker, 'The Path of Abjection', p. 34.
36. Ibid. p. 33.
37. Rimbaud, 'Genius', in *A Season in Hell & Illuminations*, p. 161.
38. Badiou, 'Rimbaud's Method: Interruption', in *Conditions*, p. 72.
39. Ross, *The Emergence*, p. 70.
40. Debord et al., 'Theses on the Paris Commune', p. 398.
41. Acker, 'Proposition One', p. 42.
42. Ross, *The Emergence*, p. 27.
43. Cited in White, *Rimbaud*, p. 43. Ross suggests that Rimbaud's connections to 'the events in Paris are not to be established by measuring geographic distance'. Ross, *The Emergence*, p. 32.
44. For a debate on Rimbaud's whereabouts during the Commune, see Starkie, *Arthur Rimbaud*, pp. 56–79.
45. For an analysis of Rimbaud's poetry produced during the Commune, see Wallace Fowlie, 'Rimbaud and the Commune', in John Hicks and Robert Tucker (eds), *Revolution & Reaction: The Paris Commune 1871* (Boston: University of Massachusetts Press, 1973), pp. 168–71.
46. Ross, *The Emergence*, p. 152.
47. See PART III in Starkie, *Arthur Rimbaud*.

48. Acker, 'The Path of Abjection', p. 31.
49. Ross, *The Emergence*, p. 9.
50. Rimbaud, 'The Impossible', in *A Season in Hell & Illuminations*, p. 47.
51. Zurbrugg, 'Kathy Acker', p. 12.
52. Acker, 'The Path of Abjection', p. 34.
53. Ibid. p. 33; author's emphasis.
54. Ibid. p. 34.
55. O'Sullivan, 'The strange temporality of the subject: Badiou and Deleuze between the finite and the infinite', p. 169.
56. Ross, *The Emergence*, p. 66.
57. 'Democracy', from *Arthur Rimbaud: Complete Works*, trans. Paul Schmidt, copyright © 1967, 1970, 1971, 1972, 1975 by Paul Schmidt, p. 92. Reprinted by permission of HarperCollins Publishers.
58. Ross, 'Democracy for Sale', p. 95; author's emphasis.
59. The phrase is Ross's, and describes the characterisation of democracy that Rancière puts forward in his *The Ignorant Schoolmaster* (1987). See Ross, 'Democracy for Sale', p. 89. See also Josiah Ober, 'The Original Meaning of "Democracy": Capacity to Do Things, Not Majority Rule', *Constellations* 15 (2008), pp. 1–9.
60. Rancière, 'Rimbaud: Voices and Bodies', p. 66.
61. Badiou, 'Rimbaud's Method: Interruption', in *Conditions*, pp. 86, 89.
62. Rimbaud, 'Bad Blood', in *A Season in Hell & Illuminations*, p. 11.
63. Rimbaud requested a copy of Johann Wolfgang von Goethe's *Faust* from a friend and writer Ernest Delahaye in a letter while writing *A Season in Hell*. The two works share many similarities.
64. Spengler, *The Decline of the West. Volume 2*, p. 464.
65. Spengler, *The Decline of the West. Volume 1*, p. 107.
66. Ibid. p. 37.
67. Spengler, *The Decline of the West. Volume 2*, p. 463; author's emphasis.
68. See Tomislav Sunic, 'History and Decadence: Spengler's Cultural Pessimism Today', *Clio* 19.1 (1989), p. 1, pp. 51–62; and Tomislav Sunic, 'Oswald Spengler and History as Destiny', in *Against Democracy and Equality: The European New Right* (London: Arktos Media, 2011), p. 91. See also H. Stuart Hughes, *Oswald Spengler: A Critical Estimate* (New York: Scribner & Sons, 1952), p. 165. Spenglerian idiom can be recognised in T. S. Eliot, the postmodern sensibility of Baudrillard and Wittgenstein, and also in the writings of figures such as F. Scott Fitzgerald and Thomas Pynchon. John Lardas's *The Bop Apocalypse* examines the influence of Spengler's philosophy of natural cycles on the Beats' imagination. See John Lardas, *The Bop Apocalypse: The Religious Visions of Kerouac, Ginsberg, and Burroughs* (Urbana and Chicago: University of Illinois Press, 2001).
69. Farrenkopf, *Prophet of Decline*, p. 54.

70. Stewart Edwards writes that 'Parisian resentment of the peace treaty [signed by Napoleon III at Sedan on 1 September 1870] was a major factor leading to the 18 March uprising'. Edwards, 'Introduction', p. 24.
71. Georges Bourgin and Gabriel Henriot, cited in Shafer, *The Paris Commune*, p. 167.
72. Colonel Stanley, cited in Edwards, 'Introduction', p. 40.
73. Ross, *The Emergence*, pp. 4, 5.
74. Cited in Ross, *The Emergence*, p. ix; author's emphasis.
75. Badiou, *Polemics*, p. 258.
76. Gluckstein, *The Paris Commune*, p. 181.
77. Cited in Harvey, *Paris*, p. 328.
78. Sigmund Neumann, cited in *OR*, p. 254.
79. Busi, 'The Failure of Revolution', p. 19.
80. Ross, *The Emergence*, p. 25.
81. Gluckstein, *The Paris Commune*, p. 35.
82. Arthur Arnould, cited in Gluckstein, *The Paris Commune*, p. 21.
83. Gluckstein, *The Paris Commune*, p. 17.
84. Badiou, cited in Hewlett, *Badiou*, p. 72.
85. Henri Lefebvre, *Critique of Everyday Life, Volume 1*, trans. John Moore (London: Verso, 1991), p. 40.
86. Peyre, 'The Commune – A Century After', p. 3.
87. Castoriadis, *The Imaginary Institution of Society*, trans. Kathleen Blamey (Cambridge: Polity, 1987), p. 183.
88. Peyre, 'The Commune – A Century After', p. 3.
89. Ross, *The Emergence*, p. 25.
90. For a reappraisal of Castoriadis's contribution to social theory, see Anthony Elliott, 'Subjectivity, Culture, Autonomy: Cornelius Castoriadis', in *Critical Visions: New Directions in Social Theory* (Lanham, MD: Rowman & Littlefield Publishers, 2003), pp. 82–104.
91. See, for example, Linda Zerilli, 'Castoriadis, Arendt and the Problem of the New', *Constellations* 9 (2002), pp. 540–53.
92. For a discussion, see Tasić, 'Mathematics and Revolutionary Theory: Reading Castoriadis after Badiou'. For Tasić, the benefit of mathematics as a basis for ontology is that, unlike the deterministic paradigm of classical mechanism, '[a] dialectic based on mathematics [. . .] would leave room for incalculably creative acts and politically radical agents that cannot be derived from a priori "laws of history"' (p. 62).
93. Castoriadis, *The Imaginary*, p. 76.
94. Ibid.
95. Castoriadis, *The Imaginary*, p. 3; author's emphasis.
96. Castoriadis, 'The Crisis of Western Societies', in *The Castoriadis Reader*, p. 263; author's emphasis.
97. Badiou with Nicholas Truong, *In Praise of Love*, p. 15.
98. Acker, 'The Path of Abjection', p. 31.
99. Dew, *Learning*, p. 123.

100. Ibid.
101. Badiou, *Ethics*, p. 78.
102. Juno, 'Kathy Acker', p. 182; author's emphasis.
103. Ibid.
104. Ibid.
105. Kennedy, 'Simulating Sex and Imagining Mothers', p. 179.
106. Acker, 'Dead Doll Prophecy', p. 27.
107. Cited in Oliver Davis, *Jacques Rancière*, p. 39.
108. Oliver Davis, *Jacques Rancière*, p. 39.

Conclusion

Acker's final text, her posthumous play *Eurydice in the Underworld* (1997), combines autobiographical material with the collective voice of responsible artists.[1] The play conveys Acker's awareness of her own impending death. Eurydice suffers from cancer, and relates her time spent in hospital, her relationship with Orpheus and, following her death, her exploration of the underworld. Acker's underworld is a composite construct – one that intersperses imagery of an afterlife with underground dissident culture.[2] Underground, Eurydice is 'free to begin travelling with three or four other girls'.[3] She meets the ghosts of artists, political activists and martyrs, including the Arab writer Assia Djebar and Russian writers who risked their lives opposing Stalin's rule. By suffusing her autobiographical revelations with the experiences of female artists, Acker places herself in their lineage and continues a responsible art. In contrast to the rational, detached, 'optic' spaces which prevail in the overworld, where, as in the hospital, 'Above, glaring lights dominate reality',[4] Eurydice's exploration of the underworld is connected, experiential, nonlinear and haptic: 'There's no more difference between what I'm seeing and who I think I am'; 'I perceived solely by feeling'.[5]

As in Acker's earlier works, the female characters summoned in the play are allotted a special role in challenging the Saturnian cliché. Women in *Eurydice* not only evoke the feminine as an abstract subversive force that liquifies hierarchical social relations, preventing the revolutionaries from hardening into the dictators they overthrew, but also refer us back to real historical agents. Thus, for Acker, women's association with revolution and fidelity to egalitarian ideals is not simply metaphorical. In the play, Eurydice identifies herself as the Russian poet Marina Tsvetaeva, and tells us about her life during the Stalinist regime; Acker draws on Nadezhda Mandelstam's memoirs, *Hope against Hope* (1971) and *Hope Abandoned* (1973).[6]

Mandelstam regarded Tsvetaeva's fate to be most 'tragic'.[7] Poverty forced her to leave her daughter in an orphanage, only to find out later that she died of malnutrition. Her poetry was unpublishable in Soviet Russia, and due to persecution and poverty she went into exile. She returned to Russia to be reunited with her husband, who was then executed by the Soviet police. As Acker writes:

> Tsvetaeva, now one of the best-known poets in the world, appealed to the head of the Union of Soviet Writers. He informed her that there was no room for her here. Later he shot himself. Had already sent her to Golitsyno where her money dwindled away. Mur, her son, begged her for food. There were only two loaves of bread. She climbed on a chair and hung herself.[8]

Eurydice discovers that 'The first thing I [Tsvetaeva] learned about Pushkin is that they wanted to kill him. Then I learned that Pushkin is – A POET.'[9] Pushkin too was forced into exile, and had to abandon his revolutionary sentiments before being allowed to return to St Petersburg by the new Tsar, Nicholas I. According to her biographer Simon Karlinsky, the young Tsvetaeva was attracted to the anarchist revolution favoured by Rosa Luxemburg and rejected the orthodox Marxist model.[10] The Stalinist regime which followed Lenin's dictatorship of the proletariat marked a definite end to experimentation in political, economic, legislative and artistic spheres. As Beth Holmgren notes, those who did not conform to the dictates of socialist realism – the state-sponsored literary doctrine – were considered criminals:

> Under his general direction, fiction writers and journalists carefully determined and recycled plots, characters and metaphors that would legitimise power and rationalize the irrational atrocity of the state's actions. An artist who wrote otherwise would be subverting an ontology thoroughly inscribed in the regime, committing an act of sabotage and so incurring the punishment of oblivion (being written out) or obliteration (the link between literary and literal in Stalinist 'aesthetics').[11]

Underscoring the inseparability of art and responsibility, Acker comments: 'Tsvetaeva said that all she could be was a poet. That there were only poets and then a dark mass, people, the ones who had murdered Pushkin.'[12]

In her resurrections of responsible artists, female and male, Acker is making a general point about artists-parrhesiasts, whose vigilance and frank recording of the betrayal of the spirit of freedom made them the victims of oppressive regimes: silenced, imprisoned, deprived of possessions, forced into exile and executed for their defiance and the role they played in society. Much as Tsvetaeva looked to other poets such as Pushkin, Blok, Bely, Pasternak and Akhmatova, Acker places herself in the tradition of parrhesia, maintaining at the point of her death a sober gaze at signs of corruption, delusion and terror, while continuing to show that possibilities are larger than the ones we are told exist.

Acker's exhortation that 'If we throw history away, we are depriving ourselves of potentialities, potentialities for actions,'[13] encapsulates the radical political impetus of her works, as I have explored throughout this study. In the Introduction I examined the ways in which the concept of revolution underwent a series of semantic shifts, ranging from its pre-modern meaning as repetition to its modern associations with linearity and novelty, to the general disenchantment with revolutionary action characteristic of postmodernism. In the dominant discourses of history, events are subjected to the laws of cause and effect, and their final outcome – namely failure – is taken to be their final 'truth'. Moreover, in modern society revolution has suffered from trivialisation and commercialisation. I turned to Deleuze and Badiou, and others, because they challenge the pervasive narratives which are used today to justify the cessation of a search for alternatives. Instead, they put forward the notion of the event, a becoming – 'a bifurcation, a deviation with respect to laws, an unstable condition which opens up the possible'.[14] Approaching Acker's political project through the prism of the event has enabled us to uncover a commitment to revolutionary change that is sometimes obscured in conventional poststructuralist criticism. In addition, we have seen that applying the notion of the event to the discussion of the relationship between the historical avant-gardes and neo-avant-gardes restores their political agenda by re-anchoring them in their historical and social contexts.

As I have attempted to show in this study, an evental approach to a radical transformation is one in which politically committed artists and theorists make it seem possible to our imagination that the world could be different. In a time when the horizons of transformation appear remote, Acker's body of work remains of great political significance. As she drew from others and from history for a repository of potentials, Acker's avant-garde provides a powerful resource for thinking the appearance of new configurations of social relations. In her own words: 'a society without dreams, without art, the actuality of dreams, is a dead society. It's the artists who make the possibilities, and people go on and make the possibilities actual.'[15]

Notes

1. Acker repeatedly rejected conventional autobiographical writing as selfish, because it 'presents a Hobbist [sic] universe which suits Reagan and Thatcher fine'. See Dunn, 'A Radical American Abroad', p. 17.
2. In her brilliant essay 'Kathy Acker's Radical Performance Writing in *Eurydice in the Underworld* and Other Texts', Catherine Rock suggests that Acker undoes the classical myth, because when Eurydice goes down into the underworld she is not only the speaking subject but also is liberated from Orpheus's 'aestheticizing gaze' and from the 'more intrusive medical gaze' (Rock, p. 200), and, more broadly, from 'being judged' (Acker, *Eurydice*, p. 19).
3. Acker, *Eurydice*, p. 15.
4. Ibid. p. 11.
5. Ibid. pp. 16, 21.
6. In both memoirs, Mandelstam aimed to restore the obliterated life of her husband Osip Mandelstam, and to promote the works of female artists active in the unofficial Soviet culture, as well as offering an incisive analysis of Stalinism.
7. Mandelstam, *Hope against Hope*, p. 416.
8. Acker, *Eurydice*, p. 20.
9. Ibid. p. 19.
10. Karlinsky, *Marina Tsvetaeva*, p. 67.
11. Holmgren, *Women's Work in Stalin's Time*, p. 7.
12. Acker, *Eurydice*, p. 20.
13. Acker, 'Writing, Identity, and Copyright in the Net Age', in *Bodies of Work*, p. 99.
14. Deleuze, 'May '68', p. 233.
15. Zurbrugg, 'Kathy Acker', p. 12.

Selected Bibliography

Acker, Kathy, *Blood and Guts in High School Plus Two: Great Expectations, and My Death My Life by Pier Paolo Pasolini* (London: Picador, 1984).

Acker, Kathy, 'Models of Our Present', *Artforum* 22.6 (February 1984), 62–5.

Acker, Kathy, 'An Informal Interview with Kathy Acker on the 23rd April, 1986', by R. J. Ellis, Carolyn Bird, Dawn Curwen, Ian Macor, Val Ogden and Charles Patrick, pp. 1–13. Held in the Kathy Acker Papers, David M. Rubenstein Rare Book and Manuscript Library, Duke University, Box 22.

Acker, Kathy, *Don Quixote: Which Was a Dream* (New York: Grove Press, 1986).

Acker, Kathy, *Empire of the Senseless* (New York: Grove Press, 1988).

Acker, Kathy, *In Memoriam to Identity* (London: Pandora, 1990).

Acker, Kathy, 'Diary: At the Edge of the New', *New Statesman & Society* 3.84 (19 January 1990), 44–5.

Acker, Kathy, *Hannibal Lecter, My Father*, ed. Sylvère Lotringer (New York: Semiotext(e), 1991).

Acker, Kathy, *Portrait of an Eye: Three Novels: The Childlike Life of the Black Tarantula by the Black Tarantula; I Dreamt I Was a Nymphomaniac: Imagining; The Adult Life of Toulouse Lautrec by Henri Toulouse Lautrec* (New York: Pantheon Books, 1992).

Acker, Kathy, *My Mother: Demonology* (New York: Grove Press, 1993).

Acker, Kathy, 'Dead Doll Prophecy', in Carol Becker (ed.), *The Subversive Imagination: Artists, Society, & Social Responsibility* (New York: Routledge, 1994), pp. 20–34.

Acker, Kathy, 'Proposition One', in Carol Becker and Ann Wiens (eds), *The Artist in Society: Rights, Roles, and Responsibilities* (Chicago: New Art Examiner Press, 1994), pp. 36–44.

Acker, Kathy, 'After the End of the Art World', in Nicholas Zurbrugg (ed.), *The Multimedia Text, Art & Design Profile* 45 (1995), pp. 7–9.

Acker, Kathy, *Pussy, King of the Pirates* (Grove Press: New York, 1996).

Acker, Kathy, 'The Path of Abjection: An Interview with Kathy Acker', in Larry McCaffery (ed.), *Some Other Frequency: Interviews with Innovative*

American Authors (Philadelphia: University of Pennsylvania Press, 1996), pp. 14–35.

Acker, Kathy, *Bodies of Work: Essays by Kathy Acker* (London: Serpent's Tail, 1997).

Acker, Kathy, *Eurydice in the Underworld* (London: Arcadia, 1997).

Acker, Kathy, *Rip-Off Red, Girl Detective and The Burning Bombing of America: The Destruction of the US* (New York: Grove, 2002).

Acker, Kathy, and Paul Buck, *Spread Wide* (Paris: Dis Voir, 2004).

Adams, Robert, *Prison Riots in Britain and the USA* (Houndmills, Basingstoke: Macmillan, 1994).

Avrich, Paul, *Anarchist Voices: An Oral History of Anarchism in America* (Princeton, NJ: Princeton University Press, 1995).

Anemone, Anthony, 'Introduction: Just Assassins?', in Anemone (ed.), *Just Assassins*, 2010), pp. 3–23.

Anemone, Anthony (ed.), *Just Assassins: The Culture of Terrorism in Russia* (Evanston: Northwestern University Press, 2010).

Arendt, Hannah, 'Totalitarian Imperialism: Reflections on the Hungarian Revolution', *Journal of Politics* 20.1 (February 1958), 5–43.

Arendt, Hannah, *On Violence* (San Diego: Harcourt Brace, 1970).

Arendt, Hannah, *The Origins of Totalitarianism* (San Diego: Harcourt Brace & Company, [1958] 1973).

Arendt, Hannah, *On Revolution* (Harmondsworth: Penguin, 1990).

Asbley, Karin, and Bill Ayers, Bernardine Dohrn, John Jacobs, Jeff Jones, Steve Tappis, Gerry Long, Home Machtinger, Mark Rudd and Terry Robbins, 'You Don't Need a Weatherman to Know Which Way the Wind Blows' (June 1969), <https://archive.org/stream/YouDontNeedAWeatherman ToKnowWhichWayTheWindBlows_925#page/n7/mode/2up> (last accessed 10 January 2019).

Assad, Maria L., *Reading with Michel Serres* (New York: State University of New York Press, 1999).

Babich, Babette, 'Sloterdijk's Cynicism: Diogenes in the Marketplace', in Stuart Elden (ed.), *Sloterdijk Now* (Cambridge: Polity, 2012), pp. 17–36.

Badiou, Alain, *Deleuze: The Clamour of Being*, trans. Louise Burchill (Minneapolis: University of Minnesota Press, 2000).

Badiou, Alain, *Saint Paul: The Foundation of Universalism*, trans. Ray Brassier (Stanford: Stanford University Press, 2003).

Badiou, Alain, *Polemics*, trans. Steve Corcoran (London: Verso, 2006).

Badiou, Alain, *Being and Event*, trans. Oliver Feltham (London: Continuum, 2010).

Badiou, Alain, *The Century*, trans. Alberto Toscano (Cambridge: Polity, 2007).

Badiou, Alain, *Conditions*, trans. Steven Corcoran (London: Continuum, 2008).

Badiou, Alain, *Logics of Worlds: Being and Event II*, trans. Alberto Toscano (London: Continuum, 2009).

Badiou, Alain, *Pocket Pantheon: Figures of Postwar Philosophy*, trans. David Macey (London: Verso, 2009).

Badiou, Alain, *Theory of the Subject*, trans. Bruno Bosteels (London: Continuum, 2009).

Badiou, Alain, 'The Idea of Communism', in Douzinas and Žižek (eds), *The Idea of Communism* (London: Verso, 2010), pp. 1–14.

Badiou, Alain, *Ethics: An Essay on the Understanding of Evil*, trans. Peter Hallward (London: Verso, 2012).

Badiou, Alain, *Philosophy for Militants*, trans. Bruno Bosteels (London: Verso, 2012).

Badiou, Alain, with Nicholas Truong, *In Praise of Love*, trans. Peter Bush (London: Serpent's Tail, 2009).

Baker, Keith Michael, and Dan Edelstein (eds), *Scripting Revolution: A Historical Approach to the Comparative Study of Revolutions* (Stanford: Stanford University Press, 2015).

Baker, Keith Michael, and Dan Edelstein, 'Introduction', in Baker and Edelstein (eds), *Scripting Revolution*, pp. 1–21.

Bakhtin, Mikhail, *Problems of Dostoevsky's Poetics*, trans. and ed. Caryl Emerson (Minneapolis: University of Minnesota Press, 1984).

de Balzac, Honoré, *Gillette or the Unknown Masterpiece*, trans. Anthony Rudolf (London: The Menard Press, 1988).

Barber, David, *A Hard Rain Fell: SDS and Why It Failed* (Jackson: University Press of Mississippi, 2008).

Barkley, Elliott James ('L.D.'), in Zinn and Arnove (eds), *Voices of a People's History of the United States*, pp. 498–9.

Bely, Andrei, *Petersburg*, trans. Robert A. Maguire and John E. Malmstad (Bloomington: Indiana University Press, 1978).

Benjamin, Walter, *Walter Benjamin: Selected Writings*, Michael W. Jennings et al. (eds), Vol. 2, Part 1 (Cambridge, MA: Harvard University Press, 2005).

Berman, Paul, *A Tale of Two Utopias: The Political Journey of the Generation of 1968* (New York: Norton, 1996).

Bew, John, *Realpolitik: A History* (Oxford: Oxford University Press, 2016).

Biao, Lin, 'Foreword to the Second Chinese Edition' (16 December, 1966), <www.marxists.org/reference/archive/lin-biao/1966/12/16.htm> (last accessed 10 January 2019).

Boniece, Sally A., 'The Spiridonova Case, 1906: Terror, Myth and Martyrdom', in Anemone (ed.), *Just Assassins*, pp. 127–62.

Bourg, Julian, *From Revolution to Ethics: May 1968 and Contemporary French Thought* (Montreal: McGill-Queen's University Press, 2007).

Bourg, Julian, 'Writing on the Wall: 1968 as Event and Representation', in Baker and Edelstein (eds), *Scripting Revolution*, pp. 287–306.

Bragg, Melvyn, Interview by Melvyn Bragg, in *Kathy Acker*, film, dir. Alan Benson (LWT, 1984).

Brande, David, 'Making Yourself a Body Without Organs: The Cartography of Pain in Kathy Acker's *Don Quixote*', *Genre* 24 (Summer 1991), 191–209.

Braund, Susanna, and Josiah Osgood (eds), *A Companion to Persius and Juvenal* (Blackwell Publishing, 2012).

Breedlove, Lynnee, 'lynnee breedlove on kathy acker – an interview', 19 August 2010, <http://remember-who-u-are.blogspot.co.uk/2010/08/lynnee-breedlove-on-kathy-acker.html> (last accessed 10 January 2019).

Briton, Crane, *The Anatomy of Revolution* (W. W. Norton & Co: New York, 1938).

Bronner, Eric, *Modernism at the Barricades: Aesthetics, Politics, Utopia* (New York: Columbia University Press, 2012).

Buchloh, Benjamin H. D., 'Allegorical Procedures: Appropriation and Montage in Contemporary Art', *Artforum* (1982), 43–56.

Bürger, Peter, *Theory of the Avant-Garde*, trans. Michael Shaw (Minneapolis: University of Minneapolis Press, 1984).

Burton, Johanna, 'Fundamental to the Image: Feminism and Art in the 1980s', in Connie Butler and Alexandra Schwartz (eds), *Modern Women: Women Artists at The Museum of Modern Art* (New York: The Museum of Modern Art, 2010), pp. 428–43.

Burton, Johanna, and Thomas Crow, David Joselit, Maria H. Loh, Howard Singerman, Carrie Springer, Elisabeth Sussman and Adam D. Weinberg, *Sherrie Levine: Mayhem* (New York: Whitney Museum of American Art/Yale University Press, 2012).

Busi, Frederick, 'The Failure of Revolution', in Hicks and Tucker (eds), *Revolution & Reaction*, pp. 14–25.

Butler, Judith, *Gender Trouble: Feminism and Subversion of Identity* (London and New York: Routledge, 1999).

Carr-Gomm, Sarah, *Francisco Goya* (New York: Parkstone International, 2012).

Castoriadis, Cornelius, *The Imaginary Institution of Society*, trans. Kathleen Blamey (Cambridge: Polity, 1987).

Castoriadis, Cornelius, *The Castoriadis Reader*, trans. and ed. David Ames Curtis (Oxford: Blackwell Publishers, 1997).

Cendrars, Blaise, *Moravagine*, trans. Alan Brown (London: Peter Owen, 1968).

de Cervantes Saavedra, Miguel, *The History and Adventures of the Renowned Don Quixote*, trans. Dr Smollett (London: W. Stratford, Crown-Court, Temple, 1811).

Chaloupka, William, *Everybody Knows: Cynicism in America* (Minneapolis: Minnesota University Press, 1999).

Chomsky, Noam, *Chomsky on Anarchism*, ed. Barry Pateman (Edinburgh: AK Press, 2005).

Connor, Steven, 'Topologies: Michel Serres and the Shapes of Thought', *Anglistik* 15 (2004), 105–17.

Cook, Alexander C., 'Mao's Little Red Book', in Cook (ed.), *Mao's Little Red Book*, p. [i].

Cook, Alexander C. (ed.), *Mao's Little Red Book: A Global History* (Cambridge: Cambridge University Press, 2014).

Crawford, Neta C., 'Human Nature and World Politics: Rethinking "Man"', *International Relations* 23.2 (June 2009), 271–88.

Davis, Angela, *An Autobiography* (New York: International Publishers, 1988).

Davis, Angela, *Are Prisons Obsolete?* (New York: Seven Stories Press, 2003).

Davis, Angela, 'Political Prisoners, Prisons, and Black Liberation', in Zinn and Arnove (eds), *Voices of a People's History of the United States*, pp. 494–8.

Davis, Oliver, *Jacques Rancière* (Cambridge: Polity, 2010).

Deaton, Rebecca, 'Kathy Acker', *Textual Practice* 6.2 (1992), 271–82.

Debord, Guy, *The Society of the Spectacle*, trans. Ken Knabb (London: Rebel Press, 2004).

Debord, Guy, and Gil J. Wolman, 'A User's Guide to Détournement', in Knabb (ed.), *Situationist International Anthology*, pp. 14–21.

Debord, Guy, Attila Kotányi and Raoul Vaneigem, 'Theses on the Paris Commune', in Knabb (ed.), *Situationist International Anthology*, pp. 398–401.

Deitcher, David, 'Sherrie Levine: Rules of the Game', in Bernhard Bürgi (ed.), *Sherrie Levine* (Zurich: B. Bürgi and B. Marbach, c. 1991), pp. 7–13.

DeKoven, Marianne, 'Gertrude Stein and Modern Painting: Beyond Literary Cubism', *Contemporary Literature* 22.1 (1981), 81–95.

Den Tandt, Christophe, 'The Rock Counterculture from Modernist Utopianism to the Development of an Alternative Music Scene', in Sheila Whiteley and Jedediah Sklower (eds), *Countercultures and Popular Music* (Farnham: Ashgate, 2014), pp. 81–93.

Deleuze, Gilles, *The Logic of Sense*, ed. Constantin V. Boundas, trans. M. Lester and C. Stivale (London: The Athlone Press, 1990).

Deleuze, Gilles, *Difference and Repetition*, trans. P. Patton (New York: Columbia University Press, 1994).

Deleuze, Gilles, *Negotiations: 1972–1990*, trans. M. Joughin (New York: Columbia University Press, 1995).

Deleuze, Gilles, and Félix Guattari *Anti-Oedipus: Capitalism and Schizophrenia*, trans. Robert Hurley, Mark Seem and Helen R. Lane (Minneapolis: University of Minnesota Press, 2000).

Deleuze, Gilles, 'May '68 Didn't Happen', trans. Ames Hodges and Mike Taormina, in David Lapoujade (ed.), *Two Regimes of Madness: Texts and Interviews 1975–1995* (New York: Semiotext[e], 2007), pp. 233–6.

Deleuze, Gilles, and Félix Guattari, *Kafka: Toward a Minor Literature*, trans. Dana Polan (Minneapolis: University of Minnesota Press, 1986).

Deleuze, Gilles, and Félix Guattari, *What is Philosophy?*, trans. Hugh Tomlinson and Graham Burchell (New York: Columbia University Press, 1994).

Deleuze, Gilles, and Félix Guattari, *A Thousand Plateaus: Capitalism and Schizophrenia*, trans. Brian Massumi (Minneapolis: University of Minnesota Press, 2005).

Deleuze, Gilles, and Claire Parnet, *Dialogues*, trans. Hugh Tomlinson and Barbara Habberjam (New York: Columbia University Press, 1987).

Desmond, William D., *Cynics* (Stocksfiedl: Acumen, 2008).

Dew, Spencer, *Learning for Revolution: The Work of Kathy Acker* (San Diego: Hyperbole Books, 2011).

di Lampedusa, Giuseppe Tomasi, *The Leopard*, trans. Archibald Colquhoun (London: Everyman's Library, 1991).

Dittmer, Lowell, *China's Continuous Revolution: The Post-liberation Epoch, 1949–1981* (Berkeley: University of California Press, 1989).

Donnelly, Jack, *Realism and International Relations* (Cambridge: Cambridge University Press, 2004).

Dostoevsky, Fyodor, *Notes from Underground*, trans. Michael R. Katz (New York: Norton, 1989).

Douzinas, Costas, and Slavoj Žižek (eds), *The Idea of Communism* (London: Verso, 2010).

Dunn, Tony, 'A Radical American Abroad', interview with Kathy Acker, *Drama* 160 (1986), pp. 15–23.

Ebbesen, Jeffrey, *Postmodernism and Its Others: The Fiction of Ishmael Reed, Kathy Acker, and Don DeLillo* (New York: Routledge, 2006).

Edwards, Stewart, 'Introduction', in Steward Edwards (ed.), *The Communards of Paris, 1871* (London: Thames and Hudson, 1973), pp. 9–43.

Ehrenreich, Barbara, 'Foreword', in Klaus Theweleit, *Male Fantasies: Volume 1*, pp. ix–xvii.

Farrenkopf, John, *Prophet of Decline: Spengler on World History and Politics* (Baton Rouge: Louisiana State University Press, 2001).

Farquharson, Alex, 'Aquatopia: The Imaginary of the Ocean Deep', in Alex Farquharson and Martin Clark (eds), *Aquatopia: The Imaginary of the Ocean Deep* (Nottingham: Nottingham Contemporary, 2013), pp. 6–11.

Finkelpearl, Tom, *What We Made: Conversations on Art and Social Cooperation* (Durham, NC: Duke University Press, 2013).

Foster, Hal, 'Some Uses and Abuses of Russian Constructivism', in Jaroslav Andel and Owen Smith (eds), *Art into Life: Russian Constructivism 1914–1932* (New York: Rizzoli, 1990), pp. 241–53.

Foster, Hal, *The Return of the Real: The Avant-Garde at the End of the Century* (Cambridge, MA: MIT Press, 1996).

Foster, Hal, *Design and Crime (And Other Diatribes)* (London: Verso, 2002).

Foster, Hal, Rosalind E. Krauss, Benjamin H. D. Buchloh and Yve-Alain Bois, *Art Since 1900: Modernism, Antimodernism, Postmodernism* (London: Thames & Hudson, 2012).

Foucault, Michel, *Power/Knowledge: Selected Interviews and Other Writings, 1972–1977*, ed. Colin Gordon (New York: Pantheon Books, 1980).

Foucault, Michel, *Fearless Speech* (Los Angeles: Semiotext(e), 2001).

Friedman, Ellen G., 'A Conversation with Kathy Acker', *Review of Contemporary Fiction* 9.3 (Fall 1989), 12–22.

Friedman, Ellen G., '"Now Eat Your Mind": An Introduction to the Works of Kathy Acker', *Review of Contemporary Fiction* 9.3 (1989), 37–49.

Gair, Christopher, *The American Counterculture* (Edinburgh: Edinburgh University Press, 2007).

Garrigós, Cristina, 'Kathy Acker's Spanish Connection: Plagiarism, Madness and Love in *Don Quixote*', in Mackay and Nicol (eds), *Kathy Acker and Transnationalism*, pp. 115–32.

Gibson, Andrew, 'Serres at the crossroads', in Niran Abbas (ed.), *Mapping Michel Serres* (Ann Arbor: The University of Michigan Press, 2008), pp. 84–98.

Gibson, Andrew, *Intermittency: The Concept of Historical Reason in Recent French Philosophy* (Edinburgh: Edinburgh University Press, 2012).

Gilmore, David, 'Introduction', in Giuseppe Tomasi di Lampedusa, *The Leopard*, trans. Archibald Colquhoun (London: Everyman's Library, 1991), pp. 3–7.

Gitlin, Todd, *The Sixties: Years of Hope, Days of Rage* (New York: Bantam Book, 1993).

Gluckstein, Donny, *The Paris Commune: A Revolution in Democracy* (London: Bookmarks, 2006).

Gordon, Daniel, '"The Perplexities of Beginning": Hannah Arendt's Theory of Revolution', in Peter Baehr and Philip Walsh (eds), *The Anthem Companion to Hannah Arendt* (London: Anthem Press, 2017), pp. 107–28.

Guyotat, Pierre, *Eden, Eden, Eden*, trans. Graham Fox (London: Creation, 2003).

Hallward, Peter, *Badiou: A Subject to Truth* (Minneapolis: University of Minnesota Press 2003).

Harvey, David, *The Condition of Postmodernity: An Enquiry into the Origins of Cultural Change* (Cambridge, MA: Blackwell, 1990).

Harvey, David, *Paris, Capital of Modernity* (London: Routledge, 2003).

Harvey, David, *A Brief History of Neoliberalism* (Oxford: Oxford University Press, 2005).

Heath, Joseph, and Andrew Potter, *The Rebel Sell: How The Counter Culture Became Consumer Culture* (Oxford: Capstone, 2006).

Hell, Richard, in Marvin J. Taylor (ed.), *The Downtown Book: The New York Art Scene, 1974–1984* (Princeton and Oxford: Princeton University Press, 2006), p. 137.

Henderson, Margaret, 'From Counterculture to Punk Culture: The Emergence of Kathy Acker's Punk Poetics', *Literature Interpretation Theory* 26 (2015), 276–97.

Hersh, Seymour M., *The Price of Power: Kissinger in the White House* (New York: Summit Books, 1983).

Hewlett, Nick, *Democracy in Modern France* (London: Continuum, 2003).

Hewlett, Nick, *Badiou, Balibar, Rancière: Rethinking Emancipation* (London: Continuum, 2007).

Hicks, John, and Robert Tucker (eds), *Revolution & Reaction: The Paris Commune 1871* (Boston: University of Massachusetts Press, 1973).

Hill, Leslie, *Marguerite Duras: Apocalyptic Desires* (London: Routledge, 2001).

Hingley, Richard, *Nihilists: Russian Radicals and Revolutionaries in the Reign of Alexander II (1855–81)* (London: Weidenfeld and Nicolson, 1967).

Hobbes, Thomas, *Leviathan*, ed. Richard Tuck (Cambridge: Cambridge University Press, [1651] 1996).

Hobsbawm, Eric, '1968 – A Retrospect', *Marxism Today* (May 1978), 130–6.

Holmgren, Beth, *Women's Work in Stalin's Time: On Lidiia Chukovskaia and Nadezhda Mandelstam* (Bloomington and Indianapolis: Indiana University Press, 1993).

Horkheimer, Max, and Theodor Adorno, *Dialectic of Enlightenment*, ed. Gunzelin Schmid Noerr, trans. Edmund Jephcott (Stanford: Stanford University Press, 2002).

Houen, Alex, *Terrorism and Modern Literature, from Joseph Conrad to Ciaran Carson* (Oxford: Oxford University Press, 2002).

Houen, Alex, *Powers of Possibility: Experimental American Writing since the 1960s* (Oxford: Oxford University Press, 2012).

Hubac-Occhipinti, Olivier, 'Anarchist Terrorists of the Nineteenth Century', in Gérard Chaliand and Arnaud Blin (eds), *The History of Terrorism: From Antiquity to Al Qaeda*, trans. Edward Schneider, Kathryn Pulver and Jesse Browner (Berkeley: University of California Press, 2007), pp. 113–31.

Hume, Kathryn, 'Voice in Kathy Acker's Fiction', *Contemporary Literature* 42.3 (2001), 485–513.

Hunt, Lynn, 'The World We Have Gained: The Future of the French Revolution', *American Historical Review* 108.1 (February 2003), 1–19.

Hussey, Andrew, *The Game of War: The Life and Death of Guy Debord* (London: Jonathan Cape, 2001).

Irigaray, Luce, *This Sex Which Is Not One*, trans. Carolyn Burke (New York: Cornell University Press, 1985).

Jackson, Gabriel, *The Spanish Republic and the Civil War 1931–1939* (Princeton: Princeton University Press, 1965).

Jackson, George, *Soledad Brother: The Prison Letters of George Jackson* (Chicago: Lawrence Hill Books, 1994).

Jackson, Jonathan Jr, 'Foreword', in George Jackson, *Soledad Brother*, pp. xiii–xxv.

Jacobs, Naomi, 'Kathy Acker and the Plagiarized Self', *Review of Contemporary Fiction*, 9.3 (Fall 1989), pp. 50–5.

James, C. L. R. *The Black Jacobins* (London: Penguin, 2001).

Jameson, Fredric, 'Periodizing the 60s', in Sonya Sahres, Anders Stephanson, Stanley Aronowitz and Fredric Jameson (eds), *The Sixties: Without Apology* (Minneapolis: University of Minnesota Press, 1985), pp. 178–209.

Johnston, Adrian, *Badiou, Žižek, and Political Transformations: The Cadence of Change* (Evanston: Northwestern University Press, 2009).

Jones, Andrew F., 'Quotation Songs: Portable Media and the Maoist Pop Song', in Cook (ed.), *Mao's Little Red Book: A Global History*, pp. 43–60.

Jorn, Asger, *Open Creation and Its Enemies*, trans. Fabian Tompsett (London: London Psychogeographical Association, 1993).

Juno, Andrea, 'Kathy Acker', in Andrea Juno and V. Vale (eds), *Angry Women* (San Francisco: Re/Search, 1991), pp. 177–85.

Junquera, Juan Jose, *The Black Paintings of Goya* (London: Scala, 1999).

Kant, Immanuel, 'Was ist Aufklärung?', in Michel Foucault, *The Politics of Truth*, ed. Sylvère Lotringer (Los Angeles: Semiotext(e), 2007), pp. 29–40.

Karlinsky, Simon, *Marina Tsvetaeva: The Woman, Her World and Her Poetry* (Cambridge: Cambridge University Press, 1985).

Katsiaficas, George, 'Marcuse as Activist: Reminiscences on His Theory and Practice', in Douglas Kellner (ed.), *Herbert Marcuse: The New Left and the 1960s* (London: Routledge, [1996] 2005), pp. 192–203.

Kavka, Gregory S., *Hobbesian Moral and Political Theory* (Princeton: Princeton University Press, 1986).

Kennedy, Colleen, 'Simulating Sex and Imagining Mothers', *American Literary History* 4.1 (Spring 1992), 165–85.

Kharpertian, Theodore, *A Hand to Turn the Time: The Menippean Satires of Thomas Pynchon* (London: Associated University Press, 1990).

Klibansky, Raymond, Erwin Panofsky and Fritz Saxl, *Saturn and Melancholy: Studies in the History of Natural Philosophy, Religion and Art* (Nendeln: Kraus Reprint, 1979).

Knabb, Ken (ed. and trans.), *Situationist International Anthology* (Berkeley: Bureau of Public Secrets, 1995).

Konstantinou, Lee, *Cool Characters: Irony and American Fiction* (Cambridge, MA: Harvard University Press, 2016).

Kraus, Chris, *After Kathy Acker: A Literary Biography* (London: Allen Lane, 2017).

Kurczynski, Karen, 'Red Herrings: Eccentric Morphologies in *Situationist Times*', in Mikkel Bolt Rasmussen and Jakob Jakobsen (eds), *Expect*

Anything Fear Nothing: The Situationist Movement in Scandinavia and Elsewhere (Copenhagen: Nebula in association with Autonomedia, 2011), pp. 131–82.

Kurlansky, Mark, *1968: The Year that Rocked the World* (London: Vintage Books, 2005).

Kuspit, Donald, *The Cult of the Avant-Garde Artist* (Cambridge: Cambridge University Press, 1993).

Lasky, Melvin Jonah, *Utopia & Revolution: On the Origins of a Metaphor* (New Brunswick, NJ: Transaction Publishers, 2004).

Les Lèvres nues 8, Brussels, 1956.

Levine, Sherrie, 'Five Comments', in Brian Wallis (ed.), *Blasted Allegories*, pp. 92–3.

Levine, Sherrie, 'After Sherrie Levine', interviewed by Jeanne Siegel in Sally Everett (ed.), *Art Theory and Criticism: An Anthology of Formalist Avant-Garde, Contextualist and Post-Modernist Thought* (Jefferson, NC: McFarland & Company, 1991), pp. 264–72.

Licht, Fred, *Goya: The Origins of the Modern Temper in Art* (London: John Murray, 1979).

Lodder, Christina, *Russian Constructivism* (New Haven, CT: Yale University Press, 1983).

Luxemburg, Rosa, *The Russian Revolution*, trans. Bertram D. Wolfe (Ann Arbor: University of Michigan Press, 1961).

Luxon, Nancy, 'Ethics and Subjectivity: Practices of Self-Governance in the Late Lectures of Michel Foucault', *Political Theory* 36: 3 (June 2008), 377–402.

Lynton, Norbert, *Tatlin's Tower: Monument to Revolution* (New Haven, CT: Yale University Press, 2009).

McCaffery, Larry, 'An Interview with Kathy Acker', *Mississippi Review* 20.1/2 (1991), 83–97.

Mackay, Polina, and Kathryn Nicol (eds), *Kathy Acker and Transnationalism* (Newcastle upon Tyne: Cambridge Scholars, 2009).

MacKenzie, Iain, 'What is a Political Event?', *Theory & Event* 11.3 (2008), 1–18.

Maerhofer, John W., *Rethinking the Vanguard: Aesthetic and Political Positions in the Modernist Debate, 1917–1962* (Newcastle upon Tyne: Cambridge Scholars, 2009).

Maguire, Robert A., and John E. Malmstad, 'Introduction', in Bely, *Petersburg*, pp. viii–xxii.

Malevich, Kazimir, *Essays on Art: 1915–1933*, vol. 2, trans. Xenia Glowaski-Prus and Arnold McMillin, ed. Troels Andersen (London: Rapp & Whiting, 1969).

Mandelstam, Nadezhda, *Hope against Hope: A Memoir*, trans. Max Hayward (London: Collins and Harvill Press, 1971).

Marcuse, Herbert, *The Aesthetic Dimension: Toward a Critique of Marxist Aesthetics* (Boston: Beacon Press, 1978).

Marcuse, Herbert, *An Essay on Liberation* (Boston: Beacon Press, [1969] 2000).

Marcuse, Herbert, 'Reflections on the French Revolution', in Douglas Kellner, ed. *Herbert Marcuse: The New Left and the 1960s* (London: Routledge, 2005), pp. 40–6.

Marcuse, Herbert, *One-Dimensional Man: Studies in the Ideology of Advanced Industrial Society* (London: Routledge, 2007).

Marshall, Peter, *Demanding the Impossible: A History of Anarchism* (London: Harper Perennial, 2008).

Marx, Karl, 'The Eighteenth Brumaire of Louis Bonaparte', trans. Terrell Carver, in Mark Cowling and James Martin (eds), *Marx's Eighteenth Brumaire: (Post)modern Interpretations* (London: Pluto Press, [1851] 2002), pp. 19–109.

Massumi, Brian, 'Translator's Foreword: Pleasures of Philosophy', in Deleuze and Guattari, *A Thousand Plateaus*, pp. ix–xv.

Matich, Olga, 'Bely, Kandinsky, and Avant-Garde Aesthetics', in Olga Matich (ed.), *Petersburg/Petersburg: Novel and City, 1900–1921* (Madison: University of Wisconsin Press, 2010), pp. 83–120.

Mazella, David, *The Making of Modern Cynicism* (Charlottesville: University of Virginia Press, 2007).

Meisner, Maurice, *Mao's China and After: A History of the People's Republic* (New York: The Free Press, 1999).

Miraldi, Robert, *Seymour Hersh: Scoop Artist* (Lincoln, NE: Potomac Books, 2013).

Naimou, Angela, '"Death-in-Life": Conflation, Decolonization, and the Zombie in *Empire of the Senseless*', in Mackay and Nicol (eds), *Kathy Acker and Transnationalism*, pp. 133–54.

Navia, Louis E., *Diogenes the Cynic: The War against the World* (New York: Humanity Books, 2005).

Norris, Christopher, *Badiou's Being and Event: A Reader's Guide* (London: Continuum, 2009).

Orwell, George, *Nineteen Eighty-Four* (London: Penguin Books, [1949] 2003).

O'Sullivan, Simon, 'The strange temporality of the subject: Badiou and Deleuze between the finite and the infinite', *Subjectivity* 27 (2009), 155–71.

Parker, Noel, *Revolutions and History: An Essay in Interpretation* (Cambridge: Polity, 1999).

Parry, Albert, *Terrorism: From Robespierre to the Weather Underground* (Mineola, NY: Dover Publications, 2006).

Paulson, Ronald, *Representations of Revolution (1789–1820)* (New Haven, CT: Yale University Press, 1983).

Peterson, John, 'Realpolitik: C'mon, get real', *Leviathan* 2.3 (May 2012), 4–5.

Peyre, Henri, 'The Commune – A Century After', in Hicks and Tucker (eds), *Revolution & Reaction*, pp. 1–4.

Phelps, Hollis, 'Absolute Beginnings . . . Almost: Badiou and Deleuze on the Event', in Roland Faber, Henry Krips and Daniel Pettus (eds), *Event and Decision: Ontology and Politics in Badiou, Deleuze, and Whitehead* (Newcastle upon Tyne: Cambridge Scholars, 2010), pp. 48–64.

Pitchford, Nicola, *Tactical Readings: Feminist Postmodernism in the Novels of Kathy Acker and Angela Carter* (Lewisburg, PA: Bucknell University Press, 2002).

Prigogine, Ilya, and Isabelle Stengers, *Order out of Chaos* (London: Flamingo, 1985).

Pynchon, Thomas, 'Introduction', in Orwell, *Nineteen Eighty-Four*, pp. v–xxv.

Rancière, Jacques, 'Rimbaud: Voices and Bodies', in Judith Butler and Frederick M. Dolan (eds), *The Flesh of Words: The Politics of Writing*, trans. Charlotte Mandell (Stanford: Stanford University Press, 2004), pp. 41–67.

Redding, Arthur F., 'Bruises, Roses: Masochism and the Writing of Kathy Acker', *Contemporary Literature* 35.2 (Summer 1994), 281–304.

Rickels, Laurence A., 'Body Bildung', *Artforum* 32.6 (February 1994), 60–3; 103–4.

Rimbaud, Arthur, *A Season in Hell & Illuminations*, trans. Bertrand Mathieu (Brockport, NY: BOA Editions, 1991).

Rimbaud, Arthur, *Arthur Rimbaud: Complete Works*, trans. Paul Schmidt (New York: Harper Perennial, 2008).

Robinson, Christopher L., 'In the Silence of the Knight: Kathy Acker's *Don Quixote* as a Work of Disenchantment', *Yearbook of Contemporary and General Literature* 47 (1999), 109–23.

Rock, Catherine, 'Kathy Acker's Radical Performance Writing in *Eurydice in the Underworld* and Other Texts', in Michael Hardin, *Devouring Institutions* (San Diego: Hyperbole Books, 2004), pp. 189–209.

Ross, Kristin, *May '68 and Its Afterlives* (Chicago, University of Chicago Press, 2002).

Ross, Kristin, *The Emergence of Social Space: Rimbaud and the Paris Commune* (London: Verso, 2008).

Ross, Kristin, 'Democracy for Sale', in Amy Allen (ed.), *Democracy in What State?* (New York: Columbia University Press, 2011), pp. 82–99.

Sartre, Jean-Paul, *Being and Nothingness*, trans. Hazel E. Barnes (New York: Washington Square Press, 1993).

Schell, Jonathan, 'Introduction', in Arendt, *On Revolution*, pp. xi–xxix.

Sciolino, Martina, 'The "Mutilating Body" and the Decomposing Text: Recovery in Kathy Acker's *Great Expectations*', in Lori Hope Lefkovitz (ed.), *Textual Bodies: Changing Boundaries of Literary Representation* (Albany: State University of New York Press, 1997), pp. 245–66.

Scott, Helen, 'Introduction to Rosa Luxemburg', in Helen Scott (ed.), *The Essential Rosa Luxemburg: Reform or Revolution and The Mass Strike* (Chicago: Haymarket Books, 2008), pp. 1–36.

Scotto, Peter, 'The Terrorist as Novelist: Sergei Stepniak-Kravchinsky', in Anemone (ed.), *Just Assassins*, pp. 97–126.

Seem, Mark, 'Introduction', in Deleuze and Guattari, *Anti-Oedipus*, pp. xv–xxiv.

Serres, Michel, *The Birth of Physics*, trans. Jack Hawkes, ed. David Webb (Manchester: Clinamen Press, 2000).

Serres, Michel, *Genesis*, trans. Genevieve James and James Nielson (Ann Arbor: University of Michigan Press, 2009).

Serres, Michel, and Bruno Latour, *Conversations on Science, Culture and Time*, trans. Roxanne Lapidus (Ann Arbor: University of Michigan Press, 2011).

Shafer, David A., *The Paris Commune: French Politics, Culture, and Society at the Crossroads of the Revolutionary Tradition and Revolutionary Socialism* (New York: Palgrave Macmillan, 2005).

Shea, Louisa, *The Cynic Enlightenment: Diogenes in the Salon* (Baltimore: Johns Hopkins University Press, 2012).

Shepard, Todd, *The Invention of Decolonization: The Algerian War and the Remaking of France* (New York: Cornell University Press, 2008).

Siegle, Robert, *Suburban Ambush: Downtown Writing and the Fiction of Insurgency* (Baltimore, MD: The Johns Hopkins University Press, 1989).

Siegle, Robert, 'Downtown Writing', in Marvin J. Taylor (ed.), *The Downtown Book: The New York Arts Scene, 1974–1984* (Princeton, NJ, and Oxford: Princeton University Press, 2006), pp. 131–53.

Silverblatt, Michael, radio interview by Michael Silverblatt, *Bookworm* (Public Radio KCRW, Los Angeles, 31 August 1992).

Sklower, Jedediah, 'Preface: Dissent within Dissent', in Sheila Whiteley and Jedediah Sklower (eds), *Countercultures and Popular Music* (Farnham: Ashgate, 2014), pp. xv–xx.

Sloterdijk, Peter, *Critique of Cynical Reason*, trans. Michael Eldred (Minneapolis: University of Minnesota Press, 1987).

Smith, Brian A., 'Badiou and Sartre: Freedom, from Imagination to Chance', in Sean Bowden and Simon (eds), *Badiou and Philosophy* (Edinburgh: Edinburgh University Press, 2012), pp. 203–23.

Snell, Robert, *Uncertainties, Mysteries, Doubts: Romanticism and the Analytic Attitude* (London: Routledge, 2013).

Spengler, Oswald, *The Decline of the West, Volume 1: Form and Actuality*, trans. Charles Francis Atkinson (New York: Alfred A. Knopf, 1926).

Spengler, Oswald, *The Decline of the West, Volume 2: Perspectives of World History*, trans. Charles Francis Atkinson (London: George Allen and Unwin, 1928).

Spies, August, 'Address of August Spies' (October 7, 1886), in Zinn and Arnove (eds), *Voices of a People's History of the United States*, pp. 219–21.

Starkie, Enid, *Arthur Rimbaud* (London: Faber and Faber, 1973).

Starr, Peter, *Logics of Failed Revolt: French Theory After May '68* (Stanford: Stanford University Press, 1995).

Stein, Gertrude, *Tender Buttons* (Los Angeles: Sun & Moon Press, 1991).

Steinberg, Mark D., 'Melancholy and Modernity: Emotions and Social Life in Russia between the Revolutions', *Journal of Social History* 41.4 (2008), 813–41.

Stepniak, Sergei, *Underground Russia: Revolutionary Profiles and Sketches from Life*, trans. from Italian (New York: Charles Scribner's Sons, 1883), p. 17. Full text available at <https://archive.org/details/undergroundruss00lavrgoog> (last accessed 10 January 2019).

Stites, Richard, *The Women's Liberation Movement in Russia: Feminism, Nihilism, and Bolshevism, 1860–1930* (Princeton: Princeton University Press, 1990).

Stosuy, Brandon, 'Introduction', in Brandon Stosuy (ed.), *Up Is Up, but So Is Down: New York's Downtown Literary Scene, 1974–1992* (New York: New York University Press), pp. 15–23.

Suri, Jeremi, *Henry Kissinger and the American Century* (Cambridge, MA: Belknap Press, 2007).

Tasić, Vladimir, 'Mathematics and Revolutionary Theory: Reading Castoriadis after Badiou', *Cosmos and History: The Journal of Natural and Social Philosophy* 8.2 (2012), 60–77.

Theweleit, Klaus, *Male Fantasies: Volume 1: Women, Floods, Bodies, History*, trans. Stephen Conway (Minneapolis: University of Minnesota Press, 2003).

Toda, Martine, Shinji Maeda and Kiyoshi Honda, 'Formant-cavity affiliation in sibilant fricatives', in Susanne Fuchs, Martine Toda and Marzena Żygis (eds), *Turbulent Sounds: An Interdisciplinary Guide* (Berlin: Walter de Gruyter, 2010), pp. 343–74.

Tucker, Marcia, 'Director's Foreword', in Wallis (ed.), *Blasted Allegories*, pp. vii–ix.

Useem, Bert, and Peter Kimball, *States of Siege: US Prison Riots, 1971–1986* (Oxford: Oxford University Press, 1991).

Vaneigem, Raoul, *The Revolution of Everyday Life*, trans. Donald Nicholson-Smith (London: Rebel Press, 2006).

Varon, Jeremy, *Bringing the War Home: The Weather Underground, the Red Army Faction, and Revolutionary Violence in the Sixties and Seventies* (Berkeley: University of California Press, 2004).

Waite, Geoff, *Nietzsche's Corps/e: Aesthetics, Politics, Prophecy, or, the Spectacular Technoculture of Everyday Life* (Durham, NC: Duke University Press, 1996).

Wallis, Brian (ed.), *Blasted Allegories: An Anthology of Writings by Contemporary Artists* (New York: New Museum of Contemporary Art, 1987).

Walsh, Richard, 'The Quest for Love and the Writing of Female Desire in Kathy Acker's *Don Quixote*', *Critique: Studies in Contemporary Fiction* 32.3 (Spring 1991), 149–79.

Wark, McKenzie, *50 Years of Recuperation of the Situationist International* (New York: Princeton Architectural Press, 2008).

Wark, McKenzie, *The Beach Beneath the Street: The Everyday Life and Glorious Times of the Situationist International* (London: Verso, 2011).

Weber, Caroline, *Terror and Its Discontents: Suspect Words in Revolutionary France* (Minneapolis: University of Minnesota Press, 2003).

White, Edmund, *Rimbaud: The Double Life of a Rebel* (London: Atlantic Books, 2009).

Wilson, Matthew, *Rules Without Rulers: The Possibilities and Limits of Anarchism* (Winchester, WA: Zero Books, 2014).

Winkler, Martin M., 'Persius and Juvenal in the Media Age', in Susanna Braund and Josiah Osgood (eds), *A Companion to Persius and Juvenal* (Blackwell, 2012), pp. 513–43.

Wolin, Richard, *The Wind from the East: French Intellectuals, the Cultural Revolution, and the Legacy of the 1960s* (Princeton: Princeton University Press, 2010).

Wollen, Peter, 'Situationists and Architecture', *New Left Review* 8 (March–April 2001), 123–39.

Young-Bruehl, Elizabeth, *Hannah Arendt: For Love of the World* (New Haven, CT: Yale University Press, 1982).

Yuknavitch, Lidia, *Allegories of Violence: Tracing the Writing of War in Late Twentieth-Century Fiction* (New York: Routledge, 2001).

Zamora, Lois Parkinson, *Writing the Apocalypse: Historical Vision in Contemporary US and Latin American Fiction* (Cambridge: Cambridge University Press, 1993).

Zedong, Mao, 'Report on an investigation of the peasant movement in Hunan', in R. Keith Schoppa, *The Columbia Guide to Modern Chinese History* (New York: Columbia University Press, 2000), pp. 286–287.

Zinn, Howard, *A People's History of the United States, 1492–Present*, Twentieth Anniversary Edition (New York: HarperCollins, 1999).

Zinn, Howard, 'Introduction', in Zinn and Arnove (eds), *Voices of a People's History of the United States*, pp. 23–8.

Zinn, Howard, and Anthony Arnove (eds), *Voices of a People's History of the United States* (New York: Seven Stories Press, 2004).

Žižek, Slavoj, *The Sublime Object of Ideology* (London: Verso, 1989).

Žižek, Slavoj, 'Only a Suffering God Can Save Us', in Slavoj Žižek and Boris Gunjević, *God in Pain: Inversions of Apocalypse* (New York: Seven Stories Press, 2000), pp. 155–92.

Žižek, Slavoj, *Enjoy Your Symptom!: Jacques Lacan in Hollywood and Out* (New York: Routledge, 2001).

Žižek, Slavoj, *Organs without Bodies: Deleuze and Consequences* (New York: Routledge, 2004).

Žižek, Slavoj, 'Passion in the Era of Decaffeinated Belief', in Michael Hoelzl and Graham Ward (eds), *Religion and Political Thought* (London: Continuum, 2006), pp. 237–42.

Žižek, Slavoj, 'How to Begin from the Beginning', in Costas Douzinas and Slavoj Žižek (eds), *The Idea of Communism* (London and New York: Verso, 2010).

Žižek, Slavoj, *Demanding the Impossible*, ed. Yong-june Park (Cambridge: Polity, 2013).

Zurbrugg, Nicholas, 'Introduction', in Nicholas Zurbrugg (ed.), *The Multimedia Text, Art & Design Profile* 45 (1995), p. 6.

Zurbrugg, Nicholas (ed.), *The Multimedia Text Art & Design Profile* 45 (1995).

Zurbrugg, Nicholas, 'Kathy Acker', in Nicholas Zurbrugg (ed.), *Art, Performance, Media: 31 Interviews* (Minneapolis: University of Minnesota Press, 2004), pp. 1–15.

Index

Page numbers in *italics* refer to illustrations.